TO THE READER

This book is presented in its original form and is part of the religious literature and works of Scientology® Founder, L. Ron Hubbard. It is a record of Mr. Hubbard's observations and research into the nature of man and each individual's capabilities as a spiritual being, and is not a statement of claims made by the author, publisher or any Church of Scientology.

Scientology is defined as the study and handling of the spirit in relationship to itself, universes and other life. Thus, the mission of the Church of Scientology is a simple one: to help the individual regain his true nature, as a spiritual being, and thereby attain an awareness of his relationship with his fellow man and the universe. Therein lies the path to personal integrity, trust, enlightenment, and spiritual freedom itself.

Scientology and its forerunner and substudy, Dianetics, as practiced by the Church, address only the "thetan" (spirit), which is senior to the body, and its relationship to and effects on the body. While the Church is free, as all churches are, to engage in spiritual healing, its primary goal is increased spiritual awareness for all. For this reason, neither Scientology nor Dianetics is offered as, nor professes to be physical healing, nor is any claim made to that effect. The Church does not accept individuals who desire treatment of physical or mental illness but, instead, requires a competent medical examination for physical conditions, by qualified specialists, before addressing their spiritual cause.

The Hubbard® Electrometer, or E-Meter, is a religious artifact used in the Church. The E-Meter, by itself, does nothing and is only used by ministers and ministers-in-training, qualified in its use, to help parishioners locate the source of spiritual travail.

The attainment of the benefits and goals of the Scientology religion requires each individual's dedicated participation, as only through one's own efforts can they be achieved.

We hope reading this book is only one step of a personal voyage of discovery into this new and vital world religion.

THIS BOOK BELONGS TO

_____

INTRODUCTION TO
SCIENTOLOGY
ETHICS

Introduction to Scientology ETHICS

L. RON HUBBARD

Bridge
Publications, Inc.

A
HUBBARD®
PUBLICATION

BRIDGE PUBLICATIONS, INC.
4751 Fountain Avenue
Los Angeles, California 90029

ISBN 978-1-4031-4490-4

IMPORTANT NOTE

In reading this book, be very certain you never go past a word you do not fully understand. The only reason a person gives up a study or becomes confused or unable to learn is because he or she has gone past a word that was not understood.

The confusion or inability to grasp or learn comes AFTER a word the person did not have defined and understood. It may not only be the new and unusual words you have to look up. Some commonly used words can often be misdefined and so cause confusion.

This datum about not going past an undefined word is the most important fact in the whole subject of study. Every subject you have taken up and abandoned had its words which you failed to get defined.

Therefore, in studying this book be very, very certain you never go past a word you do not fully understand. If the material becomes confusing or you can't seem to grasp it, there will be a word just earlier that you have not understood. Don't go any further, but go back to BEFORE you got into trouble, find the misunderstood word and get it defined.

GLOSSARY

To aid reader comprehension, L. Ron Hubbard directed the editors to provide a glossary. This is included in the Appendix, *Editor's Glossary of Words, Terms and Phrases*. Words sometimes have several meanings. The *Editor's Glossary* only contains the definitions of words as they are used in this text. Other definitions can be found in standard language or Dianetics and Scientology dictionaries.

If you find any other words you do not know, look them up in a good dictionary.

FOREWORD

 Scientologists and, indeed, the whole of Mankind are extremely fortunate to have, for the first time in history, a practical system of Ethics and Justice based solely on *reason.*

Developed by L. Ron Hubbard after decades of intensive research, here is the powerful technology by which one ensures survival and freedom despite the dwindling spiral of civilization. It provides the means whereby individuals can become more ethical and regain their infinite ability to survive.

This new edition of *Introduction to Scientology Ethics* contains all one needs to effectively use Ethics Technology in one's daily existence. This *is* the basic Ethics Handbook. And with it, one can honestly reverse *any* deteriorating trend.

While data and technology concerning Suppressive Persons and Potential Trouble Sources is contained in this volume, the entire wealth of this technology is only to be found in various *PTS/SP Courses* that include all Bulletins, Policy Letters and lectures on the subject.

Additionally, while this volume provides the fundamentals of Ethics for application to one's own post and life, the *Hubbard Ethics and Justice Specialist Course* contains the complete body of technology and is the required training for Ethics Officers in Church Organizations.

However, all that is needed for the individual Scientologist to both advance personal survival on an individual basis, as well as avail oneself of the broad array of the first Justice System based on compassion and honesty, *is* contained in this volume.

Man's greatest weapon is his reason. Ethics *are* reason.

Thus, it is our sincere hope that you avail yourself of this valuable data, understand it fully and put it to effective use.

—The Editors

CONTENTS

THE CONDITIONS FORMULAS

C H A P T E R   1 1

THE THIRD PARTY

C H A P T E R   1 2

THE SCIENTOLOGY JUSTICE CODES AND THEIR APPLICATION

C H A P T E R   1 3

SCIENTOLOGY JUSTICE PROCEDURES

THE BASICS
OF ETHICS

THE BASICS
OF ETHICS

hroughout the ages, Man has struggled with the subjects of right and wrong and ethics and justice.

The dictionary defines *ethics* as "the study of the general nature of morals and of the specific moral choices to be made by the individual in his relationship with others."

The same dictionary defines *justice* as "conformity to moral right or to reason, truth or fact," or "the administration of law."

As you can see, these terms have become confused.

All philosophies from time immemorial have involved themselves with these subjects. And they never solved them.

That they have been solved in Dianetics and Scientology is a breakthrough of magnitude. The solution lay, first, in their *separation*. From there it could go forward to a workable technology for each.

Ethics consists simply of the actions an individual takes on himself. It is a personal thing. When one is ethical or "has his ethics in," it is by his own determinism and is done by himself.

Justice is the action taken on the individual by the group when he fails to take these actions himself.

HISTORY

These subjects are, actually, the basis of all philosophy. But in any study of the history of philosophy, it is plain that they have puzzled philosophers for a long time.

The early Greek followers of Pythagoras (Greek philosopher of the sixth century B.C.) tried to apply their mathematical theories to the subject of human conduct and ethics. Some time later, Socrates (Greek philosopher and teacher, 470?–399 B.C.) tackled the subject. He demonstrated that all those who were claiming to show people how to live were unable to defend their views or even define the terms they were using. He argued that we must know what courage, and justice, law and government are before we can be brave or good citizens or just or good rulers. This was fine but he then refused to provide definitions. He said that all sin was ignorance but did not take the necessary actions to rid Man of his ignorance.

Socrates' pupil, Plato (Greek philosopher, 427?–347 B.C.), adhered to his master's theories but insisted that these definitions could only be defined by pure reason. This meant that one had to isolate oneself from life in some ivory tower and figure it all out—not very useful to the man in the street.

Aristotle (Greek philosopher, 384–322 B.C.) also got involved with ethics. He explained unethical behavior by saying that Man's rationality became overruled by his desire.

This chain continued down the ages. Philosopher after philosopher tried to resolve the subjects of ethics and justice.

4

Unfortunately, until now, there has been no workable solution, as evidenced by the declining ethical level of society.

So you see it is no small breakthrough that has been made in this subject. We have defined the terms, which Socrates omitted to do, and we have a workable technology that anyone can use to help get himself out of the mud. The natural laws behind this subject have been found and made available for all to use.

ETHICS

Ethics is so native to the individual that when it goes off the rails he will always seek to overcome his own lack of ethics.

He knows he has an ethics blind spot the moment he develops it. At that moment he starts trying to put ethics in on himself and, to the degree that he can envision long-term survival concepts, he may be successful—even though lacking the actual tech of Ethics.

All too often, however, the bank is triggered by an out-ethics situation and, if the individual has no tech with which to handle it analytically, his "handling" is to mock-up motivators. In other words, he tends to believe or pretend that something was done to him that prompted or justified his out-ethics action and at that point he starts downhill.

It is *not* his attempt to get his ethics in that does him in. It is the automaticity of the bank which kicks in on him and his use of a bank mechanism at this point which sends him down the chute. When that happens, nobody puts him down the chute harder, really, than he does himself. And, once on the way down, without the basic technology of Ethics, he has no way of climbing back up the chute—he just caves himself in directly and deliberately. And even though he has a lot of complexities in his life, and he has other people doing him in, it all starts with his lack of knowledge of the technology of Ethics.

This, basically, is one of the primary tools he uses to dig himself out.

BASIC NATURE OF MAN

No matter how criminal an individual is, he will be trying, one way or another, to put ethics in on himself.

This explains why Hitler invited the world to destroy Germany. He had the whole war won before September 1939, before he declared war. The Allies were giving him everything he wanted; he had one of the finest intelligence organizations that ever walked; he had Germany well on the way to getting her colonies back and the idiot declared war! And he just caved himself and Germany right in. His brilliance was going at a mad rate in one direction and his native sense of ethics was causing him to cave himself in at a mad rate in the other direction.

The individual who lacks any Ethics Technology is unable to put in ethics on himself and restrain himself from contra-survival actions, so he caves himself in. And the individual is not going to come alive unless he gets hold of the basic tech of Ethics and applies it to himself and others. He may find it a little unpalatable at first, but when you're dying of malaria you don't usually complain about the taste of the quinine: you may not like it, but you sure drink it.

JUSTICE

When the individual fails to put in his own ethics, the group takes action against him and this is called justice.

I have found that Man cannot be trusted with justice. The truth is, Man cannot really be trusted with "punishment." With it he does not really seek discipline, he wreaks injustice. He dramatizes his inability to get his own ethics in by trying to get others to get their ethics in: I invite you to examine what laughingly passes for "justice" in our current society.

Many governments are so touchy about their divine rightness in judicial matters that you hardly open your mouth before they burst into uncontrolled violence. Getting into police hands is a catastrophe in its own right in many places, even when one is merely the plaintiff, much less the accused. Thus, social disturbance is at maximum in such areas.

When the tech of Ethics isn't known, justice becomes an end-all in itself. And that just degenerates into a sadism. Governments, because they don't understand ethics, have "ethics committees" but these are all worded in the framework of justice. They are even violating the derivation of the word *ethics*. They write justice over into ethics continuously with medical ethics committees, psychological ethics committees, Congressional committees, etc. These are all on the basis of justice because they don't really know what ethics is. They call it ethics but they initiate justice actions and they punish people and make it harder for them to get their own ethics in.

Proper justice is expected and has definite use. When a state of discipline does not exist the whole group caves in. It has been noted continually that the failure of a group began with a lack of or loss of discipline. Without it, the group and its members die. But you must understand ethics *and* justice.

The individual can be trusted with ethics and when he is taught to put his own ethics in, justice no longer becomes the all-important subject that it is made out to be.

BREAKTHROUGH

The breakthrough in Scientology is that we *do* have the basic technology of Ethics. For the first time Man *can* learn how to put his own ethics in and climb back up the chute.

This is a brand-new discovery. Before Scientology it had never before seen the light of day, anywhere. It marks a turning point in the history of philosophy. The individual can learn this technology, learn to apply it to his life and can then put his own ethics in, change conditions and start heading upwards toward survival under his own steam.

I hope you will learn to use this technology very well for your own sake, for the sake of those around you and for the sake of the future of this culture as a whole.

ETHICS,
JUSTICE AND
THE DYNAMICS

SURVIVAL

T he Dynamic Principle of Existence is: SURVIVE!

No behavior or activity has been found to exist without this principle. It is not new that life is surviving. It is new that life has as its entire dynamic urge *only* survival.

It is as though, at some remarkably distant time, the Supreme Being gave forth a command to all life: "Survive!" It was not said how to survive nor yet how long. All that was said was "Survive!" The reverse of "Survive!" is "Succumb." And that is the penalty for not engaging in survival activities.

An individual survives or succumbs in ratio to his ability to acquire and hold the wherewithal of survival. The security of a good job, for instance, means some guarantee of survival—other threats to existence not becoming too overpowering. The man who makes a good living can afford better clothing against the weather, a sounder and better home, medical care for himself and his family, good transportation and, what is important, the respect of his fellows. All these things are survival.

THE EIGHT DYNAMICS

s one looks out across the confusion which is life or existence to most people, one can discover eight main divisions.

There could be said to be eight urges (drives, impulses) in life.

These we call *dynamics*.

These are motives or motivations.

We call them *the eight dynamics*.

There is no thought or statement here that any one of these eight dynamics is more important than the others. While they are categories (divisions) of the broad game of life, they are not necessarily equal to each other. It will be found amongst individuals that each person stresses one of the dynamics more than the others, or may stress a combination of dynamics as more important than other combinations.

The purpose in setting forth this division is to increase an understanding of life by placing it in compartments. Having subdivided existence in this fashion, each compartment can be inspected (as itself and by itself) in its relationship to the other compartments of life.

In working a puzzle, it is necessary to first take pieces of similar color or character and place them in groups. In studying a subject, it is necessary to proceed in an orderly fashion.

To promote this orderliness, it is necessary to assume (for our purposes) these eight arbitrary compartments of life.

The First Dynamic is the urge toward existence as one's self. Here we have individuality expressed fully. This can be called the *Self Dynamic*.

The Second Dynamic is the urge toward existence as a sexual activity. This dynamic actually has two divisions. Second Dynamic (a) is the sexual act itself. And the Second Dynamic (b) is the family unit, including the rearing of children. This can be called the *Sex Dynamic*.

The Third Dynamic is the urge toward existence in groups of individuals. Any group, or part of an entire class, could be considered to be a part of the Third Dynamic. The school, the society, the town, the nation are each *part* of the Third Dynamic and each one *is* a Third Dynamic. This can be called the *Group Dynamic*.

The Fourth Dynamic is the urge toward existence as or of Mankind. Whereas one race would be considered a Third Dynamic, all the races would be considered the Fourth Dynamic. This can be called the *Mankind Dynamic*.

The Fifth Dynamic is the urge toward existence of the animal kingdom. This includes all living things, whether vegetable or animal, the fish in the sea, the beasts of the field or of the forest, grass, trees, flowers or anything directly and intimately motivated by *life*. This can be called the *Animal Dynamic*.

The Sixth Dynamic is the urge toward existence as the physical universe. The physical universe is composed of Matter, Energy, Space and Time. In Scientology we take the first letter of each of these words and coin a word—MEST. This can be called the *Universe Dynamic*.

The Seventh Dynamic is the urge toward existence as or of spirits. Anything spiritual, with or without identity, would come under the heading of the Seventh Dynamic. This can be called the *Spiritual Dynamic*.

The Eighth Dynamic is the urge toward existence as infinity. This is also identified as the Supreme Being. This is called the Eighth Dynamic because the symbol of infinity, ∞, stood upright makes the numeral 8. This can be called the *Infinity* or *God Dynamic*.

Scientologists usually call these by number.

A further manifestation of these dynamics is that they could best be represented as a series of concentric circles, wherein the First Dynamic would be the center and each new dynamic would be successively a circle outside it.

The basic characteristic of the individual includes his ability to so expand into the other dynamics. But when the Seventh Dynamic is reached in its entirety, one will only then discover the true Eighth Dynamic.

As an example of use of these dynamics, one discovers that a baby at birth is not perceptive beyond the First Dynamic. But as the child grows and interests extend, the child can be seen to embrace other dynamics.

As a further example of use, a person who is incapable of operating on the Third Dynamic is incapable at once of being a part of a team and so might be said to be incapable of a social existence.

As a further comment upon the eight dynamics, no one of these dynamics from one to seven is more important than any other one of them in terms of orienting the individual.

The abilities and shortcomings of individuals can be understood by viewing their participation in the various dynamics.

GRADIENT SCALE OF RIGHT AND WRONG

 he word *gradient* is meant to define "lessening or increasing degrees of condition." The difference between one point on a gradient scale and another point could be as different or as wide as the entire range of the scale itself. Or it could be as tiny as to need the most minute discernment for its establishment.

Terms like *good* and *bad, alive* and *dead, right* and *wrong* are used only in conjunction with gradient scales.

On the scale of right and wrong, everything above zero or center would be more and more right, approaching an infinite rightness; and everything below zero or center would be more and more wrong, approaching an infinite wrongness. The gradient scale is a way of thinking about the universe which approximates the actual conditions of the universe more closely than any other existing logical method.

The resolution of all problems is a study in rightness and wrongness. The entire problem of getting right answers and wrong answers is a problem of degrees of rightness and wrongness.

Acts or solutions are either more right than wrong (in which case they are right) or more wrong than right (in which case they are wrong).

An ultimate wrongness for the organism would be death—not only for the organism itself, but for all involved in its dynamics. An ultimate rightness for the organism would be survival to a reasonable term for himself, his children, his group and Mankind.

An ABSOLUTE WRONGNESS would be the extinction of the Universe and all energy and the source of energy—the infinity of complete death. An ABSOLUTE RIGHTNESS would be the immortality of the individual himself, his children, his group, Mankind and the Universe and all energy—the infinity of complete survival.

GRAPH OF LOGIC

(Simplified for illustration)

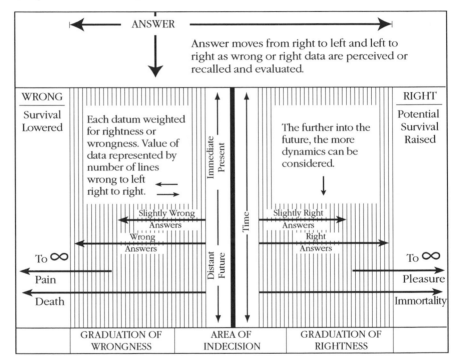

| | GRADUATION OF WRONGNESS | AREA OF INDECISION | GRADUATION OF RIGHTNESS | |

If a man, a group, a race or Mankind does its thinking on a sufficiently rational plane, it survives. And survival, that dynamic thrust through time toward some unannounced goal, is pleasure. Creative and constructive effort is pleasure.

If a man, a group or a race or Mankind does its thinking on a sufficiently irrational plane—out of lack of data, warped viewpoint or simply aberration—the survival is lessened; more is destroyed than is created. That is pain. That is the route toward death. That is evil.

Logic is not good or bad in itself, it is the name of a computation procedure—the procedure of the mind in its effort to attain solutions to problems.

ETHICS, JUSTICE AND THE DYNAMICS

very being has an infinite ability to survive. How well he accomplishes this is dependent on how well he uses ethics on his dynamics.

Ethics Tech exists for the individual.

It exists to give the individual a way to increase his survival and thus free himself from the dwindling spiral of the current culture.

ETHICS

The whole subject of ethics is one which, with the society in its current state, has become almost lost.

Ethics actually consists of rationality toward the highest level of survival for the individual, the future race, the group, Mankind and the other dynamics taken up collectively.

Ethics are reason.

Man's greatest weapon is his reason.

The highest ethic level would be long-term survival concepts with minimal destruction, along all of the dynamics.

An optimum solution to any problem would be that solution which brought the greatest benefits to the greatest number of dynamics. The poorest solution would be that solution which brought the greatest harm to the most number of dynamics.

Activities which brought minimal survival to a lesser number of dynamics and damaged the survival of a greater number of dynamics could not be considered rational activities.

18

One of the reasons that this society is dying and so forth, is that it's gone too far out-ethics. Reasonable conduct and optimum solutions have ceased to be used to such an extent that the society is on the way out.

By *out-ethics* we mean an action or situation in which an individual is involved, or something the individual does, which is contrary to the ideals, best interests and survival of his dynamics.

For a man to develop a weapon capable of destroying all life on this planet (as has been done with atomic weapons and certain drugs designed by the US Army) and place it in the hands of the criminally insane politicians is obviously not a survival act.

For the government to actively invite and create inflation to a point where a depression is a real threat to the individuals of this society is a non-survival action to say the least.

This gets so batty that in one of the South Pacific societies, infanticide became a ruling passion. There was a limited supply of food and they wanted to keep down the birthrate. They began using abortion and if this didn't work, they killed the children. Their Second Dynamic folded up. That society has almost disappeared.

These are acts calculated to be destructive and harmful to the survival of the people of the society.

Ethics are the actions an individual takes on himself in order to accomplish optimum survival for himself and others on all dynamics. Ethical actions are survival actions. Without a use of ethics we will not survive.

We know that the Dynamic Principle of Existence is SURVIVE!

At first glance that may seem too basic. It may seem too simple. When one thinks of survival, one is apt to make the error of thinking in terms of "barest necessity." That is not survival. Survival is a graduated scale, with infinity or immortality at the top and death and pain at the bottom.

GOOD AND EVIL, RIGHT AND WRONG

Years ago I discovered and proved that Man is basically good. This means that the basic personality and the basic intentions of the individual, toward himself and others, are good.

When a person finds himself committing too many harmful acts against the dynamics, he becomes his own executioner. This gives us the proof that Man is basically good. When he finds himself committing too many evils, then, causatively, unconsciously or unwittingly, Man puts ethics in on himself by destroying himself and he does himself in without assistance from anybody else.

This is why the criminal leaves clues on the scene, why people develop strange incapacitating illnesses and why they cause themselves accidents and even decide to have an accident. When they violate their own ethics, they begin to decay. They do this all on their own, without anybody else doing anything.

The criminal who leaves clues behind is doing so in hopes that someone will come along to stop him from continuing to harm others. He is *basically* good and does not want to harm others. And in the absence of an ability to stop himself outright, he attempts to put ethics in on himself by getting thrown in prison where he will no longer be able to commit crimes.

Similarly, the person who incapacitates himself with illness or gets himself in an accident is putting ethics in on himself by lessening his ability to harm and maybe even by totally removing himself from the environment that he has been harming. When he has evil intentions, when he is being "intentionally evil," he still has an urge to also stop himself. He seeks to suppress them and when he cannot do so directly, he does so indirectly. Evil, illness and decay often go hand in hand.

Man is basically good. He is basically well intentioned. He does not want to harm himself or others. When an individual does harm the dynamics, he will destroy himself in an effort to save those dynamics. This can be proven and has been proven in innumerable cases. It is this fact which evidences that Man is basically good.

On this basis we have the concepts of right and wrong.

When we speak of ethics, we are talking about right and wrong conduct. We are talking about good and evil.

Good can be considered to be any constructive survival action. It happens that no construction can take place without some small destruction, just as the tenement must be torn down to make room for the new apartment building.

To be good, something must contribute to the individual, to his family, his children, his group, Mankind or life. To be good, a thing must contain construction which outweighs the destruction it contains. A new cure which saves a hundred lives and kills one is an acceptable cure.

Good is survival. Good is being more right than one is wrong. Good is being more successful than one is unsuccessful, along constructive lines.

Things are good which complement the survival of the individual, his family, children, group, Mankind, life and MEST.

Acts are good which are more beneficial than destructive along these dynamics.

Evil is the opposite of good, and is anything which is destructive more than it is constructive along any of the various dynamics. A thing which does more destruction than construction is evil from the viewpoint of the individual, the future race, group, species, life or MEST that it destroys.

When an act is more destructive than constructive, it is evil. It is out-ethics. When an act assists succumbing more than it assists survival, it is an evil act in the proportion that it destroys.

Good, bluntly, is survival. Ethical conduct is survival. Evil conduct is non-survival. Construction is good when it promotes survival.

Construction is evil when it inhibits survival. Destruction is good when it enhances survival.

An act or conclusion is as right as it promotes the survival of the individual, future race, group, Mankind or life making the conclusion. To be entirely right would be to survive to infinity.

An act or conclusion is wrong to the degree that it is non-survival to the individual, future race, group, species or life responsible for doing the act or making the conclusion. The most wrong a person can be on the First Dynamic is dead.

The individual or group which is, on the average, more right than wrong (since these terms are not absolutes, by far) should survive. An individual who, on the average, is more wrong than right will succumb.

While there could be no absolute right or absolute wrong, a right action would depend upon its assisting the survival of the dynamics immediately concerned, a wrong action would impede the survival of the dynamics concerned.

Let us look at how these concepts of right and wrong fit into our current society.

This is a dying society. Ethics have gone so far out and are so little understood that this culture is headed for succumb at a dangerous rate.

A person is not going to come alive, this society is not going to survive, unless Ethics Tech is gotten hold of and applied.

When we look at Vietnam, inflation, the oil crisis, corruption of government, war, crime, insanity, drugs, sexual promiscuity, etc., we are looking at a culture on the way out. This is a direct result of individuals failing to apply ethics to their dynamics.

It actually starts with individual ethics.

Dishonest conduct is non-survival. Anything is unreasonable or evil which brings about the destruction of individuals, groups or inhibits the future of the race.

The keeping of one's word, when it has been sacredly pledged, is an act of survival, since one is then trusted, but only so long as he keeps his word.

To the weak, to the cowardly, to the reprehensibly irrational, dishonesty and underhanded dealings, the harming of others and the blighting of their hopes seem to be the only way of conducting life.

Unethical conduct is actually the conduct of destruction and fear. Lies are told because one is afraid of the consequences should one tell the truth. Destructive acts are usually done out of fear. Thus, the liar is inevitably a coward and the coward inevitably a liar.

The sexually promiscuous woman, the man who breaks faith with his friend, the covetous pervert are all dealing in such non-survival terms that degradation and unhappiness are part and parcel of their existence.

It probably seems quite normal and perfectly all right to some, to live in a highly degraded society full of criminals, drugs, war and insanity, where we are in constant threat of the total annihilation of life on this planet.

Well, let me say that this is not normal and it is not necessary. It *is* possible for individuals to lead happy productive lives without having to worry about whether or not they are going to be robbed if they walk outside their door or whether Russia is going to declare war on the United States. It is a matter of ethics. It is simply a matter of individuals applying ethics to their lives and having their dynamics in communication and surviving.

MORALS

Now we have ethics as survival. But what of such things as morals, ideals, love? Don't these things go above "mere survival"? No, they do not.

Romantic novels and television teach us that the hero always wins and that good always triumphs. But it appears that the hero doesn't always win and that good does not always triumph.

On a shorter view we can see villainy triumphing all about us. The truth of the matter is that the villainy is sooner or later going to lose. One cannot go through life victimizing one's fellow beings and wind up anything but trapped—the victim himself.

However, one doesn't observe this in the common course of life. One sees the villains succeeding everywhere, evidently amassing money, cutting their brother's throat, receiving the fruits of the courts and coming to rule over men.

Without looking at the final consequence of this, which is there just as certainly as the sun rises and sets, one begins to believe that evil triumphs whereas one has been taught that only good triumphs. This can cause the person himself to have a failure and can actually cause his downfall.

As for ideals, as for honesty, as for one's love of one's fellow man, one cannot find good survival for one or for many where these things are absent.

The criminal does not survive well. The average criminal spends the majority of his adult years caged like some wild beast and guarded from escape by the guns of good marksmen.

A man who is known to be honest is awarded survival—good jobs, good friends. And the man who has his ideals, no matter how thoroughly he may be persuaded to desert them, survives well only so long as he is true to those ideals.

Have you ever seen a doctor who, for the sake of personal gain, begins to secretly attend criminals or peddle dope? That doctor does not survive long after his ideals are laid aside.

Ideals, morals, ethics, all fall within this understanding of survival. One survives so long as he is true to himself, his family, his friends, the laws of the universe. When he fails in any respect, his survival is cut down.

In the modern dictionary, we find that *ethics* are defined as "morals" and *morals* are defined as "ethics." These two words are *not* interchangeable.

Morals should be defined as a code of good conduct laid down out of the experience of the race to serve as a uniform yardstick for the conduct of individuals and groups.

Morals are actually laws.

The origin of a moral code comes about when it is discovered through actual experience that some act is more non-survival than pro-survival. The prohibition of this act then enters into the customs of the people and may eventually become a law.

In the absence of extended reasoning powers, moral codes, so long as they provide better survival for their group, are a vital and necessary part of any culture.

Morals, however, become burdensome and protested against when they become outmoded. And although a revolt against morals may have as its stated target the fact that the code no longer is as applicable as it once was, revolts against moral codes generally occur because individuals of the group or the group itself has gone out-ethics to a point where it wishes to practice license against these moral codes, not because the codes themselves are unreasonable.

If a moral code were thoroughly reasonable, it could, at the same time, be considered thoroughly ethical. But only at this highest level could the two be called the same.

The ultimate in reason is the ultimate in survival.

Ethical conduct includes the adherence to the moral codes of the society in which we live.

JUSTICE

When an individual fails to apply ethics to himself and fails to follow the morals of the group, justice enters in.

It is not realized generally that the criminal is not only anti-social but is also anti-self.

A person who is out-ethics, who has his dynamics out of communication, is a potential or active criminal, in that crimes against the pro-survival actions of others are continually perpetrated. *Crime* might be defined as the reduction of the survival level along any one of the eight dynamics.

Justice is used when the individual's own out-ethics and destructive behavior begin to impinge too heavily on others.

In a society run by criminals and controlled by incompetent police, the citizens reactively identify any justice action or symbol with oppression.

But we have a society full of people who do not apply ethics to themselves, and in the absence of true ethics one cannot live with others and life becomes miserable. Therefore we have justice, which was developed to protect the innocent and decent.

When an individual fails to apply ethics to himself and follow the moral codes, the society takes justice action against him.

Justice, although it unfortunately cannot be trusted in the hands of Man, has as its basic intention and purpose the survival and welfare of those it serves. Justice, however, would not be needed when you have individuals who are sufficiently sane and in-ethics that they do not attempt to blunt others' survival.

Justice would be used until a person's own ethics render him fit company for his fellows.

ETHICS, JUSTICE AND YOUR SURVIVAL

In the past, the subject of ethics has not really been mentioned very much. Justice was, however. Justice systems have long been used as a substitute for ethics systems. But when you try to substitute ethics for justice, you get into trouble.

Man has not had an actual workable way of applying ethics to himself. The subjects of ethics and justice have been terribly aberrated.

We now have the tech of Ethics and Justice straightened out. This is the only road out on the subject that Man has.

People have been trying to put ethics in on themselves for eons without knowing how. Ethics evolved with the individual's attempts at continued survival.

When a person does something which is out-ethics (harms his and others' survival), he tries to right this wrong. Usually he just winds up caving himself in. (*Caved in* means mental and/or physical collapse to the extent that the individual cannot function causatively.)

They cave themselves in because, in an effort to restrain themselves and stop themselves from committing more harmful acts, they start withdrawing and withholding themselves from the area they have harmed. A person who does this becomes less and less able to influence his dynamics and thus becomes a victim of them. It is noted here that one must have done to other dynamics those things which other dynamics now seem to have the power to do to him. Therefore he is in a position to be injured and he loses control. He can become, in fact, a zero of influence and a vacuum for trouble.

This comes about because the person does not have the basic tech of Ethics. It has never been explained to him. No one ever told him how he could get out of the hole he's gotten himself into. This tech has remained utterly unknown.

So he has gone down the chute.

Ethics is one of the primary tools a person uses to dig himself out with.

Whether he knows how to or not, every person will try to dig himself out. It doesn't matter who he is or what he's done, he is going to be trying to put ethics in on himself, one way or the other.

Even with Hitler and Napoleon, there were attempts at self-restraint. It's interesting in looking at the lives of these people how thoroughly they worked at self-destruction. The self-destruction is their attempt at applying ethics to themselves. They worked at this self-destruction on several dynamics.

They can't put ethics in on themselves, they can't restrain themselves from doing these harmful acts, so they punish themselves. They realize they are criminals and cave themselves in.

All beings are basically good and are attempting to survive as best they can. They are attempting to put ethics in on their dynamics.

Ethics and justice were developed and exist to aid an individual in his urge towards survival. They exist to keep the dynamics in communication. The tech of Ethics is the actual tech of survival.

An individual's dynamics will be in communication to the degree that he is applying ethics to his life. If one knows and applies Ethics Tech to his life, he can keep the dynamics in communication and continuously increase his survival.

That is why ethics exists—so that we can survive like we want to survive, by having our dynamics in communication.

Ethics are not to be confused with justice. Justice is used only after a failure of the individual to use ethics on himself. With personal ethics in across the dynamics, Third Dynamic justice disappears as a primary concern. That's where you get a world without crime.

A man who steals from his employer has his Third Dynamic out of communication with his First Dynamic. He is headed for a prison sentence, or unemployment at best, which is not what one would call optimum survival on the First and Second Dynamic (not to mention the rest of them). He probably believes he is enhancing his survival by stealing, yet if he knew the tech of Ethics he would realize he is harming himself as well as others and will only end up further down the chute.

The man who lies, the woman who cheats on her husband, the teenager who takes drugs, the politician who is involved in dishonest dealings, all are cutting their own throats. They are harming their own survival by having their dynamics out of communication and not applying ethics to their lives.

It may come as a surprise to you, but a clean heart and clean hands are the only way to achieve happiness and survival.

The criminal will never make it unless he reforms; the liar will never be happy or satisfied with himself until he begins dealing in truth.

The optimum solution to any problem presented by life would be that which leads to increased survival on the majority of the dynamics.

Thus we see that a knowledge of ethics is necessary to survival.

The knowledge and application of ethics is the way out of the trap of degradation and pain.

We can, each and every one of us, achieve happiness and optimum survival for ourselves and others by using Ethics Tech.

WHAT HAPPENS IF THE DYNAMICS GO OUT-ETHICS

It is important to remember that these dynamics comprise life. They do not operate singly without interaction with the other dynamics.

Life is a group effort. None survive alone.

If one dynamic goes out-ethics, it goes out of communication with (to a greater or lesser degree) the other dynamics. In order to remain in communication, the dynamics must remain in-ethics.

Let us take the example of a woman who has totally withdrawn from the Third Dynamic. She won't have anything to do with any groups or the people of her town. She has no friends. She stays locked in her house all day thinking (with some misguided idea of independence or individuality) that she is surviving better on her First Dynamic. Actually she is quite unhappy and lonely and lives in fear of other human beings. To ease her misery and boredom, she begins to take sedatives and tranquilizers which she becomes addicted to and then starts drinking alcohol as well.

She is busy "solving" her dilemma with further destructive actions. You can see how she has driven her First, Second and Third Dynamics out of communication. She is actively destroying her survival on her dynamics. These actions are out-ethics in the extreme, and it would not be surprising if she eventually killed herself with the deadly combination of sedatives and alcohol.

Or let us take the man who is committing destructive acts on the job. These acts need not be large, they can be as simple as showing up late for work, not doing as professional a job on each product as he is capable of, damaging equipment or hiding things from his employer. He does not have to be overtly engaged in the total destruction of the company to know that he is committing harmful acts.

Now, this man finds himself sliding more and more out-ethics as time goes along. He feels he must hide more and more and he does not know how to stop this downward spiral. Very likely it never even occurred to him that he could stop it. He is lacking the tech of Ethics. He probably doesn't realize that his actions are driving his dynamics out of communication.

This may affect his other dynamics in various ways. He will probably be a bit miserable and, since he is basically good, he will feel guilt. He goes home at night and his wife says cheerily, "How was your day?" and he cringes a little and feels worse. He starts drinking to numb the misery. He is out of communication with his family. He is out of communication on his job. His performance at work worsens. He begins to neglect himself and his belongings. He no longer gets joy out of life. His happy and satisfying life slips away from him. Because he does not know and apply Ethics Tech to his life and his dynamics, the situation goes quite out of his control. He has unwittingly become the effect of his own out-ethics. Unless he gets his life straightened out by using ethics, he will undoubtedly die a miserable man.

Now I ask you, what kind of life is that? Unfortunately, it is all too common in our current times.

A person cannot go out-ethics on a dynamic without it having disastrous consequences on his other dynamics.

It is really quite tragic, the tragedy being compounded by the fact that it is so unnecessary. If Man only knew the simple tech of Ethics, he could achieve for himself the self-respect, personal satisfaction and success that he only believes himself capable of dreaming of, not attaining.

Man is seeking survival. Survival is measured in pleasure. That means, to most men, happiness, self-respect, the personal satisfaction of a job well done and success. A man may have money, he may have a lot of personal belongings, etc., but he will not be happy unless he actually has his ethics in and knows he came by these things honestly. These rich political and financial criminals are not happy. They may be envied by the common man for their wealth, but they are very unhappy people who more often than not come to grief eventually through drug or alcohol addiction, suicide or some other means of self-destruction.

Let us look at the all-too-common current occurrence of out-ethics on the Second Dynamic. This is generally thought to be perfectly acceptable behavior.

It is easy to see how Second Dynamic out-ethics affects the other dynamics.

Let us say we have a young woman who is somewhat happily married and decides to have an affair with her boss, who happens to be a good friend of her husband. This is quite obviously out-ethics, as well as against the law, although an amazing number of people would find this sort of behavior acceptable or mildly objectionable at most.

This is quite a destructive act, however. She will suffer from guilt; she will feel deceitful and unhappy because she knows she has committed a bad act against her husband. Her relationship with him will certainly suffer and since her boss is experiencing much the same thing in his home, she and her boss will begin to feel bad towards each other as they begin to target each other for their misfortune. Their dynamics end up quite messed up and out of communication. She will feel unhappy on her First Dynamic as she has abandoned her own moral code. Her Second Dynamic will be out of communication and she may even begin to find fault with and dislike her husband. The situation at work is strained as she is now out of communication with her boss and her fellow workers. Her boss has ruined his relationship and friendship with her husband. She is so embroiled in these three dynamics that they go totally out of communication with her Fourth, Fifth and Sixth Dynamics. This is all the result of ethics going out on a single dynamic.

The repercussions spread insidiously to all the dynamics.

Our survival is assured only by our knowledge and application of ethics to our dynamics in order to keep them in communication.

Through ethics we can achieve survival and happiness for ourselves and for planet Earth.

HONESTY

DEFINITIONS

Moral:

Able to know right from wrong in conduct; deciding and acting from that understanding.

Moral Code:

An agreed-upon code of right and wrong conduct. It is that series of agreements to which a person has subscribed to guarantee the survival of the group. The origin of a moral code comes about when it is discovered through actual experience that some act is more non-survival than pro-survival. The prohibition of this act then enters into the customs of the people and may eventually become a law.

Overt:

A harmful act or a transgression against the moral code of a group is called an "overt act" or an "overt." When a person does something that is contrary to the moral code he has agreed to, or when he omits to do something that he should have done per that moral code, he has committed an overt act. An overt act violates what was agreed upon.

It is an act by the person or individual leading to the injury, reduction or degradation of another, others or their beingness, persons, possessions, associations or dynamics. (See *The Eight Dynamics.*) It can be intentional or unintentional.

An overt act is not just injuring someone or something. An overt act is an act of omission or commission which does the least good for the least number of dynamics or the most harm to the greatest number of dynamics.

Overt of Omission:

A failure to act resulting in the injury, reduction or degradation of another or others or their beingness, persons, possessions or dynamics.

Motivator:

An act received by the person or individual causing injury, reduction or degradation of his beingness, person, associations or dynamics.

A motivator is called a "motivator" because it tends to prompt an overt. It gives a person a motive or reason or justification for an overt.

When a person commits an overt or overt of omission with no motivator, he tends to believe or pretends that he has received a motivator which does not in fact exist. This is a *false motivator*. Beings suffering from this are said to have "motivator hunger" and are often aggrieved over nothing.

Overt Act–Motivator Sequence:

When a person commits an overt, he will then believe he's got to have a motivator or that he has had a motivator. For instance, if he hits somebody, he will tell you immediately that he has been hit by the person even when he has not been.

Or simply when one has a motivator, he is liable to hang himself by committing an overt.

If Joe hits Bill, he now believes he should be hit by Bill. More importantly, he will actually get a somatic to prove he *has* been hit by Bill, even though Bill hasn't hit him. He will make this law true regardless of the actual circumstances. And people go around all the time justifying, saying how they've been "hit by Bill, hit by Bill, hit by Bill."

Withhold:

> An unspoken, unannounced transgression against a moral code by which the person is bound is called a "withhold." A withhold is an overt act that a person committed that he or she is not talking about. It is something that a person believes that if revealed will endanger his self-preservation. Any withhold comes *after* an overt.

Responsibility:

> The nonrecognition and denial of the right of intervention between oneself and any being, idea, matter, energy, space, time or form, and the assumption of full right of determination over it.

> Full Responsibility is not *fault,* it is recognition of being *cause.*

> Responsibility means the state, quality or fact of being responsible. And "responsible" means legally or ethically accountable for the care or welfare of another; involving personal accountability or ability to act without guidance or superior authority; being the source or cause of something; capable of making moral or rational decisions on one's own and therefore answerable for one's behavior; able to be trusted or depended upon (reliable); based upon or characterized by good judgment or sound thinking.

> Responsibility (Process): a process which addresses one's ability to be responsible.

Irresponsibility:

> Denial of past participation, agreement or authorship.

> *Overt acts* proceed from *irresponsibility.* Therefore, when responsibility declines, overt acts can occur. When responsibility declines to zero, then a person doing overt acts no longer conceives them to be overt acts.

Justification:

A social mechanism a person uses when he has committed an overt act and withheld it. It is a means by which a person can relieve himself of consciousness of having done an overt act by trying to *lessen the overt*. This is done by finding fault or displacing blame. It is explaining away the most flagrant wrongnesses.

The reasons overts are not overts to people are *justifications*.

BLOW-OFFS

cientology technology includes the factual explanation of departures, sudden and relatively unexplained, from sessions, posts, jobs, locations and areas.

This is one of the things Man thought he knew all about and therefore never bothered to investigate. Yet this, amongst all other things, gave him the most trouble. Man had it all explained to his own satisfaction and yet his explanation did not cut down the amount of trouble which came from the feeling of "having to leave."

For instance, Man has been frantic about the high divorce rate, about the high job turnover in plants, about labor unrest and many other items all stemming from the same source—sudden departures or gradual departures.

We have the view of a person who has a good job, who probably won't get a better one, suddenly deciding to leave, and going. We have the view of a wife, with a perfectly good husband and family, up and leaving it all. We see a husband, with a pretty and attractive wife, breaking up the affinity and departing.

In Scientology, we have the phenomenon of preclears in session or students on courses deciding to leave and never coming back. And that gives us more trouble than most other things all combined.

Man explained this to himself by saying that things were done to him which he would not tolerate and therefore he had to leave. But if this were the explanation, all Man would have to do would be to make working conditions, marital relationships, jobs, courses and sessions all very excellent and the problem would be solved.

But on the contrary, a close examination of working conditions and marital relationships demonstrates that improvement of conditions often worsens the amount of blow-off, as one could call this phenomenon. Probably the finest working conditions in the world were achieved by Mr. Hershey (of chocolate bar fame) for his plant workers. Yet they revolted and even shot at him. This, in its turn, led to an industrial philosophy that the worse workers were treated, the more willing they were to stay—which in itself is as untrue as the better they are treated, the faster they blow-off.

One can treat people so well that they grow ashamed of themselves (knowing they don't deserve it) that a blow-off is precipitated. And certainly one can treat people so badly that they have no choice but to leave. But these are extreme conditions and in between these we have the majority of departures: The auditor is doing his best for the preclear and yet the preclear gets meaner and meaner and blows the session. The wife is doing her best to make a marriage and the husband wanders off on the trail of a tart. The manager is trying to keep things going and the worker leaves. These, the unexplained, disrupt organizations and lives and it's time we understood them.

PEOPLE LEAVE BECAUSE OF THEIR OWN OVERTS AND WITHHOLDS.

40

That is the factual fact and the hardbound rule. A man with a clean heart can't be hurt. The man or woman who must-must-must become a victim and depart is departing because of his or her own overts and withholds. It doesn't matter whether the person is departing from a town or a job or a session. The cause is the same.

Almost anyone, no matter his position, can remedy a situation, no matter what's wrong, if he or she really wants to. When the person no longer wants to remedy it, his own overt acts and withholds against the others involved in the situation have lowered his own ability to be responsible for it. Therefore he or she does not remedy the situation. Departure is the only apparent answer.

To justify the departure, the person blowing off dreams up things done to him in an effort to minimize the overt by degrading those it was done to. The mechanics involved are quite simple.

It is an irresponsibility on our part, now that we know this, to permit this much irresponsibility. When a person threatens to leave a town, post, job, session or class, the only kind thing to do is to get off that person's overt acts and withholds. To do less sends the person off with the feeling of being degraded and having been harmed.

It is amazing what trivial overts will cause a person to blow. I caught a staff member one time just before he blew and traced down the original overt act against the organization to his failure to defend the organization when a criminal was speaking viciously about it. This failure to defend accumulated to itself more and more overts and withholds, such as failing to relay messages, failure to complete an assignment, until it finally utterly degraded the person into stealing something of no value. This theft caused the person to believe he had better leave.

It is a rather noble commentary on Man that *when a person finds himself,* as he believes, *incapable of restraining himself from injuring a benefactor, he will defend the benefactor by leaving.* This is the real source of the blow-off. If we were to better a person's working conditions in this light, we would see that we have simply magnified his overt acts and made it a certain fact that he would leave. If we punish, we can bring the value of the benefactor down a bit and thus lessen the value of the overt. But improvement and punishment are, neither one, answers. The answer lies in Scientology and processing the person up to a high-enough responsibility to take a job or a position and carry it out without all this weird hocus-pocus of "I've got to say you are doing things to me so I can leave and protect you from all the bad things I am doing to you." That's the way it is and it doesn't make sense not to do something about it now that we know.

Before a person may draw his last paycheck from an organization he is leaving of his own volition, he must write down all his overts and withholds against the organization and its related personnel and have these checked out on an E-Meter.*

To do less than this is cruelty itself. The person is blowing himself off with his own overts and withholds. If these are not removed, then anything the organization or its people do to him goes in like a javelin and leaves him with a dark area in his life and a rotten taste in his mouth. Further, he goes around spouting lies about the organization and its related personnel. And every lie he utters makes him just that much sicker. By permitting a blow-off without clearing it, we are degrading people. For I assure you (and with some sorrow) people have not often recovered from overts against Scientology, its organizations and related persons. They don't recover because they know in their hearts, even while they lie, that they are wronging people who have done and are doing enormous amounts of good in the world and who definitely do not deserve libel and slander. Literally, it kills them. And if you don't believe it, I can show you the long death list.

The only evil thing we are doing is to be good, if that makes sense to you. For by being good, things done to us out of carelessness or viciousness are all out of proportion to the evil done to others. This often applies to people who are not Scientologists. I had an electrician who robbed HCO of money with false bills and bad workmanship. One day, he woke up to the fact that the organization he was robbing was helping people everywhere, far beyond his ability to ever help anyone. Within a few weeks, he contracted TB and was dying in a London hospital. Nobody took off the overts and withholds when he left. And it was actually killing him—a fact which is no fancy on my part. There is something a little terrifying in this sometimes. I once told a bill collector what and who we were and that he had wronged a good person. And a half-hour later, he threw a hundred grains of Veronal down his throat and was lugged off to the hospital, a suicide.

42

Today, policy requires that staff receive a Leaving Staff Confessional before departing staff.

This campaign is aimed straightly at cases and getting people cleared. It is aimed at preserving staffs and the lives of persons who believe they have failed us.

Uneasy lies the head that has a bad conscience. Clean it up and run Responsibility on it and you have another better person. And if anybody feels like leaving, just examine the record and sit down and list everything done to and withheld from me and the organization and send it along. We'll save a lot of people that way.

And on our parts, we'll go along being as good a manager, as good an organization and as good a field as we can be. And we'll get rid of all our overts and withholds, too.

Think it will make an interesting new view?

Well, Scientology specializes in those.

JUSTIFICATION

hen a person has committed an overt act and then withholds it, he or she usually employs the social mechanism of justification.

We have all heard people attempt to justify their actions and all of us have known instinctively that justification was tantamount to a confession of guilt. But not until now have we understood the exact mechanism behind justification.

Short of Scientology auditing, there was no means by which a person could relieve himself of consciousness of having done an overt act except to try to *lessen the overt.*

Some churches used a mechanism of confession. This was a limited effort to relieve a person of the pressure of his overt acts. Later, the mechanism of confession was employed as a kind of blackmail, by which increased contribution could be obtained from the person confessing. Factually, this is a limited mechanism to such an extent that it can be extremely dangerous. Religious confession does not carry with it any real stress of responsibility for the individual but, on the contrary, seeks to lay responsibility at the door of the Divinity—a sort of blasphemy in itself. Confession, to be nondangerous and effective, must be accompanied by a full acceptance of responsibility. All overt acts are the product of irresponsibility on one or more of the dynamics.

Withholds are a sort of overt act in themselves, but have a different source. Oddly enough, we have just proven conclusively that Man is basically good—a fact which flies in the teeth of old religious beliefs that Man is basically evil. Man is good to such an extent that when he realizes he is being very dangerous and in error, he seeks to minimize his power. And if that doesn't work and he still finds himself committing overt acts, he then seeks to dispose of himself either by leaving or by getting caught and executed. Without this computation, police would be powerless to detect crime—the criminal always assists himself to be caught. Why police punish the caught criminal is the mystery. The caught criminal wants to be rendered less harmful to the society and wants rehabilitation. Well, if this is true, then why does he not unburden himself? The fact is this: unburdening is considered by him to be an overt act. People withhold overt acts because they conceive that telling them would be another overt act. It is as though thetans were trying to absorb and hold out of sight all the evil of the world. This is wrongheaded. By withholding overt acts, these are kept afloat in the universe and are themselves, as withholds, entirely the cause of continued evil. Man is basically good, but he could not attain expression of this until now. Nobody but the individual could die for his own sins—to arrange things otherwise was to keep Man in chains.

In view of these mechanisms, when the burden became too great, Man was driven into another mechanism—the effort to lessen the size and pressure of the overt. He or she could only do this by attempting to reduce the size and repute of the terminal. Hence, Not-isness. Hence when a man or a woman has done an overt act, there usually follows an effort to reduce the goodness or importance of the target of the overt. Hence the husband who betrays his wife must then state that the wife was no good in some way. Thus the wife who betrayed her husband had to reduce the husband to reduce the overt. This works on all dynamics. In this light, most criticism is justification of having done an overt.

This does not say that all things are right and that no criticism anywhere is ever merited. Man is not happy. He is faced with total destruction unless we toughen up our postulates. And the overt act mechanism is simply a sordid game condition Man has slipped into without knowing where he was going. So there are rightnesses and wrongnesses in conduct and society and life at large, but random, carping 1.1 criticism, when not borne out in fact, is only an effort to reduce the size of the target of the overt so that one can live (he hopes) with the overt. Of course, to criticize unjustly and lower repute is itself an overt act and so this mechanism is not, in fact, workable.

Here we have the source of the dwindling spiral. One commits overt acts unwittingly. He seeks to justify them by finding fault or displacing blame. This leads him into further overts against the same terminals, which leads to a degradation of himself and, sometimes, those terminals.

Scientologists have been completely right in objecting to the idea of punishment. Punishment is just another worsening of the overt sequence and degrades the punisher. But people who are guilty of overts demand punishment. They use it to help restrain themselves from (they hope) further violation of the dynamics. It is the victim who demands punishment and it is a wrongheaded society that awards it. People get right down and beg to be executed. And when you don't oblige, the woman scorned is sweet-tempered by comparison. I ought to know—I have more people try to elect me an executioner than you would care to examine. And many a preclear who sits down in your pc chair for a session is there just to be executed. And when you insist on making such a pc better, why you've had it. For they start on this desire for execution as a new overt chain and seek to justify it by telling people you're a bad auditor.

When you hear scathing and brutal criticism of someone which sounds just a bit strained, know that you have your eye on overts against that criticized person and, next chance you get, pull the overts and remove just that much evil from the world.

We have our hands here on the mechanism that makes this a crazy universe, so let's just go for broke on it and play it all the way out.

RESPONSIBILITY

In order to make up one's mind to be responsible for things, it is necessary to get over the idea that one is being forced into responsibility.

The power of choice is still senior to responsibility. What one does against his will operates as an overt act against oneself. But where one's will to do has deteriorated to unwillingness to do anything, lack of will is itself an aberration.

There is nothing wrong, basically, with doingness. But where one is doing something he is unwilling to do, aberration results. One does, in such a case, while unwilling to do. The result is doingness without responsibility.

In the decline of any state into slavery (as in Greece) or into economic strangulation of the individual (as in our modern Western society), doingness is more and more enforced and willingness to do is less and less in evidence. At length, people are doing without being responsible. From this results bad workmanship, crime, indigence and its necessities for welfarism. At length, there are so many people who are unwilling to do that the few left have to take the full burden of the society upon their backs. Where high unwillingness to do exists, democracy is then impossible, for it but votes for the biggest handout.

Where high unwillingness to do exists, then, we have a constant restimulation of all the things one is really unwilling to do, such as overt acts. Forcing people who do not want to work to yet work, restimulates the mechanism of overt acts with, thereby, higher and higher crime ratio, more and more strikes and less and less understanding of what it is all about.

The individual who has done something *bad* that he was not willing to do, then identifies anything he does with any unwillingness to do—when, of course, he has done this many times. Therefore all doingness becomes bad. Dancing becomes bad. Playing games becomes bad. Even eating and procreation become bad. And all because unwillingness to do something bad has evolved and identified into unwillingness to do.

The person who has done something bad restrains himself by withholding doingness in that direction. When at length he conceives he has done many, many bad things, he becomes a total withhold. As you process him, you encounter the recurring phenomenon of his realization that he has not been as bad as he thought he was. And that's the wonderful part of it. People are never as bad as they think they are and, certainly, other people are never as bad as one thinks they have been.

The basic wonder is that people police themselves. Out of a concept of good, they conceive themselves to be bad and after that seek every way they can to protect others from self. A person does this by reducing his own ability. He does it by reducing his own activity. He does this by reducing his own knowingness.

Where you see a thetan who sleeps too much and does too little, where you see a person who conceives bad doingness on every hand, you see a person who is safeguarding others from the badness of himself or herself.

Now, there is another extreme. A person who must do because of economic or other whips and yet, because of his own concept of his own badness, dares not do, is liable to become criminal. Such a person's only answer to doingness is to do without taking any responsibility. And this, when you examine the dynamics, falls easily into a pattern of dramatized overt acts. Here you have a body that is not being controlled, where most knowledge is obscured and where responsibility for others or even self is lacking. It is an easy step from criminality to insanity, if indeed there is any step at all. Such people cannot be policed, since being policed admits of some obedience. Lacking control, there is no ability to obey and so they wind up simply hating police and that is that.

Only when economic grips are so tight or political pressure is so great, as it is in Russia, do we get high criminality and neurotic or psychotic indexes. Whenever doing is accompanied by no will to do, irresponsibility for one's own acts can result.

Basically, then, when one is processing a pc, one is seeking to rehabilitate a willingness to do. In order to accomplish this, one must remove from the case the unwillingness to have done certain things and must rehabilitate the ability to withhold—on the pc's own determinism, not by punishment—further bad actions. Only then will the pc be willing to recover from anything wrong with the pc, since anything wrong with the pc is self-imposed in order to prevent wrongdoing at some past time.

Responsibility *can* be rehabilitated on any case.

HONEST PEOPLE HAVE RIGHTS, TOO

fter you have achieved a high level of ability you will be the first to insist upon your rights to live with honest people.

When you know the technology of the mind, you know that it is a mistake to use "individual rights" and "freedom" as arguments to protect those who would only destroy.

Individual rights were not originated to protect criminals, but to bring freedom to honest men. Into this area of protection then dived those who needed "freedom" and "individual liberty" to cover their own questionable activities.

Freedom is for honest people. No man who is not himself honest can be free—he is his own trap. When his own deeds cannot be disclosed then he is a prisoner; he must withhold himself from his fellows and is a slave to his own conscience. Freedom must be deserved before any freedom is possible.

To protect dishonest people is to condemn them to their own hells. By making "individual rights" a synonym for "protect the criminal" one helps bring about a slave state for all; for where "individual liberty" is abused, an impatience with it arises which at length sweeps us all away. The targets of all disciplinary laws are the few who err. Such laws unfortunately also injure and restrict those who do not err. If all were honest, there would be no disciplinary threats.

There is only one way out for a dishonest person—facing up to his own responsibilities in the society and putting himself back into communication with his fellow man, his family, the world at large.

By seeking to invoke his "individual rights" to protect himself from an examination of his deeds, he reduces just that much the future of individual liberty—for he himself is not free. Yet he infects others who are honest by using *their* right to freedom to protect himself.

Uneasy lies the head that wears a guilty conscience. And it will lie no more easily by seeking to protect misdeeds by pleas of "freedom means that you must never look at me." The right of a person to survive is directly related to his honesty.

Freedom for Man does not mean freedom to injure Man. Freedom of speech does not mean freedom to harm by lies.

Man cannot be free while there are those amongst him who are slaves to their own terrors.

The mission of a techno-space society is to subordinate the individual and control him by economic and political duress. The only casualty in a machine age is the individual and his freedom.

To preserve that freedom, one must not permit men to hide their evil intentions under the protection of that freedom. To be free, a man must be honest with himself and with his fellows. If a man uses his own honesty to protest the unmasking of dishonesty, then that man is an enemy of his own freedom.

We can stand in the sun only so long as we do not let the deeds of others bring the darkness.

Freedom is for honest men. Individual liberty exists only for those who have the ability to be free.

Today, in Scientology, we know the jailer—the person himself. And we can restore the right to stand in the sun by eradicating the evil men do to themselves.

So do not say that an investigation of a person or the past is a step toward slavery. For, in Scientology, such a step is the first step toward freeing a man from the guilt of self.

Were it the intention of the Scientologist to punish the guilty, then and only then would a look into the past of another be wrong.

But we are not police. Our look is the first step toward unlocking the doors—for they are all barred from *within*.

Who would punish when he could salvage? Only a madman would break a wanted object when he could repair it—and we are not mad.

The individual must not die in this machine age—rights or no rights. The criminal and madman must not triumph with their newfound tools of destruction.

The least free person is the person who cannot reveal his own acts and who protests the revelation of the improper acts of others. On such people will be built a future political slavery where we all have numbers—and our guilt—unless we act.

It is fascinating that blackmail and punishment are the keynotes of all dark operations. What would happen if these two commodities no longer existed? What would happen if all men were free enough to speak? Then and only then would you have freedom.

On the day when we can fully trust each other, there will be peace on Earth.

Don't stand in the road of that freedom. Be free, yourself.

CLEAN HANDS MAKE A HAPPY LIFE

or the first time in the soggy stream that's history to the human race, it's possible that happiness exists.

This goal, repeated many times and sought so heavily, has been ungraspable as sun motes, unattainable as a loved one's sigh.

What makes Mankind, basically good beings all, such strangers far to happiness?

The rich man geysers out his wealth. The poor man peers in every crack. But wealth buys nought and crevices are bare. The child hopes he will realize it when grown and, grown, wishes he were happy as a child.

We grasp it but, like gossamer, it's nought. We marry a most perfect girl or man and then throughout our lives weep to make the other make us glad.

Often sought, but seldom found, there are no riches, gems or palaces as valued as mere happiness.

But listen! Here is happiness, just at our fingertips, awaiting only magic words "Start Session" to begin its quest.

But like we walk through rain toward a banquet hall, our happiness in processing is gained by passing through the phantom shadows of our "sins."

What has made all Man a pauper in his happiness?

Transgressions against the mores of his race, his group, his family!

We care but little what these mores were or are. It was transgression did the trick.

We agree to fixed moralities and then, unthinking, we transgress, or with "good cause" offend, and there we are, the first dull bars of misery draw stealthily behind us.

And as we wander on, transgressing more, agreeing to new mores and then transgressing those, we come into that sunless place, the prison of our tears and sighs and might-have-beens, unhappiness.

Mutual action is the key to all our overt acts. Agreement to what ought to be and then a shattering of the troth works all the spell that's needed for a recipe of misery.

There must be pain. So we agreed. For pain restrains and warns, shuts off, forbids. But goodness now must then consist of bringing in no pain.

Mutual motion is agreed. And then we disagree and part and so are tied no more—tied not save back there in our minds, with scars of broken faith. The faith we broke, and said it had to be.

We all agree to feel the sun and then protest it burns. We all agree to kiss and love and then are startled that such pain can follow in that wake.

Mutual motion is all right—until we act in cruelty to the rest.

Tied by agreements and coactions, we dare be cruel to that to which the hard steel clasps of promises have bound us.

And so in being cruel to part of self—extended self as in a couple or a group—we then find pain in self with great surprise.

The overt act sequence is simple now to grasp. The scope is limited. But it began when we first had a cruel impulse to others bound to us by mores or coacts.

Why does one suffer pain in his own arm when he or she has struck another's limb?

Because the cruel impulse has been a break of bond with others where pledge once lived.

The only overt act that can bring pain to self is that cruel act which then transgresses things to which we had agreed.

Share action with a group or person in your life, agree to mutually survive by some specific code and then be cruel to them and so transgress and you'll have pain.

All Mankind lives and each man strives by codes of conduct mutually agreed. Perhaps these codes are good, perhaps they're bad, it's only evident they're codes. Mores bind the race.

Coaction then occurs. Thought and motion in accord. A oneness, then, of purpose and survival so results.

But now against that code there is transgression. And so because the code was held, whatever code it was, and Man sought comfort in Man's company, he held back his deed and so entered then the bourne in which no being laughs or has a freedom in his heart.

So down the curtains come across the brightness of the day and dull-faced clouds enmist all pleasant circumstance. For one has evilly transgressed and may not speak of it for fear *all* happiness will die.

And so we shut ourselves from off the light and enter gray-faced gloom. And seal within our deepest vault the reasons why we dare not face our friends.

And afterwards we go on making others guilty with the rest when, like some scrawny scarecrow of a priest whose tattered filthy robes are rough with sacrificial blood, we point the way to Hell for those who kill.

And deep within us secret gnawings ache. And then at last we cannot even cry.

The road to Hell—Man's very good at painting ugly signs that point its course and way.

The road to Heaven—Man's often sent but never yet arrived—more like he found the "other place."

But now a road that's wide has opened up—in Scientology.

The meter and the Process Check, when done by auditors with skill, can open up transgression's rush and loose a cascade out until Hell's spent.

And day will once more have a drop of dew upon the morning rose.

YOU CAN
BE RIGHT

ightness and wrongness form a common source of argument and struggle.

The concept of rightness reaches very high and very low on the Tone Scale.

And the effort to be right is the last conscious striving of an individual on the way out. I-am-right-and-they-are-wrong is the lowest concept that can be formulated by an unaware case.

What *is* right and what *is* wrong are not necessarily definable for everyone. These vary according to existing moral codes and disciplines and, before Scientology, despite their use in law as a test of "sanity," had no basis in fact but only in opinion.

In Dianetics and Scientology a more precise definition arose. And the definition became as well the true definition of an overt act. An overt act is not just injuring someone or something: an overt act is an act of omission or commission which does the least good for the least number of dynamics or the most harm to the greatest number of dynamics. (See *The Eight Dynamics*.)

Thus a wrong action is wrong to the degree that it harms the greatest number of dynamics. And a right action is right to the degree that it benefits the greatest number of dynamics.

Many people think that an action is an overt simply because it is destructive. To them, all destructive actions or omissions are overt acts. This is not true. For an act of commission or omission to be an overt act, it must harm the greater number of dynamics.

A failure to destroy can be, therefore, an overt act. Assistance to something that would harm a greater number of dynamics can also be an overt act.

An overt act is something that harms broadly. A beneficial act is something that helps broadly. It can be a beneficial act to harm something that would be harmful to the greater number of dynamics.

Harming everything and helping everything alike can be overt acts. Helping certain things and harming certain things alike can be beneficial acts.

The idea of not harming anything and helping everything are alike rather mad. It is doubtful if you would think helping enslavers was a beneficial action and equally doubtful if you would consider the destruction of a disease an overt act.

In the matter of being right or being wrong, a lot of muddy thinking can develop. There are no absolute rights or absolute wrongs. And being right does not consist of being unwilling to harm and being wrong does not consist only of not harming.

There is an irrationality about "being right" which not only throws out the validity of the legal test of sanity, but also explains why some people do very wrong things and insist they are doing right.

The answer lies in an impulse, inborn in everyone, to *try to be right*. This is an insistence which rapidly becomes divorced from right action. And it is accompanied by an effort to make others wrong, as we see in hypercritical cases. A being who is apparently unconscious is *still* being right and making others wrong. It is the last criticism.

We have seen a "defensive person" explaining away the most flagrant wrongnesses. This is "justification" as well. Most explanations of conduct, no matter how far-fetched, seem perfectly right to the person making them since he or she is only asserting self-rightness and other-wrongness.

We have long said that that which is not admired tends to persist. If no one admires a person for being right, then that person's "brand of being right" will persist, no matter how mad it sounds. Scientists who are aberrated cannot seem to get many theories. They do not because they are more interested in insisting on their own odd rightnesses than they are in finding truth. Thus we get strange "scientific truths" from men who should know better, including the late Einstein. Truth is built by those who have the breadth and balance to see also where they're wrong.

You have heard some very absurd arguments out among the crowd. Realize that the speaker was more interested in *asserting* his or her own rightness than in *being right*.

A thetan *tries* to be right and *fights* being wrong. This is without regard to being right *about* something or to do actual right. It is an *insistence* which has no concern with a rightness of conduct.

One tries to be right *always*, right down to the last spark.

How, then, is one ever wrong?

It is this way: One does a wrong action, accidentally or through oversight. The wrongness of the action or inaction is then in conflict with one's necessity to be right. So one then may continue and repeat the wrong action to prove it is right.

This is a fundamental of aberration. All wrong actions are the result of an error followed by an insistence on having been right. Instead of righting the error (which would involve being wrong) one insists the error was a right action and so repeats it.

As a being goes downscale, it is harder and harder to admit having been wrong. Nay, such an admission could well be disastrous to any remaining ability or sanity.

For rightness is the stuff of which survival is made. And as one approaches the last ebb of survival, one can only insist on having been right—for to believe for a moment one has been wrong is to court oblivion.

The last defense of any being is "I was right." That applies to anyone. When that defense crumbles, the lights go out.

So we are faced with the unlovely picture of asserted rightness in the face of flagrant wrongness. And any success in making the being realize their wrongness results in an immediate degradation, unconsciousness, or at best a loss of personality. Pavlov, Freud, psychiatry alike never grasped the delicacy of these facts and so evaluated and punished the criminal and insane into further criminality and insanity.

All justice today contains in it this hidden error—that the last defense is a belief in personal rightness regardless of charges and evidence alike, and that the effort to make another wrong results only in degradation.

But all this would be a hopeless impasse leading to highly chaotic social conditions were it not for one saving fact:

All repeated and "incurable" wrongnesses stem from the exercise of a last defense: "trying to be right." Therefore the compulsive wrongness can be cured no matter how mad it may seem or how thoroughly its rightness is insisted upon.

Getting the offender to admit his or her wrongness is to court further degradation and even unconsciousness or the destruction of a being. Therefore the purpose of punishment is defeated and punishment has minimal workability.

But by getting the offender off the compulsive repetition of the wrongness, one then cures it.

But how?

By rehabilitating the ability to be right!

This has limitless application—in training, in social skills, in marriage, in law, in life.

Example: A wife is always burning dinner. Despite scolding, threats of divorce, anything, the compulsion continues. One can wipe this wrongness out by getting her to explain what is *right* about her cooking. This may well evoke a raging tirade in some extreme cases. But if one flattens the question, that all dies away and she happily ceases to burn dinners. Carried to classic proportions, but not entirely necessary to end the compulsion, a moment in the past will be recovered when she accidentally burned a dinner and could not face up to having done a wrong action. To be right she thereafter had to burn dinners.

Go into a prison and find one sane prisoner who says he did wrong. You won't find one. Only the broken wrecks will say so out of terror of being hurt. But even they don't believe they did wrong.

A judge on a bench, sentencing criminals, would be given pause to realize that not one malefactor sentenced really thought he had done wrong and will never believe it, in fact, though he may seek to avert wrath by saying so.

The do-gooder crashes into this continually and is given his loses by it.

But marriage, law and crime do not constitute all the spheres of living where this applies. These facts embrace all of life.

The student who can't learn, the worker who can't work, the boss who can't boss are all caught on one side of the right–wrong question. They are being completely one-sided. They are being "last-ditch-right." And opposing them, those who would teach them are fixed on the other side "admit-you-are-wrong." And out of this we get not only no-change but actual degradation where it "wins." But there are no wins in this imbalance, only loses for both.

Thetans on the way down don't believe they are wrong because they don't dare believe it. And so they do not change.

Many a preclear in processing is only trying to prove himself right and the auditor wrong, particularly the lower case levels, and so we sometimes get no-change sessions.

And those who won't be audited at all are totally fixed on *asserted rightness* and are so close to gone that any question of their past rightness would, they feel, destroy them.

I get my share of this when a being, close to extinction and holding contrary views, grasps for a moment the rightness of Scientology and then in sudden defense asserts his own "rightnesses," sometimes close to terror.

It would be a grave error to go on letting an abuser of Scientology abuse. The route is to get him or her to explain how *right* he or she is without explaining how wrong Scientology is, for to do the last is to let them commit a serious overt. "What is right about your mind" would produce more case change and win more friends than any amount of evaluation or punishment to make them wrong.

You can be right. How? By getting another to explain how he or she is right—until he or she, being less defensive now, can take a less compulsive point of view. You don't have to agree with what they think. You only have to acknowledge what they say. And suddenly they *can* be right.

A lot of things can be done by understanding and using this mechanism. It will take, however, some study of this material before it can be gracefully applied—for all of us are reactive to some degree on this subject. And those who sought to enslave us did not neglect to install a right–wrong pair of items on the far back track. But these won't really get in your way.

As Scientologists, we are faced by a frightened society who think they would be wrong if we were found to be right. We need a weapon to correct this. We have one here.

And you can be right, you know. I was probably the first to believe you were, mechanism or no mechanism. The road to rightness is the road to survival. And every person is somewhere on that scale.

You can make yourself right, amongst other ways, by making others right enough to afford to change their minds. Then a lot more of us will arrive.

O/W WRITE-UPS

 t has been longstanding knowledge in Scientology that in the presence of overts and withholds no gains occur.

An overt act is an act of omission or commission which does the least good for the least number of dynamics or the most harm to the greatest number of dynamics. Overts are the biggest reason a person restrains and withholds himself from action.

Man is basically good. When people commit overts and then withhold them, it is because they conceive that telling them would be another overt act. By withholding overt acts, these are kept afloat in the universe and are themselves, as withholds, entirely the cause of continued evil.

A person who has overts and withholds becomes less able to influence his dynamics and falls out of communication with those people and things he has committed overts against.

Writing up one's overts and withholds offers a road out. By confronting the truth an individual can experience relief and a return of responsibility.

BASIC THEORY

The theory behind the action of writing up one's overts and withholds is contained in the Scientology Axioms, published in their entirety in the book *Scientology 0-8: The Book of Basics.*

Axiom 38 is particularly applicable:

1: *Stupidity is the unknownness of consideration.*

2: Mechanical Definition: *Stupidity is the unknownness of time, place, form and event.*

1: Truth is the exact consideration.

2: Truth is the exact time, place, form and event.

Thus we see that failure to discover Truth brings about stupidity.

Thus we see that the discovery of Truth would bring about an As-isness by actual experiment.

Thus we see that an Ultimate Truth would have no time, place, form or event.

Thus, then, we perceive that we can achieve a persistence only when we mask a truth.

Lying is an alteration of time, place, event or form.

Lying becomes Alter-isness, becomes stupidity.

(The blackness of cases is an accumulation of the case's own or another's lies.)

Anything which persists must avoid As-isness. Thus, anything to persist must contain a lie.

Writing up one's overts and withholds can accomplish an As-isness and thereby relieve a person of the burden of his transgressions.

FORMAT FOR WRITING O/Ws

When people do O/W write-ups, abuses can occur if the specifics of the action are not known and followed.

The first step before one undertakes the action of an O/W write-up is to word clear exactly how such write-ups are done.

Experience has proven that people have run into trouble on O/W write-ups when the format (including the key words and terms) was not word cleared before embarking on the action.

time: the moment of an event, process or condition. A definite moment, hour, day or year as indicated or fixed by a clock or calendar; a precise instant or date; the period during which something (as an action) exists or continues.

place: the location of occurrence or action; a specific location; a particular position or point in space.

form: the arrangement of things. The particular character, nature or structure of a thing.

event: something that happens or comes to pass; a distinct incident; a thing that takes place.

Format:

The format for writing up one's overts of omission, overts of commission or withholds is as follows:

1. Write down the overt or withhold.

2. Then state explicitly the specifics regarding the action or inaction, including:

   a. time

   b. place

   c. form

   d. event.

One has to get the time, place, form and event and one has to get a "done" (or one fails to get an As-isness).

Example:

"1. I hit a friend's car when backing out of my parking space at work and caused about five hundred dollars worth of damage to his car.

"2. On the 30th of June 1980, when I was leaving work, I was backing out of my parking space and hit the back end of my friend Joe's car. There was no one else around and the parking lot was almost empty. I drove away, without leaving a note or telling Joe, knowing that I caused about five hundred dollars damage to his car which he had to pay for."

Example:

"1. I cheated on my wife (Sally) by seeing another woman and never told her about this.

"2. Three years ago, when I was first married to Sally, I cheated on her by seeing another woman. I have never told Sally about this. One morning in June 1980, I had told Sally I would take her to the movies that night. On my way home from work, when I was at Jones' Department Store, I saw an old girlfriend of mine (Barbara). I asked Barbara to go out to dinner with me that night and she accepted (she did not know that I was married). I told her I would pick her up at 8:00 P.M. that night. When I got home from the store, I told Sally I had to go back to work to get some things done and would not be able to go to the movies with her. I then went out to dinner with Barbara in another city (at the 'Country Inn') so I would not risk seeing any of my friends."

———

Writing up one's overts and withholds is a simple procedure that has unlimited application.* O/W write-ups can bring about great relief and enable a person to achieve greater happiness.

*The complete technology of O/W write-ups is contained in HCO Policy Letters and is required study for organizational staff administering such.

HONESTY AND CASE GAIN

ISHONESTY CAN PREVENT CASE GAIN.

Case gain depends entirely upon the person's ability to view the truth of something in order to bring about an As-isness.

This ability is gained or regained on a gradient scale. The Grade Chart is designed to assist one to view gradiently larger areas of truth at each level. As one progresses up the Chart, his ability to view the truth of things improves and expands. The accumulated masses and burdens and problems and falsities of a lifetime or lifetimes are dissolved and vanished, leaving the being free and clean and in control of his life and environment.

But to receive help as a pc or pre-OT, one has to be honest with his auditor.

Dishonest people have withholds, and withholds stack up mass and bring about stupidity. They cut the person's reach and his ability to perceive. They hold in place the masses that imprison and pin the being at the level of Homo sapiens—and a miserable Homo sapiens, at that! Who is such a person really fooling?

Thus, one can bar his own way up the Bridge by dishonesty.

I always feel a bit sad when I see somebody doing himself in this way. It is so pointless.

One sees this in those who, for whatever irrational reason, cling knowingly to withholds and wind up critical, nattery and generating hostility. If one finds himself feeling hounded or persecuted, he should ask himself what his condition is on the First Dynamic instead of going around persuading others to do him in.

How precious, after all, are one's dishonesties, withholds and falsities in the face of the real freedom there is to be gained?

One *can* be honest. He will find it a happier, more comfortable existence when he is.

And more important—he'll find the route to stable case gain is now open to him.

HONESTY OPENS THE DOOR TO CASE GAIN.

That is the route to sanity. It is the route up the Bridge to OT and real freedom. With honesty, one can make it and make it all the way!

Why settle for anything less?

STATISTICS
AND THE
CONDITIONS
OF EXISTENCE

THE CONDITIONS STATES OF OPERATION

n organization or its parts or an individual passes through various states of existence. These, if not handled properly, bring about shrinkage and misery and worry and death. If handled properly they bring about stability, expansion, influence and well-being.

These, arranged from highest to lowest, are:

Power
Power Change
Affluence
Normal Operation
Emergency
Danger
Non-Existence
Liability
Doubt
Enemy
Treason
Confusion

The formulas for these are apparently monitoring formulas for livingness.

The first thing to know about them is that each step in a formula is in exact sequence and must be done in *that* sequence. It is totally fatal to reverse the order of sequence of two or more actions.

Example: In Emergency, economize before you promote. If the sequence is disordered, the final result is a smaller org or less influential person.

A key datum is that if the formulas are not known or not correctly applied, an organism emerges from each crisis smaller.

The next thing to know is that one knows what formula to apply only by closely and continually inspecting statistics. By *statistics* is meant numbers of things, measurement of volume, all relative to time. A statistic not compared to the same type of statistic earlier will not predict any future statistic. A single statistic is meaningless. Statistics are always worse than, the same as or better than they were at an earlier period. Graphing and the reading of graphs is a vital necessity, then, in monitoring an org, department or person and applying Condition Formulas to it.

This is much easier than it appears. If you made $1,000 last week and only $200 this week, you obviously are slipping, if you made $1,100 this week you are pretty stable, if you made $5,000 this week you are affluent. All compared to the $1,000 you made last week.

What is the Code of Conduct you should use to stay healthy under these *conditions*? These are the Condition Formulas.

The third thing to know is that one can wreck an org or department or person by applying the wrong Condition Formula. The person is in Emergency Condition. One applies the Condition of Affluence or Power or anything but the Emergency Formula and the person will go bust. The universe is made that way. The *right* condition must be applied.

A vital thing to realize is that the formulas of conditions exist. They are part and parcel of any activity in this universe and now that they are known they must be complied with. This takes about 90 percent of chance out of business operation or personal economics. The variables are only how well one estimates the situation and how energetic one is in applying the formulas.

The next thing to know is that the proper application of the proper formula works. It works no matter how stupidly it is applied only so long as the *right* formula is applied and the exact sequence of steps is taken. Brilliance only shows up in the *speed* of recovery or expansion. Very brilliant applications show up in overnight, sound expansions. Dull applications, given only that they are correct, show up in slower expansions. In other words, nobody has to be a screaming genius to apply them or dream up the necessary ideas in them. One only has to estimate the condition accurately and *act* energetically in applying its steps in exact order. The brighter the ideas, the faster the expansion, that's all. The expansion or gain is itself inevitable. However, if the dullness includes adding needless steps, then one may fail. And if one is so stupid that a wrong estimate is made of conditions and a wrong formula is applied and applied with its steps in wrong sequence, then one jolly well deserves to fail!

Another thing to know is that these conditions apply to a universe, a civilization, an org, a portion of an org or a person alike.

The next thing to know is that knowing the formulas carries the responsibility of using them. Otherwise one could be accused of willful suicide! For these *are* the formulas. And they *do* work like magic.

If these formulas are not known or used, expansion is totally a matter of chance or fate regardless of how good one's ideas are.

STATISTICS
WHAT THEY ARE

hat is a *statistic*? A statistic is a number or amount *compared* to an earlier number or amount of the same thing. Statistics refer to the quantity of work done or the value of it in money.

A *down statistic* means that the current number is less than it was.

An *up statistic* means the current number is more than it was.

We operate on statistics. These show whether or not a staff member or group is working or not working as the work produces the statistic. If he doesn't work effectively, the statistic inevitably goes down. If he works effectively, the statistic goes up.

NEGATIVE STATISTICS

Some things go up in statistic when they are bad (like car accidents). However, we are not using negative statistics. We only use things that mean good when they go up or mean bad when they go down.

STATISTIC GRAPHS

A *graph* is a line or diagram showing how one quantity depends on, compares with or changes another. It is any pictorial device used to display numerical relationships.

A graph is not informative if its vertical scale results in graph line changes that are too small. It is not possible to draw the graph at all if the line changes are too large.

If the ups and downs are not plainly visible on a graph, then those interpreting the graph make errors. What is shown as a flat-looking line really should be a mountain range.

By *scale* is meant the number of anything per vertical inch of graph.

The way to do a scale is as follows:

Scale is different for every statistic.

1. Determine the lowest amount one expects a particular statistic to go—this is not always zero.

2. Determine the highest amount one can believe the statistic will go in the next three months.

3. Subtract (1) from (2).

4. Proportion the vertical divisions as per (3).

Your scale will then be quite real and show up its rises and falls.

Here is an *incorrect* example.

We take an org that runs at $5,000 per week. We proportion the vertical marks of the graph paper of which there are 100 so each one represents $1,000. This when graphed will show a low line, quite flat, no matter what the org income is doing and so draws no attention from executives when it rises and dives.

This is the *correct* way to do it for Gross Income for an org averaging $5,000/week.

1. Looking over the old graphs of the past 6 months we find it never went under $2,400. So we take $2,000 as the lowest point of the graph paper.

2. We estimate this org should get up to $12,000 on occasion in the next 3 months, so we take this as the top of the graph paper.

3. We subtract $2,000 from $12,000 and we have $10,000.

4. We take the 100 blocks of vertical and make each one $100, starting with $2,000 as the lowest mark.

Now we plot Gross Income as $100 per graph division.

This will look right, show falls and rises very clearly and so will be of use to executives in interpretation.

Try to use easily computed units like 5, 10, 25, 50, 100, and show the scale itself on the graph (1 div = 25).

The element of hope can enter too strongly into a graph. One need not figure a scale for more than one graph at a time. If you go onto a new piece of graph paper, figure the scale all out again and, as the org rises in activity, sheet by sheet the scale can be accommodated. For example it took 18 months to get one org's statistics up by a factor of 5 (5 times the income, etc.) and that's several pieces of graph paper, so don't let scale do more than represent current expectancy.

On horizontal time scale, try not to exceed 3 months as one can get that scale too condensed too, and also too spread out where it again looks like a flat line and misinforms.

Correct scaling is the essence of good graphing.

INCORRECTLY SCALED GRAPH

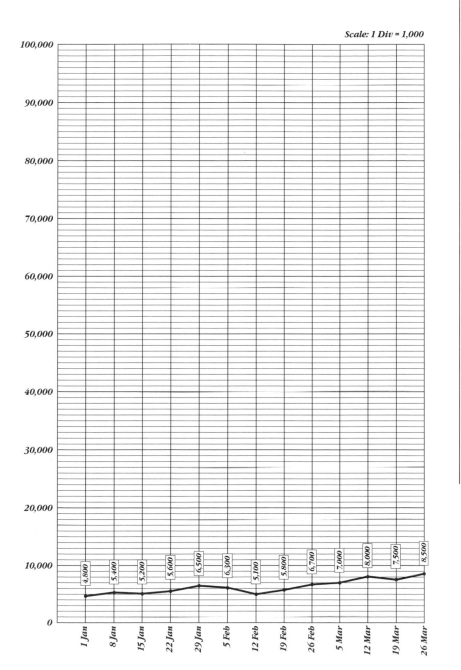

Scale: 1 Div = 1,000

CORRECTLY SCALED GRAPH

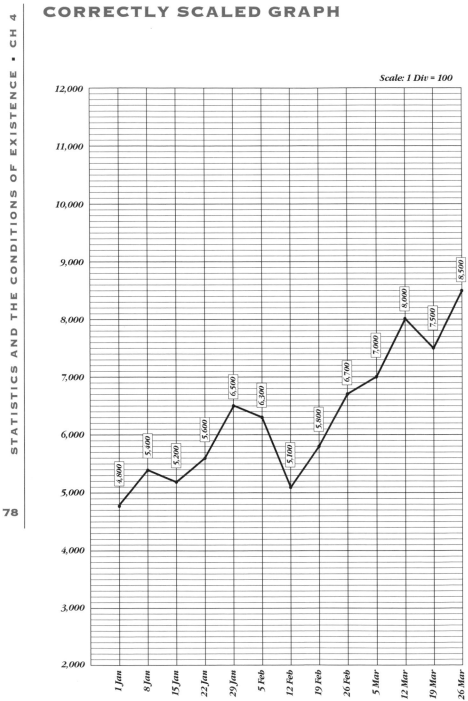

Scale: 1 Div = 100

12,000
11,000
10,000
9,000
8,000
7,000
6,000
5,000
4,000
3,000
2,000

4,800
5,400
5,200
5,600
6,500
6,300
5,100
5,800
6,700
7,000
8,000
7,500
8,500

1 Jan 8 Jan 15 Jan 22 Jan 29 Jan 5 Feb 12 Feb 19 Feb 26 Feb 5 Mar 12 Mar 19 Mar 26 Mar

READING STATISTICS

One can determine the condition of a stat by its slant on a graph.

Steep near vertical down: **Non-Existence**

Down: **Danger**

Slightly down or level: **Emergency**

Slightly up: **Normal**

Steeply up: **Affluence**

Steep near vertical down: **Non-Existence**

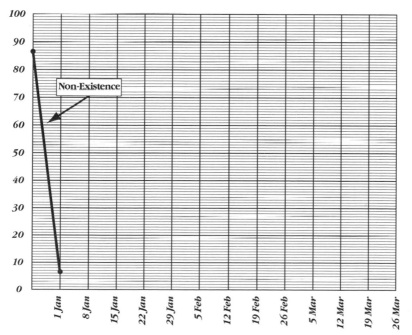

Down: Danger

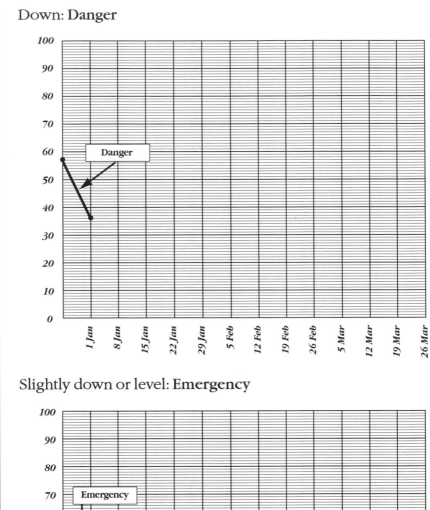

Slightly down or level: Emergency

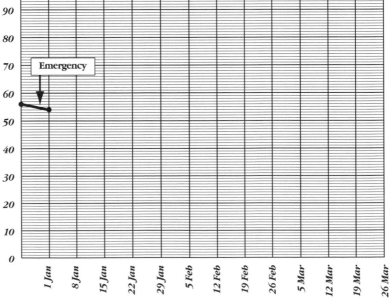

Slightly down or level: **Emergency**

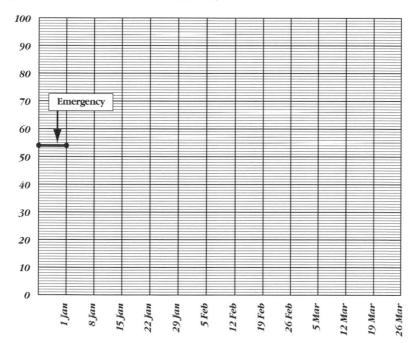

Slightly up: Normal

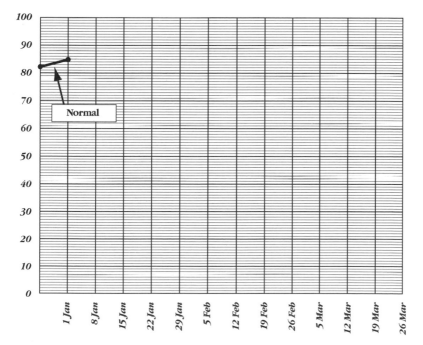

Steeply up: **Affluence**

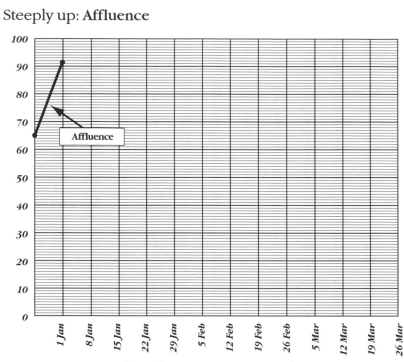

As Power is a *trend* (see later, *Statistic Trends, Stat Interpretation*), it is not judged by a single line on a graph. **Power** is a Normal trend maintained in a high, high range. Thus a Power Condition must be determined by more than one week's worth of stats.

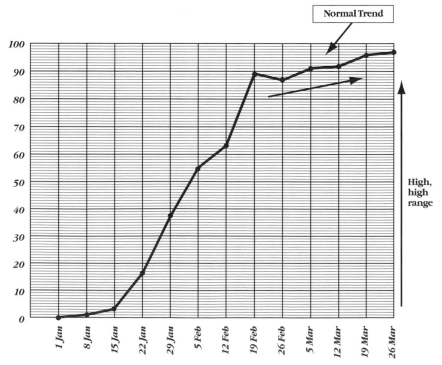

"UPSIDE DOWN" GRAPHS

he technology of graphing stats includes stats that should be graphed "upside down."

There are several ways to handle it, but a graph which when it goes down is good news and when it goes up is bad news has to be graphed differently than other graphs. Otherwise conditions can get misassigned to it.

One of the ways to handle this is to reverse the numbers on the left side of the graph so that zero is at the top. It is simply a matter of graphing the graph "upside down" so far as the numerical vertical scale on the left is concerned.

Example: Graphed in the usual way, with zero at the bottom of the graph, a decrease in disbursements could be erroneously labeled as "Emergency." If it was graphed "upside down," with zero at the top of the scale, then proper conditions could be assigned to it. When such a graph goes up, less money is being disbursed and when it goes down more money is being disbursed and you will find that the Conditions Formulas apply to it.

With disbursements graphed in this way, one could keep check on the cost of an operation. It certainly doesn't become an Emergency when the cost of an operation decreases.

One must look and determine whether an increasing number or amount of something is good or bad.

If this were put on a regular scale it would look like this:

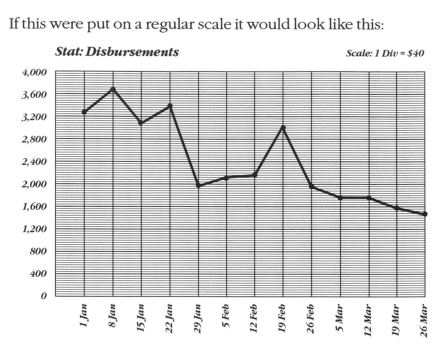

Stat: Disbursements   *Scale: 1 Div = $40*

Graphed in this way, with zero at the bottom of the graph, one could erroneously label the condition as Emergency.

Here the graph has been scaled "upside down," with zero at the top. This gives an accurate picture and shows the correct condition is Normal.

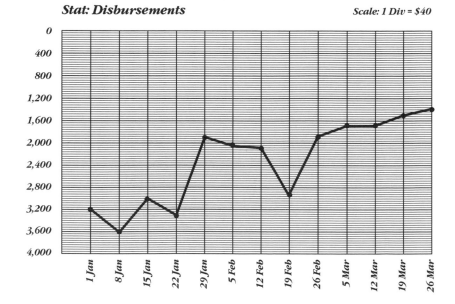

Stat: Disbursements   *Scale: 1 Div = $40*

STATISTIC TRENDS
STAT INTERPRETATION

he interpretation of statistics includes *trend*.

Trend means the tendency of statistics to average out up, level or down over several weeks or even months as long as the situation remains.

The closer one is to the scene of the stat, the more rapidly it can be adjusted and the smaller the amount of time per stat needed to interpret it.

One can interpret one's own personal statistic hour to hour.

A division head can interpret on a basis of day to day.

An Executive Secretary needs a few days' worth of stat.

An Executive Director would use a week's worth of stat.

A more remote governing body would use a *trend* (which would be several weeks) of divisional stats to interpret.

In short, the closer one is to a statistic, the easier it is to interpret it and the easier it is to change it.

One knows he had no stat on Monday—he didn't come to work. So Tuesday he tries to make up for it.

At the other end of the scale, a Continental Executive Council would have to use a trend of weeks to see what was going on.

READING STAT TRENDS

A *trend* is an inclination toward a general course or direction.

Trends can be anything from Danger to Power, depending on the slant and its steepness. It is also possible to have a Non-Existence trend.

Note: On the graphs below the dotted lines have been drawn in simply and only to show the trend—the general course or direction—these statistics are taking over a period of weeks. They are given here to educate one in the relationship between trend lines and conditions and for no other purpose. One does *not* in actuality determine a trend by drawing a dotted line or any kind of line through the graph. A trend is determined by looking. It is done with the eye. One must visually average the peaks and valleys of a stat and one looks at the period of time overall and determines the pitch or slant of the graph.

A **Non-Existence** *trend* would look like this:

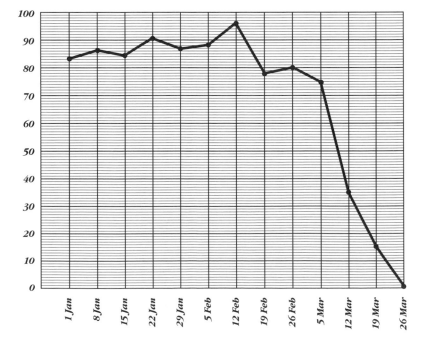

This would also be a **Non-Existence** *trend:*

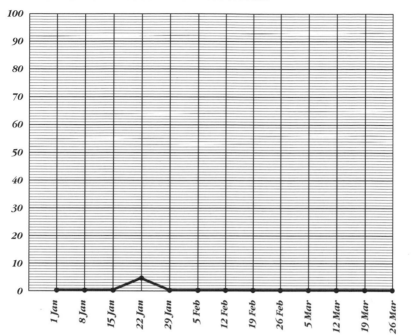

This would be a **Danger** *trend:*

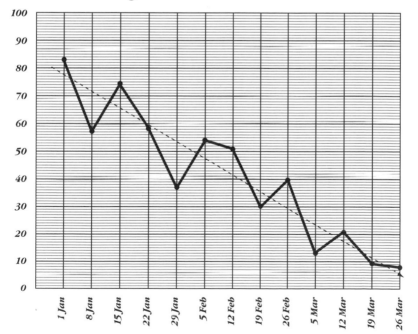

This would be an **Emergency** *trend:*

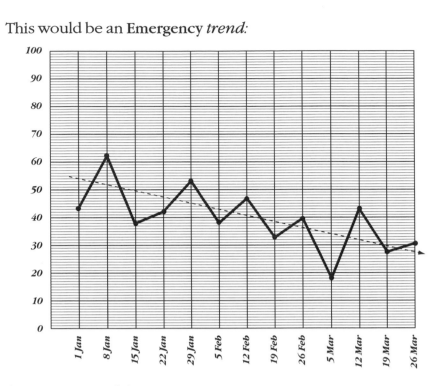

As you can see, it is not so steep.

This would also be an **Emergency** *trend* as it will collapse—nothing stays level long.

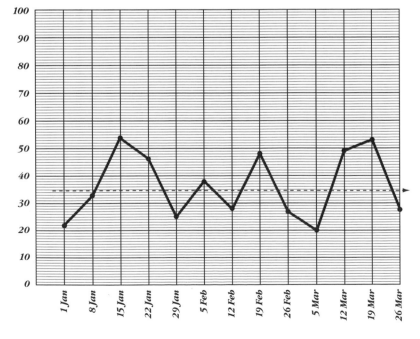

This would be a **Normal** *trend:*

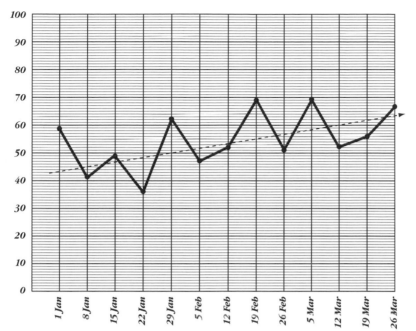

Any slight rise above level is Normal.

This would be an **Affluence** *trend:*

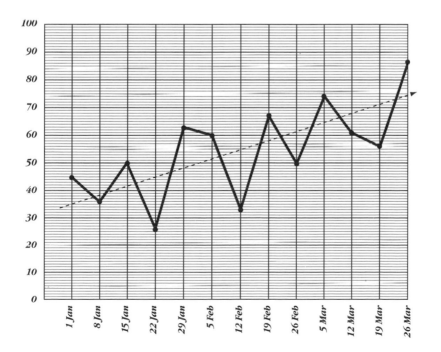

This would also be an **Affluence** *trend:*

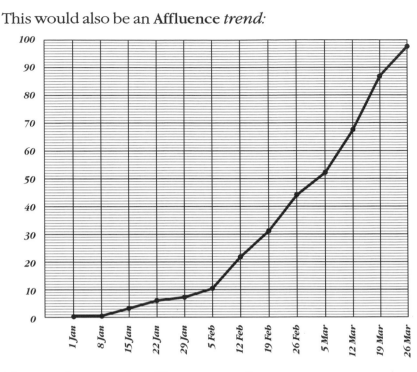

The graph is steeply Affluence trending.

This graph shows an **Affluence going into Power:**

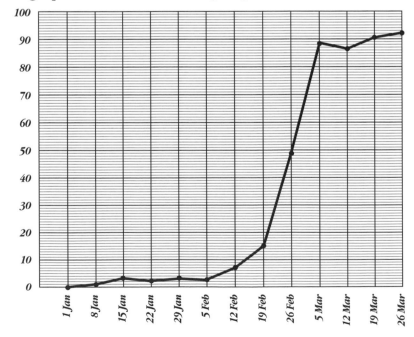

The Affluence *trend* has peaked at a new high range. Power is a Normal *trend* that is being maintained in a very, very high range.

A single day or week's graph goes into **Affluence** differently:

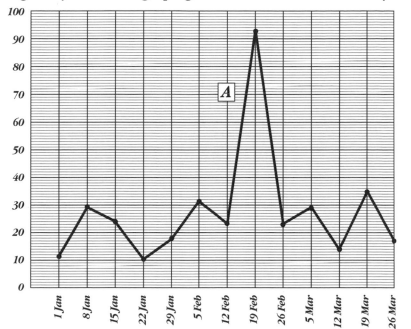

Point A is the single Affluence. The *trend* however is barely Normal as the single surge did not maintain itself.

THE
CONDITIONS
FORMULAS

CONDITION OF CONFUSION

he lowest condition is a Condition of Confusion.

In a Condition of Confusion, the being or area will be in a state of random motion. There will be no real production, only disorder or confusion.

In order to get out of Confusion, one has to find out where he is.

It will be seen that the progress upward would be, in Confusion, find out *where* you are; in Treason, find out *that* you are; and for Enemy, find out *who* you are.

CONFUSION FORMULA

The formula for Confusion is:

FIND OUT *WHERE* YOU ARE.

Note: It is important that the person who is in Confusion be cleared up on the definition of *confusion.* (This is done before the formula itself is started.)

Definitions:

1. Any set of factors or circumstances which do not seem to have any immediate solution.

   More broadly:

   A confusion in this universe is random motion. If you were to stand in heavy traffic, you would be likely to feel confused by all the motion whizzing around you. If you were to stand in a heavy storm with leaves and papers flying by, you would be likely to feel confused.

A confusion is only a confusion so long as *all* particles are in motion. A confusion is only a confusion so long as *no* factor is clearly defined or understood.

Confusion is the basic cause of stupidity.

A confusion could be called an "uncontrolled randomness." Only those who can exert some control over that randomness can handle confusions. Those who cannot exert control actually breed confusions.

2. All a confusion is, is unpatterned flow. The particles collide, bounce off each other and stay *in* the area. Thus there is no product, as to have a *product* something must flow *out*.

The additional formula for the Condition of Confusion is:

1. Locational* on the area in which one is.

2. Comparing where one is to other areas where one was.

3. Repeat step 1.

EXPANDED CONFUSION FORMULA

Where a person is in Confusion and his own MEST or the MEST of his post is messed up or in a state of disorder, then the Expanded Confusion Formula is done.

The Expanded Confusion Formula consists of all the steps given above for the Confusion Formula with the following additions:

4. The Order versus Disorder Checklist (see *Order versus Disorder*) lists all the points that need to be checked for and handled in order to get the basics of organization in on an individual or area, and all these points are checked for and handled as part of the Expanded Confusion Formula.

*A Locational is done by walking around with the person, both indoors and out-of-doors, using the commands: "Look at that (indicated object). Thank you," using objects such as a chair, a tree, a car, the floor, the ceiling, a house, etc. The person running the Locational would point at the object each time. It is simply run until the person visibly brightens up and has a cognition.

Each point is checked and any handling needed for that point is done right away before continuing with the checklist.

5. Repeat Step 1 (Locational).

Where a Condition of Confusion exists, all these steps can be done to handle the condition. On the other hand, if someone has a huge win on the first steps and comes out of Confusion, one would not force him to do all the other steps and keep him in the condition when he has actually come out of it. He would still handle the points on Order versus Disorder, but this must *not* be used to keep someone in a Condition of Confusion and refuse to upgrade him when he has come out of the condition.

The purpose of the formula is to get someone located in his present time environment, knowing where he is and where the various things he needs to operate with are, so that he is no longer in a Condition of Confusion.

For someone who is actually in a Condition of Confusion, this can be a huge win and it will start him on the road to Power. It can be a turning point in his life.

The formula is complete when the person has made it out of Confusion, knows where he is, has established order in his area and knows the basics of how to operate out of that area.

When this end result has been achieved, the person will be ready to be upgraded and move on up through the other conditions. The fact that he has not completed all steps of the formula must not be used as a reason to keep someone in Confusion when he has honestly made it out of that condition.

Lack of this condition sometimes brings about an assignment of Treason in which the person cannot actually find out that he is and so occasionally does not make it on up the conditions.

Many more persons are in this condition than is generally realized.

With the expansion of the formula, anybody who is in this condition can really make it out of Confusion and on up through the other conditions.

Doing Confusion fully and properly gives one a very firm footing so that he can make it up the conditions and be truly successful in his area.

GROUP CONFUSION FORMULA

Correct application of the Condition Formulas by a group is vital to its survival and expansion, and this includes the lower conditions and their formulas.

A group in the Condition of Confusion will be in a state of random motion; its staff will be stumbling around and running into walls, with no real production. When such an organization or group is assigned Confusion, it does *not* apply the formula "Find out *where* you are." This is a First Dynamic formula.

The formula to be applied by a group which is in the Condition of Confusion is:

FIND OUT *WHAT* YOU ARE.

Once this formula is complete, the group would apply the Treason Formula and continue up the conditions, eventually arriving at Power. Each formula is applied *for the group,* not as a personal or First Dynamic formula.

CONDITION OF TREASON

 reason is defined as betrayal after trust.

The formula for Treason is very correctly and factually "Know *that* you are."

It will be found, gruesomely enough, that a person who accepts a post or position and then doesn't function as it, will inevitably upset or destroy some portion of an org.

By not knowing that he is the _____ (post name), he is committing treason in fact.

The results of this can be found in history. A failure to be what one has the post or position name of will result in a betrayal of the functions and purposes of a group.

Almost all organizational upsets stem from this one fact:

A person in a group who, having accepted a post, does not know *that* he is a certain assigned or designated beingness is in Treason against the group.

TREASON FORMULA

The formula for the Condition of Treason is:

FIND OUT *THAT* YOU ARE.

CONDITION OF ENEMY

hen a person is an avowed and knowing enemy of an individual, a group, project or org, a Condition of Enemy exists.

ENEMY FORMULA

The formula for the Condition of Enemy is just one step:

FIND OUT *WHO* YOU REALLY ARE.

CONDITION OF DOUBT

When one cannot make up one's mind as to an individual, a group, org or project, a Condition of Doubt exists.

DOUBT FORMULA

The formula is:

1. Inform oneself honestly of the actual intentions and activities of that group, project or org, brushing aside all bias and rumor.

2. Examine the statistics of the individual, group, project or org.

3. Decide on the basis of "the greatest good for the greatest number of dynamics" whether or not it should be attacked, harmed or suppressed or helped.

4. Evaluate oneself or one's own group, project or org as to intentions and objectives.

5. Evaluate one's own or one's group, project or org's statistics.

6. Join or remain in or befriend the one which progresses toward the greatest good for the greatest number of dynamics and announce the fact publicly to both sides.

7. Do everything possible to improve the actions and statistics of the person, group, project or org one has remained in or joined.

8. Suffer on up through the conditions in the new group if one has changed sides, or the conditions of the group one has remained in if wavering from it has lowered one's status.

CONDITION OF LIABILITY

elow Non-Existence there is the Condition of Liability. The being has ceased to be simply non-existent as a team member and has taken on the color of an enemy.

It is assigned where careless or malicious and knowing damage is caused to projects, orgs or activities. It is adjudicated that it is malicious and knowing because orders have been published against it or because it is contrary to the intentions and actions of the remainder of the team or the purpose of the project or org.

It is a *liability* to have such a person unwatched as the person may do or continue to do things to stop or impede the forward progress of the project or org and such a person cannot be trusted. No discipline or the assignment of conditions above it has been of any avail. The person has just kept on messing it up.

The condition is usually assigned when several Dangers and Non-Existences have been assigned or when a long unchanged pattern of conduct has been detected.

When all others are looking for the reason mail is getting lost, such a being would keep on losing the mail covertly.

The condition is assigned for the benefit of others so they won't get tripped up trusting the person in any way.

LIABILITY FORMULA

The formula of Liability is:

1. Decide who are one's friends.

2. Deliver an effective blow to the enemies of the group one has been pretending to be part of despite personal danger.

3. Make up the damage one has done by personal contribution far beyond the ordinary demands of a group member.

4. Apply for reentry to the group by asking the permission of each member of it to rejoin and rejoining only by majority permission. And if refused, repeating (2) and (3) and (4) until one is allowed to be a group member again.

CONDITION OF NON-EXISTENCE
(NEW POST FORMULA)

Every new appointee to a post begins in Non-Existence, whether obtained by new appointment, promotion or demotion.

He is normally under the delusion that now he is *"THE _____"* (new title). He tries to start off in Power Condition as he is usually very aware of his new status or even a former status. But in actual fact *he* is the only one aware of it. All others, except perhaps the Personnel Officer, are utterly unaware of him as having his new status.

Therefore he begins in a state of Non-Existence. And if he does not begin with the Non-Existence Formula as his guide, he will be using the wrong condition and will have all kinds of trouble.

NON-EXISTENCE FORMULA

The Non-Existence Formula is:

1. Find a comm line.

2. Make yourself known.

3. Discover what is needed or wanted.

4. Do, produce and/or present it.

A new appointee taking over a going concern often thinks he had better make himself known by changing everything whereas he (a) is not well enough known to do so and (b) hasn't any idea of what is needed or wanted yet. And so he makes havoc.

Sometimes he assumes he knows what is needed or wanted when it is only a fixed idea with him and is only his idea and not true at all and so he fails at his job.

Sometimes he doesn't bother to find out what is really needed or wanted and simply assumes it or thinks he knows when he doesn't. He soon becomes "unsuccessful."

Now and then a new appointee is so "status happy" or so insecure or so shy that even when his boss or his staff comes to him and tells him what is needed or wanted, he can't or doesn't even acknowledge and really does go into Non-Existence for keeps.

Sometimes he finds that what he is *told* is needed or wanted needs reappraisal or further investigation. So it is always safest for him to make his own survey of it and operate on it when he gets his own firm reality on what is needed or wanted.

If the formula is applied intelligently the person can expect to get into a zone of bypass where people are still doing his job to fill the hole his predecessor may have left. This is a Danger Condition—but it is the next one higher than Non-Existence on the scale. If he defends his job and does his job and applies the Danger Formula, he will come through it.

He can then expect to find himself in Emergency Condition. In this, he must follow the Emergency Formula with his post and he will come through *it*.

He can now expect to be in Normal Operation and if he follows the formula of that, he will come to Affluence. And if he follows *that* formula, he will arrive at Power. And if he applies the Power Formula, he will stay there.

So it is a long way from Power that one starts his new appointment and if he doesn't go *up* the scale from where he really is at the start, he will of course fail.

This applies to groups, to organizations, to countries as well as individuals.

It also applies when a person fails at his job. He has to start again at Non-Existence and he will build up the same way condition by condition.

Most failures on post are occasioned by failures to follow the conditions and recognize them and apply the formula of the condition one is in when one is in it and cease to apply it when one is out of it and in another.

This is the secret of holding a post and being successful on a job or in life.

NON-EXISTENCE FORMULA EXPANDED

Many staff misapply the new post Non-Existence Formula or the Non-Existence Formula by stats and then wonder why they seem to continue in trouble.

Executives sometimes wonder why certain staff personnel never seem to be able to do anything right and out of exasperation go into a Phase I and wind up handling the whole area themselves.

The answer is a misapplication of and not really doing the Non-Existence Formula on post.

Experience has shown that even experienced executives and staff members have not in fact ever come out of Non-Existence. And where the org runs at all, it is carried on the back of one or two key seniors.

The phrase "find a communication line" is shortened down by too many to locating somebody's in-basket and dropping a "needed and wanted" request in it. This is not really finding a communication line.

To handle *any* post, you have to have *information* and furnish *information*. Where this is not done, the person finds himself doing projects that get rejected, projects that have to be redone, restraints put on his actions and finds himself sinking down the conditions. He gets in bad with his seniors *because he doesn't acquire and doesn't furnish* the vital information of *what is going on*.

It is the duty of any staff member, new on post or not, *to round up the communication lines that relate to his post, find out who needs vital information from him* and *get those lines in in in* as a continuing action.

When a person fails to do just that, he never comes out of Non-Existence. He isn't even up to Danger because nobody knows they are even bypassing him. In other words, when a staff member does not do that, in the eyes of the organization, he is simply a *zero*.

Orders being issued by him usually wind up *cancelled* when discovered by some senior because they are not real. Joe was already handling it. Bill's schedule was thrown out by it. Treasury yells, "How come this expensive Dev-T!"

Pretty soon, when staff hears it's so-and-so's order they just ignore it.

The bright hopes of such a staff member usually wind up as hopes he will be able to get transferred, the sooner the better. Everybody is agin him.

But what really happened?

He never applied the Non-Existence Formula for real and so he stayed in Non-Existence. His actions do not coordinate because he does *not have the lines to give or receive information*.

It is really and factually not up to anyone else to round up his lines for him any more than it is up to others to do his breathing for him. The inhale and exhale of an organization is the take and give of *vital information and particles*.

Any staff member who finds himself in apparent Non-Existence, Liability or worse, should rush around and find the comm lines that apply to his activity and post and insist that he be put on those lines.

Sometimes he is balked by security measures. Messages going out and coming in in code are not likely to be pried out of communicators, secretaries or the mail office with ease.

Well, there's a thing called a security pledge. One signs it and if the information is not safeguarded by the person, he's for it. The bulk of such information does not relate to his post anyway. But some of it may.

Such a staff member or executive has to write down what information he has to have to handle his post and what information others have to have from him to do their jobs.

And then arrange comm lines so that he is an info addressee from communicators on those lines.

Senior executives such as division heads or heads of an org do have a responsibility for briefing staff. But they are usually also faced with security problems as well as a wish to look good. And their data is general for the whole division or org. It does include specifics like "Mrs. Zikes is arriving at 1400 hours" or "The telephone company rep says the bill must be paid by 1200 hours today or we got no phones."

Havoc and Phase I occur where the bulk of the staff has omitted to get themselves on important comm lines and keep those lines flowing. Do not send to find why the stats are down if 90 percent of your staff is in Non-Existence or worse! Simply because they never really found any comm lines.

EXPANDED NON-EXISTENCE FORMULA

Therefore the Expanded Non-Existence Formula is:

1. Find and get yourself on every comm line you will need in order to give and obtain information relating to your duties and materiel.

2. Make yourself known, along with your post title and duties, to every terminal you will need for the obtaining of information and the giving of data.

3. Discover from your seniors and fellow staff members and any public your duties may require you to contact, what is needed and wanted from each.

4. Do, produce and present what each needs and wants that is in conformation with policy.

5. Maintain your comm lines that you have and expand them to obtain other information you now find you need on a routine basis.

6. Maintain your origination lines to inform others what you are doing exactly, but only those who actually need the information.

7. Streamline what you are doing, producing and presenting so that it is more closely what is really needed and wanted.

8. With full information being given and received concerning your products, do, produce and present a greatly improved product routinely on your post.

I can guarantee that if you do this—and write your info concisely so it is quick to grasp and get your data in a form that doesn't jam your own lines—you will start on up the conditions for actual and in due course arrive in Power.

CONDITION OF DANGER

hen the formula for handling a Danger Condition is not done, an org or activity or person cannot easily get above that condition thereafter.

A prolonged State of Emergency or threats to viability or survival or a prolonged single-handing will not improve unless the actual Danger Formula is applied.

DANGER FORMULA

The formula follows:

1. Bypass (ignore the junior or juniors normally in charge of the activity and handle it personally).

2. Handle the situation and any danger in it.

3. Assign the area where it had to be handled a Danger Condition.

4. Assign each individual connected with the Danger Condition a First Dynamic Danger Condition and enforce and ensure that they follow the formula completely. And if they do not do so, do a full Ethics Investigation and take all actions indicated.

5. Reorganize the activity so that the situation does not repeat.

6. Recommend any firm policy that will hereafter detect and/or prevent the condition from recurring.

The senior executive present acts and acts according to the formula above.

A Danger Condition is normally assigned when:

1. An Emergency Condition has continued too long.

2. A statistic plunges downward very steeply.

3. A senior executive suddenly finds himself or herself wearing the hat of head of the activity because it is in trouble.

FIRST DYNAMIC FORMULA

The formula is converted for the First Dynamic to:

1st 1. Bypass habits or normal routines.

1st 2. Handle the situation and any danger in it.

1st 3. Assign self a Danger Condition.

1st 4. Get in your own *personal ethics* by finding what you are doing that is out-ethics and use self-discipline to correct it and get honest and straight.

1st 5. Reorganize your life so that the dangerous situation is not continually happening to you.

1st 6. Formulate and adopt firm policy that will hereafter detect and prevent the same situation from continuing to occur.

JUNIOR DANGER FORMULA

Where a Danger Condition is assigned to a junior, request that he or she or the entire activity write up his or her overts and withholds and any known out-ethics situation and turn them in at a certain stated time on a basis that the penalty for them will be lessened but if discovered later after the deadline it will be doubled.

This done, require that the junior and the staff that had to be bypassed and whose work had to be done for them or continually corrected, each one write up and fully execute the *First Dynamic Danger Formula* for himself personally and turn it in.

When production has again increased, the Danger Condition should be formally ended and an Emergency Condition assigned and its formula should be followed.

CONDITION OF EMERGENCY

ne applies the Condition of Emergency when:

1. Statistics of an org, department or portion of an org or a person are seen to be *declining*.

2. *Unchanging* statistics of an org or a portion of an org or a person.

EMERGENCY FORMULA

1. Promote. That applies to an organization. To an individual you had better say "produce." That's the first action regardless of any other action, regardless of anything else, that is the first thing they have to put their attention on.

   Exactly what is *promotion*? Well, look it up in the dictionary. It is making things known. It is getting things out. It is getting oneself known, getting one's products out.

2. Change your operating basis. If, for instance, you went into a Condition of Emergency and then you didn't change your operation after you had promoted, you will just head for another Condition of Emergency. So that has to be part of it. You had better change your operating basis because that operating basis led you into an Emergency.

3. Economize.

4. Prepare to deliver.

5. Stiffen discipline. Part of the Condition of Emergency contains this little line of "you have got to stiffen discipline" or "you have got to stiffen ethics."

To an individual, this would simply mean not go down to the pub every Friday night. Stiffen up the discipline. Stay home and burn the midnight oil, do one's homework, etc. Be a little more regular on the job, work a little harder, don't goof quite so much, don't make so many mistakes. All of this would be part of stiffening discipline.

Organizationally, suppose the activity doesn't come out of emergency when a State of Emergency is assigned. Regardless of what caused the emergency, in spite of the fact that they have been labeled a State of Emergency, suppose the activity just doesn't come out of emergency. They have been directed to "follow the formula," they have been told to "snap and pop" and "get that thing straightened out," yet they are still found to be goofing and the statistic continues to go down. What do you do? There is only one thing left to do and that is discipline. Because life itself is going to discipline the individual.

So the rule of the game is if a State of Emergency is ignored and the steps are not taken successfully ("not taken successfully" is different than "not taken"), then you get an announcement that the condition has been continued. And if the condition is continued beyond a specified period of time, it has to walk forward into an ethics matter. Because how else could you straighten out that activity? There must be somebody goofing like crazy, sitting on most of the comm lines. You've got some ethical problem involved with it, somebody who won't function, somebody who has got the brakes on so that you can smell the smoke. And so you walk forward into an ethical situation.

CONDITION OF NORMAL

ou could call Normal a "condition of stability" and it probably should be called a condition of stability, except for this one little factor: This universe does not admit of a static state. It won't admit a no-increase, no-decrease. You cannot have a condition in this universe where there is no increase and no decrease. That's a totally stable condition and there is no such thing in this universe, from one end of it to the other. There isn't anything that always remains the same.

The Condition of Normal Operation, then, is not one of "stability," because it can't be. Normal Operation must be a routine or gradual increase. And there must be a regular, routine, gradual increase. And if there is no gradual increase, there will not be a condition of stability. You cannot have a total, even state of existence which does not eventually fall on its head. The second you get this even state in this universe, it starts to deteriorate. So a state of stability would eventually deteriorate. To prevent a deterioration, you must have an increase. That increase doesn't have to be spectacular, but it has to be something. There has to be a bit of an increase there.

NORMAL FORMULA

1. Don't change anything. The way you maintain an increase is when you are in a state of Normal Operation, you don't change anything.

2. Ethics are very mild. The justice factor is quite mild and quite reasonable. There are no savage actions taken particularly.

114

3. Every time a statistic betters, look it over carefully and find out *what* bettered it. And then do that without abandoning what you were doing before. Those are the only changes you make.

4. Every time a statistic worsens slightly, quickly find out *why* and remedy it.

And you just jockey those two factors: the statistic bettering, the statistic worsening. You will find out, inevitably, some change has been made in that area where a statistic worsens. Some *change* has been made and you better get that change off the lines in a hurry. And when you find that a statistic is bettering, you better find out *how* it is bettering.

CONDITION OF AFFLUENCE

hen you have a line going steeply up on a graph, that's Affluence. Whether it's up steeply for one week or up steeply from its last point week after week after week, it's Affluence.

When you've got an Affluence, regardless of how you did it, the Affluence Formula applies.

You *must* apply the Affluence Formula or you will be in trouble. Anyone dealing with Affluence should be aware of the following peculiarities about it.

Affluence is the most touchy condition there is. Misname it or handle it off formula and it can kill you! It is, strangely enough, the most dangerous of all conditions in that if you don't spot it and apply the formula, you spatter all over the street! Spot and handle it right and it's a rocket ride.

AFFLUENCE FORMULA

1. Economize. Now the first thing you must do in Affluence is economize and then make very, very sure that you don't buy anything that has any future commitment to it. Don't buy anything with any future commitments, don't hire anybody with any future commitments—nothing. That is all part of that economy. Clamp it down.

2. Pay every bill. Get every bill that you can possibly scrape up from anyplace, every penny you owe anywhere under the sun, moon and stars and pay them. Pull everything down in all directions until you have got it down to as close to zero as you can get or at zero.

3. Invest the remainder in service facilities. Make it more possible to deliver.

4. Discover what *caused* the Condition of Affluence and strengthen it.

ACTION AFFLUENCE FORMULA

When an Affluence exists based on a statistic measuring one's actions, and disrelated to finance, this is the formula to apply.

1. *Economize* on needless or dispersed actions that did not contribute to the present condition. Economize financially by knocking off all *waste*.

2. Make every action count and don't engage in any useless actions. Every new action to contribute and be of the same kind as *did* contribute.

3. Consolidate all gains. Any place we have gotten a gain, we keep it. Don't let things relax or go downhill or roller coaster. Any advantage or gain we have, keep it, maintain it.

4. Discover for yourself what *caused* the Condition of Affluence in your immediate area and strengthen it.

CONDITION OF POWER

Power stat is a stat in a very high range; a brand-new range in a Normal trend.

A Power stat is not just a stat that is steeply up for a long time. Nor is Power simply a very high stat. Power is not a one-week thing. Power is a *trend.*

Definition: *Power* is a Normal in a stellar range so high that it is total abundance, no doubt about it. It is a stat that has gone up into a whole new, steeply high range and maintained that range and now, in that new high range, is on a Normal trend.

Operating in this new range, you may get a slight dip in that stat now and then. But it is still Power.

There is another datum that is of importance if one is to correctly recognize and understand this condition:

Why do we call it Power?

Because there is such an abundance of production there that momentary halts or dips can't pull it down or imperil its survival.

And *that* is *Power.*

The question could be asked, "How much work can one guy do?" Or, "How many bricks can a guy lay in a day?"

Of course, a person can only work so many hours in a day. He can only get so much individual production in a day. But he can get enough production in a day to support himself. He can get his production up into such abundance that he can take some time off. That depends on his efficiency and brightness.

At a certain peak of Affluence, he will hit how many bricks he can lay. By increasing practice and efficiency, he can keep that level of production going in a Normal.

If he's laying so many bricks that nobody is ever going to think of firing him, why, he's in Power. That's a Power Condition for an individual.

POWER FORMULA

1. Don't disconnect. The first law of a Condition of Power is *don't disconnect.* That will bring about catastrophe for both you and anybody else.

   You'll find out that people whine and complain about this. How about the big boy? He's been a local boy in some town and all of a sudden he becomes a big boy. He's highly powerful on Wall Street and he never again speaks to any of his friends in the old home town. Those people resent that so much that it's almost impossible to speak to them. That is to say, if you've been in an area where you've been very well known and you suddenly become a celebrity or something like that, these people won't believe that you want to talk to them, you see? They're so used to having the formula violated. You get the idea? In other words, beings in the universe fully expect that you're going to violate the first position of the Power Condition, which is "don't disconnect." They think you're going to disconnect.

   No! Power! Position of Power! Don't disconnect. Even though you're promoted to general from colonel of a regiment, don't be such a fool as to think that you can totally disconnect from that regiment. Because the only way you *can't* disconnect from the regiment is *to* disconnect from it. You can't just deny your connections. What you've got to do is take *ownership* and *responsibility* for your connections.

2. Write up your own post.

   Now, the Condition of Power is the guy going into a Condition of Power or the organization going into a Condition of Power.

And the Condition of Power Change is actually a fellow assuming a condition which has been held from Power. You get the difference? You're replacing Bill, who was in a Condition of Power. Now, when he moves off, disconnects, then the Power Change is who took over. The first thing an upgrade of the Power has got to do is make a record of all the post's lines. That's the only way he will ever be able to disconnect. And then the assumption of this state of Power, Power Change, is governed by its own formula.

Now, for instance, I'll show you how this applies big and small. Supposing you were a very, very successful Receptionist in an organization and you were so successful that you were made the Registrar. Well, actually, that is an upgrade of Power. Now, you don't permit the person who takes over the post to operate in a condition of Power Change unless you make a total record of your post.

So, on a Condition of Power, the first thing you have to do is write up your whole post. You'll find out if you don't write up your whole post, you're going to be stuck with a piece of that post for time immemorial. And a year or so later, somebody will still be coming to you asking you about that post which you occupied because you didn't write up your post. So by writing up your post, you make it possible for the next fellow to assume that state of Power Change—of *changing nothing*—because you've shown what was there so he knows what *not* to change. But if you didn't write it up, then he could change it. That's the surest way in the world to be snapped in against some old post that you have held and that's how never to get away from a post. And you say, "These new people that take over these Reception posts are no good and they don't care." Now, let's make sure before we start being too critical: Did we ever write up this post? Did we ever really leave the post? Did we leave it in a condition that it could be left? And then, did we just negate the whole post after we left it or did we occasionally walk by and say, "How's the post coming?"

It's no sudden disconnection. That's what it really amounts to. Don't go disconnecting. And the responsibility is write the post up and get it into the hands of the guy that's going to take care of it. Now if the other guy doesn't take care of it, that's his track, that's not yours.

Do all you can to make the post occupiable. Sooner or later somebody is going to come along and occupy the post properly.*

*See The Responsibilities of Leaders for more on the Condition of Power.

CONDITION OF POWER CHANGE

here are only two circumstances which require replacement: the very successful one or the very unsuccessful one.

What a song it is to inherit a successful pair of boots. There is nothing to it. Just step in the boots and don't bother to walk. And this is somehow or another considered reprehensible by people. You are supposed to "strike out on your own," you are supposed to "put your own personality on the post." No! Put on the boots, but don't walk, man! If it was in a Normal State of Operation, which it normally would have been in for anybody to have been promoted out of it, you just don't change anything.

Power Change: *don't change anything.*

You just sit around for a while. You know immediately that all of the pressure points in the organization are going to come to you at once. The fellow who had the position before you had all these pressure points, but he must have resisted them successfully because they still exist. See? So, anybody wants anything signed that your predecessor didn't sign, don't sign it. That's an easy rule to follow, isn't it? This absolutely is the laziest position that anybody could ever occupy. And that's the only way it can be occupied—with total laziness. *Don't do anything!*

Keep your eyes open, learn the ropes and, depending on how big the organization is, after a certain time, see how it's running and run it as Normal Operating Condition. If it's not in anything but a Normal Operating Condition, just apply the Normal Operating Condition to it. Besides the little routine that's done, go around

122

and snoop around and find out what made it a little bit better that week and reinforce that. And find out what worsened a little bit and take that out. Just sniff around. By that time, you're so well acquainted with the operation, you know everybody by his first and last names, you know this, that and the other thing, you know where all the papers are, you know the favorite dodges and you've seen all these things happen and, frankly, the operation will just keep on moving on up. It will move ahead very successfully.

Go through the exact same routine of every day that your predecessor went through, sign nothing that he wouldn't sign, don't change a single order. Look through the papers that have been issued—these are the orders that are extant—and get as busy as the devil just enforcing those orders and your operation will increase and increase and increase and increase.

The keynote of the State of Power Change is study the org, Policy Letters, lines, patterns and activity and *issue no orders* that are not routine—change nothing, innovate nothing. Write up fully post just left. Mainly observe on post just taken over. Learn the new post before doing anything.

One takes over a *new* post or a collapsed post in Non-Existence. *But* a going concern is taken over by the Power Change Formula.

POWER CHANGE FORMULA

The formula of the Power Change Condition is:

When taking over a new post change nothing until you are thoroughly familiar with your new zone of power.

POWER CHANGE VIOLATION REPAIR FORMULA

A Danger Condition can be brought about by a violation of the Power Change Condition.

An example was in some transfers to form the heads of a few orgs.

None of these orgs except one were higher than Emergency. There had been a false condition. The rule is that when a false condition is assigned, the org will drop one lower than the one it is actually in.

These orgs then compounded the felony by their new heads violating the Power Change Formula almost without exception.

The new heads of orgs and some juniors, who were given new senior posts, introduced new changes, violating Power Change.

Not being briefed in and not following existing successful patterns, three of these orgs were trying to operate with greatly changed patterns, losing touch with former actions.

Power Change should have been followed by the heads and seniors. They should have studied what was going on previously.

Therefore, those who had a Power Change must apply the Power Change Violation Repair Formula:

1. Observe, question and draw up a list of what was previously successful in your area or zone of control.

2. Observe and draw up a list of all those things that were unsuccessful in your area in the past.

3. Get the successful actions *in*.

4. Throw the unsuccessful actions out.

5. Knock off frantically trying to cope or defend.

6. Sensibly get back in a working structure.

CONDITION FORMULAS, APPLICATION AND REMEDIES

CONDITIONS HANDLINGS

ne has to *do* the steps of a Condition Formula in order to improve one's condition.

And those doingnesses, which will bring about a changed condition, will then be reflected in one's statistics.

A communication I received from a staff member illustrates this perfectly.

This staff member had, for years, started each new week with a battle plan that encompassed the exact actions she had worked out to take on her post, in order to actually apply the steps of the formula for the condition she was in.

Whatever her condition at the end of the week, she did a weekly Conditions Formula write-up, worked out how she would apply the formula steps in relation to her post, and added those actions at the beginning of her battle plan. Other battle plan targets would also be included, but the weekly condition handling steps were always a part of it. This brought good results statisticwise.

When she ceased to do this and began simply battle planning needed actions without taking the condition into account, her application of the formulas on a routine basis also dropped out. The result was she suddenly found herself with crashed statistics and faced with post and production situations which needed resolving fast. And she experienced the phenomenon of feeling there was "no handling apparent" for the situation.

Of course, if one doesn't do the steps to handle a condition (the formula), then one has "no handling" for the condition!

Needless to say, this staff member, upon spotting what had happened, resumed doing her weekly formula write-ups at once!

I think there may be staff members who don't do any part of this. Aside from possibly not knowing what their stat is or what the org stat really is, they don't finish their week by assigning it a condition and writing up the formula. And so, of course, they wind up not doing the handling for the condition they're in.

There are undoubtedly some staff who think they don't have to do so if it is not in a *lower* condition. Yet they are upsetting their higher conditions by not doing so.

There is a law that holds true in this universe whereby if one does not correctly designate the condition he is in and apply its formula to his activities or if he assigns and applies the wrong condition, then the following happens: He will inevitably drop one condition below the condition he is *actually* in. Thus, if one incorrectly says he is in Power and tries to apply that formula when he is *actually* in Non-Existence, he will inevitably drop to Liability. If one incorrectly states he is in Normal when he is *actually* in Emergency, he will drop to Danger. Thus it is vital to accurately and honestly ascertain the condition one is in and apply that formula and actually do it. Otherwise one can go the route and drop down the conditions without ever understanding why. Whole nations do this and it is one of the reasons for the decline of civilizations. And while one is not a nation, one is still important enough to properly handle conditions.

And remember that it is not enough to do this as a simple administrative exercise; one actually has to *do* the formulas if he ever expects his condition to improve.

The way to never be faced with post situations for which there seems to be "no handling" is to routinely and regularly ascertain and apply the Conditions Formulas to one's post and activities.

COMPLETING CONDITIONS FORMULAS

he Ethics Conditions Formulas flow, one to the next, with the first step of one formula directly following the final step of the previous formula.

But what do you do if your stat graph indicates you've moved up a condition before you even have a chance to finish a formula? Do you just drop that formula and start on the next one? The answer is *"No."* One completes the formula he has begun.

I'll give you an example. An ED in looking over his stats sees that they are in Emergency. He immediately sees to it that the *"Promote"* step of the Emergency Formula is begun. Once that is well in hand, he begins to *"Change his operating basis."* He gets Reges onto daily drilling and puts three new auditors into his HGC.

But before he has a chance to do each of the remaining steps of the Emergency Formula, the income and delivery statistics move up into Normal Operation.

What does he do? Well, he is now in a Condition of Normal by stats. But the Normal Formula would also cause him to complete the Emergency Formula, because in the Normal Formula you drop out what is unsuccessful and you push what was successful; what was successful here was the Emergency Formula. Thus, this ED can get continued improvement on the graph by *completing* the Emergency Formula as the actions on the Emergency Formula are what got him to Normal so quickly. So he would push them until they were completed fully. This doesn't mean he is still in an Emergency Condition—the stats are now rising and the condition *is* Normal. It's a bit of an oddball thing.

As another example, suppose someone is doing a Junior Danger Formula. The person goes step by step through the procedure and writes up his or her overts and withholds and any known out-ethics situation and starts applying the First Dynamic Danger Formula. But before he completes the formula, his stats rise. It would be dangerous indeed for this person to not finish the Danger Formula (e.g., getting done the "Reorganize your life" and "Formulate and adopt firm policy" steps of the Danger Formula).

That one's stats rise before completing a formula doesn't mean he can't go into the higher condition his stats now indicate. However, it would be a grave fault not to complete the undone steps of an earlier formula. So, as in the above examples, one has to complete the earlier formula, then complete the next formula and continue on as his graph dictates.

Completing a formula is very vital. One doesn't just name a formula. He gets it *completed.*

DANGER CONDITION
RESPONSIBILITIES OF DECLARING

YPASS = Jumping the proper terminal in a chain of command.

If you declare a Danger Condition, you of course must do the work necessary to handle the situation that is dangerous.

This is also true backwards. If you start doing the work of a post on a bypass, you will of course unwittingly bring about a Danger Condition. Why? Because you unmock the people who should be doing the work.

Further, if you habitually do the work of others on a bypass, you will of course inherit all the work. This is the answer to the overworked executive. He or she bypasses. It's as simple as that. If an executive habitually bypasses, he or she will then become overworked.

Also the Condition of Non-Existence will occur.

So the more an executive bypasses, the harder he works. The harder he works on a bypass, the more the section he is working on will disappear.

So purposely or unwittingly working on a bypass, the result is always the same—Danger Condition.

If you *have* to do the work on a bypass, you *must* get the condition declared and follow the formula.

If you declare the condition, you must also do the work.

You must get the work being competently done, by new appointment or transfer or training or case review. And the condition is *not* over when the Hearings are over. It is over when that portion of the org has visibly statistically recovered.

So there are great responsibilities in declaring a Danger Condition. These are outweighed in burdensomeness by the fact that if you *don't* declare one on functions handled by those under you which go bad, it will very soon catch up with you yourself; willy-nilly and declared or not, *you* will go into a Danger Condition personally.

There's the frying pan—there's the fire. The cheerful note about it is that if the formula is applied, you have a good chance of not only rising again but also of being bigger and better than ever.

And that's the first time *that* ever happened to an executive who started down the long slide. There's hope!

There is one further footnote on a Danger Condition. I have carefully studied whether or not HCOBs and Policy Letters and actions by me were bypasses. And a search of statistics refutes it as when I give the most attention to all echelons of an org, wherever the org is, its statistics rise and when I don't they fall. Therefore we must assume that advice is not a bypass, nor is a general order by me.

Where there is disagreement on a command channel I am trying to forward, *then* a bypass occurs.

So we can assume correctly on experience and statistics that Danger Conditions occur only when there are fundamental disagreements on a command channel.

If you yourself then ferret out the disagreeable ones of those under your orders, you will clear your command lines.

Review can always find disagreements when they exist with a meter.

Where Danger Conditions are declared, the declaring executive should make an effort to find the disagreement with himself, policy, the org or Scientology as a basic Review action on persons found responsible for a Danger Condition. The only errors are not to look for them and not to find *all* the disagreements the person has on the subject of his superiors and post, policy, technology or orders.

This is why a low leadership-survey-grade person can be counted on to put wherever he is in Danger. His disagreements are too many and he doesn't execute and thereby secretly puts his superior into bypassing and a Danger Condition inevitably occurs.

It needn't occur. We have the data, now.

HANG-UP
AT DOUBT

t can occur that a person working up through the lower ethics conditions can get hung up at Doubt and not be able to complete the formula.

In such instances, a PTS condition (see *The Basics of Suppression*) or false data may be found to exist.

PTS

In the Doubt Formula, one follows the steps of the formula and by doing so is then able to make up his mind as to the individual, group, org or project the condition is being applied to. But if he's PTS, he is stuck in a problem and is unable to come to a decision.

When a person is faced with suppression, whether the actual suppression exists in present time or is a past suppression restimulated in present time, he is facing a counter-postulate.

A problem is a postulate–counter-postulate resulting in indecision. The first manifestation of and the first consequence of a problem is indecision.

Therefore a PTS condition can hang one up at Doubt.

FALSE DATA

False data can also cause a hang-up on the Doubt Formula.

In one case, a person who couldn't get through Doubt was found to be PTS to someone from an earlier group he'd been in. This SP had fed him a bunch of false data on the tech of doing his post and on what the purpose of his post was. In present time, he was still stuck with this suppressive false data—it was part of his PTSness. In addition to the usual de-PTSing actions done, the false data was cleaned up and he was then able to get through Doubt.

HANDLING

On somebody who hangs up at Doubt, the Ethics Officer or whoever is handling him should check for a PTS condition or false data.

It can be one or the other or both.

A PTS condition is of course located and handled as per the existing materials on PTS Tech.

Getting rid of the guy's false data would have to be done by someone who had checked out on the HCOB describing it.

RESULTS

When the Ethics Conditions Formulas are correctly and standardly applied, the results can be nothing short of miraculous.

With this discovery you'll get the results smoother and faster.

Use it.

ORDER VERSUS DISORDER

rder is defined as a condition in which everything is in its proper place and performs its proper function.

A person with a personal sense of order knows *what* the things in his area are, he knows *where* they are, he knows *what* they are for. He understands their value and relationship to the whole.

A personal sense of order is essential in getting out products in an area.

An orderly typist, for instance, would have all the materials requiring typing, she would have ample paper and carbons within arm's reach, she would have her correction fluid to hand, etc. With all preparatory actions done, she would sit down to type with an operational typewriter and would know what that typewriter was and what it was for.

She would be able to sit down and get her product, with no wasted motion or stops.

But let's say you had a carpenter who couldn't find his hammer and he didn't even know what a hammer was for and he couldn't find his chisel because when he picked it up he put it down and couldn't find it again and then he didn't know where his nails were. You give him a supply of lumber and he doesn't know what it's for, so he doesn't categorize it where he can put his hands on it.

How many houses do you think he would build?

The actual fact of the case is that a disordered person, operating in a disorganized area, makes a ten-minute cycle into a three-week cycle (believe it, this is true) simply because he couldn't find his ruler, lost his eraser, broke his typewriter, dropped a nut and couldn't find it again and had to send off to Seattle for another one, etc., etc., etc.

BASICS

In working with a group of nonproductive technicians, I discovered something interesting: out-basics. I actually found a lower undercut to what we generally think of when we say "basics."

These technicians had reportedly researched a key piece of equipment and had it all sorted out. But I found that they didn't even know the basic fundamental of what that machine was supposed to do and what they were supposed to be doing in their area!

That told me at once that they had no orderly files, no research data. They were losing things.

Now, if they were losing things, that opened the door to another basic: they couldn't have known where things were. They put down a tool over there and then when they needed it again they would have to look all over the place because they hadn't put it down where it belonged.

Their work was not organized so that it could be done and the tools were not known.

So I checked this out. Were they logging the things they were using in and out so they could find them again? Were they putting things away when they were done with them? No, they weren't.

This is simply the basic admin coupled with the knowledge of what the things one is working with are. It's orderliness and knowing what things are, knowing what they are for and where they are, etc. That's the undercut.

If people don't have a true knowledge of what the things they're working with are, if there are omitted tools, inoperational tools, if they don't know what their tools are supposed to do, if there are no files or, if once used, files are not reassembled and put back in the file drawer, if things get lost and people don't know where things are and so on, they will be running around spending three or four hours trying to locate a piece of paper. That isn't production.

If a person can't tell you what the things he works with are, what they're for and where they are, he isn't going to get out any product. He doesn't know what he's doing.

It's like the carpenter trying to build a house without knowing what he's got to build it with, without understanding his tools and raw materials and the basic actions he must take to get his product. That's what was holding up production in the area: disorderliness. And the basics were out.

This is actually far *below* knowing the tech of the area—the actual techniques used to get the product. The person doesn't even know what his tools and equipment are or what they're supposed to do. He doesn't know whether they are operational or inoperational. He doesn't know that when you use a tool, you return it to its proper place; when you have a despatch, you put it in a file where it can be retrieved. It undercuts even knowing the orders and Policy Letters relevant to his hat.

What are the basics that are missing? The basics of sitting down to the table that one is supposed to sit down to, to do the work! The basics of knowing what the tools, materials and equipment he works with *are* and what he's supposed to *do* with them to get his product—those are the basics that are missing.

We are down to a real reason why a person cannot turn out products. This is what is holding up such a person's production. It is well below knowing the technique of his job. Out-basics.

Does the guy know where the file is? When he finishes with that file, does he leave it scattered all over the place or does he put it back together and into the file where it can be found?

Now a person who's working will have papers all over the place, but does he know where they are and is he then going to reassemble them and put them back in order or is he going to just leave them there and pile some more papers on top of them?

If you find Project No. 2 scattered on top of Project No. 1, you know something about that area. Basics are out.

This is a little piece of tech and with that piece of tech you've got insight. You would have to have an overall picture of what the area would look like when properly ordered and organized—how it would be organized to get optimum production. Then you could inspect the area and spot what's going on. You would inspect on the basis of: How does the area compare with how it should be organized? You would find out if the personnel didn't know what the things in their area were or what they were for, you would see if they knew the value of things in the area or if there were altered importances, omitted files or filing, actions being done out of sequence, inoperational tools or equipment, anything added to the scene that was inapplicable to production, etc. In other words, you can inspect an area by outpoints against this one factor of orderliness.

This sort of out-basics and disorderliness cuts production down to nothing. There just won't be any production at all. There will be no houses built.

What we are talking about here is an orderly frame of mind. A person with a sense of order and an understanding of what he is doing sits down to write a story or a report and he'll have his paper to hand, he'll have it fixed up with carbons and he'll have his reference notes to hand. And before he touches the typewriter, he'll familiarize himself with what the scene is. He'll do the necessary preparatory work in order to get his product.

Now someone else might sit down, write something, then dimly remember there was a note someplace and then look for an hour to find where that note was and then not be able to find it and then decide that it's not important anyway and then come back and forth a few times and finally find out he's typed it all up without a carbon.

———————

There is a handling for this. Anyone trying to handle a person or an area that doesn't understand the basics of what they're dealing with and is in an utter state of disorder, must get a firm reality on the fact that *until the basics are learned and the disorder handled, the area will not produce satisfactorily.*

The following inspection is used in determining and handling the state of such an area.

INSPECTION

This inspection is done in order to determine an area's knowledge of basics and its orderliness. It can be done by an area's senior for the purpose of locating and correcting disordered areas. It is for use by anyone who is in the business of production and getting products.

The full inspection below would be done, clipboard in hand, with full notes made and *then* handlings would be worked out based on what was found in the inspection (according to the Handling section below and the suggested handlings given in parentheses below).

1. *Does he know what organization, firm or company he's in? Does he know what his post or job is?*

   This is a matter of: Does he even know where he is? Does he know what the organization or company he works for is? Does he know what the post he is holding is?

   (If he is so confused and disoriented that he doesn't even know the company or org he's in or doesn't know what his post is, he needs to apply the Expanded Confusion Formula and then work up through the conditions. Of course, the person would also need to be instant hatted on his post—the organization, his post title, his relative position on the org board, what he's supposed to produce on his post, etc. If he is doing this handling as part of his Expanded Confusion Formula, simply have him get the instant hatting and carry on with his Confusion Formula.)

2. *Ask the person what his product is.*

   Does he know? Can he tell you without comm lag or confusion?

   You may find out that he has no idea of what his product is or that he has a wrong product or that he has confusions about his product. Maybe he doesn't even know he's supposed to get out products?

   (If this is the case, he must find out what his product is. If the person's product is given in policy references, he should look these up. If his product is not covered in tech or policy references, he'll have to work out what it is.)

3. *Can he rattle off a list of the basic actions, in proper sequence, necessary to get out his product or does he hem and haw on it?*

   Does he know what to do with his product once it is completed?

   He may try to tell you what he does each day or how he handles this or that and what troubles he's having with his post. You note this, but what you're interested in is does he know the basic actions he has to take to get out his product? And does he know what to do with the product once it is complete?

   (If he can't rattle off the sequence of actions 1, 2, 3, then he'd better clay demo the basic actions, in proper sequence, necessary to get out his product and then drill these actions until he can rattle them off in his sleep. If he does not know what to do with his product once completed, then he'd need to find out and then drill handling the completed product.)

4. *Ask him what his tools are that enable him to get this product.*

Note his reaction. Can he name his tools at all? Does he include the significant tools of his area? Does he include his hat pack as a tool?

(If he doesn't know what his tools are, he'd better find out what he's operating with and what it does. A good workman knows his tools so well he can use them blindfolded, standing on his head and with one arm tied behind his back.)

5. *Ask him to show you his tools.*

Are his tools present in the work area or does he have them out of reach, down the hall or in some other room?

(He may have to reorganize his work space to get his tools within easy reach and to get in some basics of organization. The purpose of such organization would be to make production easier and faster.)

6. *Ask him to tell you what each of his tools are.*

Can he define them? Does he know what each of them are and what they are for?

(If he doesn't know, he'd better find out.)

7. *Ask him to tell you what the relationship is between each one of his tools and his product.*

(If he can't do this, have him clay demo the steps he takes to get out his products with each tool he uses, so he sees the relationship between each tool and his product.)

8. *Ask him to name off the raw materials he works with. Ask him to show you his materials.*

Does he know what his raw materials are? Are they in his work area? Are they in order? Does he know where to get them?

(He may have to find out what the raw materials of his post are [by defining them] and where they come from. He should drill procuring and handling them and then run Reach and Withdraw on them.)

9. *Does he have a file cabinet? Files? Ask him what they are.*

Does he know what they are for? Does he know what a despatch is, etc?

(He may have to be brought to an understanding of what files, file cabinets, despatches, etc., *are* and what they have to do with him and his product. He may have to clay demo the relationship between these things. He will have to set up a filing system.)

10. *Does he have a system for locating things?*

Ask to see it. Check his files. Does he have logs? Does he log things out and correct the logs when he puts them back? Are the comm baskets labeled? Does he have a specific place for supplies? Ask him to find something in his files. How long does it take?

Does he have an orderly collection of references or a library containing the materials of his field? Is it organized so as to be usable?

(If he has no system for locating things, have him set one up. Have him establish a filing system, a logging system, label the comm baskets, arrange supplies, etc. Get a reference library set up and organized. Drill using the system he has.)

11. *When he uses an item, does he put it back in the same place? Does he put it back where others can find it?*

He'll probably tell you, yes, of course he does. Look around. Are objects and files lying about? Is the place neat or is it a mess? Ask him to find you something. Does he know right where it is, or does he have to search around? Is there an accumulation of unhandled particles around?

(Have him clay demo why it might be advantageous to put things back in the same place he found them. Drill him on putting things back when he's finished with them. Have him clean up the place, handling any accumulation of unhandled particles.)

12. *If feasible, actually go with the person to his personal living area.*

Is the bed made? Is the area clean? Are things put away? How much dirty laundry does he have? Is it stowed in a bag or hamper or is it strewn about the place? People who had disorderly personal MEST, one for one, were *not* getting out any products on post—they had no sense of order.

(If his personal quarters are a mess, have him—on his own time, of course—straighten up his personal area and keep it that way on a daily basis. This will teach him what order *is*.)

HANDLING

Some areas, of course, will be found to be in excellent order and will pass the inspection. These will most likely be high production areas.

Other areas will be found to have only a few points out which would correct easily with the above handlings. These will probably be areas where some production is occurring.

Where personnel have a concept of what order is and why it is important, they will usually be eager to correct the points of disorder that have turned up on the investigation and may need no further urging, drilling or correction, but will quickly set about remedying outpoints. For many bright and willing staff members, just reading the material herein will be enough to get them to straighten out their areas right away.

There is, however, a sector which has no concept of order and may not have the slightest notion of why anyone would bother with it. You will most likely find them in apathy, overwhelm or despair with regard to their post areas. No matter what they do, they simply cannot get their products out in adequate quantity and quality. They try and try and try, but everything seems to be working against them.

When you find such a situation, know that the area is in Confusion. You are trying to handle an area which is in a confirmed, dedicated Condition of Confusion.

Such an area or individual would require the application of the Expanded Confusion Formula including the handlings above. So if these things confirm in an area, you must use the Expanded Confusion Formula and the handlings given above to full completion. Because, frankly, such an area or individual *is* in a Condition of Confusion and will remain in Confusion until the Expanded Confusion Formula, including the full handlings from the inspection, are applied.

Once out of Confusion, the person would have to be brought up through the rest of the conditions.

CAUTION

The Condition of Confusion is a very low condition and should never be assigned where it is not warranted. Where one or two points on the above inspection were found to be out in an area, and where these corrected easily, there would be no purpose in assigning Confusion to that area. In fact, it may worsen an area to assign an incorrect condition.

But where you have a long-term situation of no or few products combined with a state of disorder, know that the area or individual is in a Condition of Confusion and that the application of the Confusion Formula plus the handlings given here will bring the area out of the muck and up to square one where it can *begin* producing.

Note: If the inspection is done on a person or area and some of the points are found to be out and handlings are done, but no Condition of Confusion is assigned, the area must be reinspected about a week later. This way you will detect if an actual Condition of Confusion was missed, as the area will have lapsed back into disorderliness or will have worsened.

SUMMARY

A knowledge of the basics of an area and having orderliness in an area are essential to production.

When you find a fellow who is a light-year away from the basics and doesn't have a clue on the subject of order and he's flying way up in the sky someplace instead of just trying to put together what he's supposed to put together or do what he's supposed to do, you've got your finger on his Why for no production.

With the inspection and handlings given here, we can now handle any degree of disorderliness and disorganization.

And order will reign.

Nonproductive areas become capable of producing.

Already-producing areas increase their production.

And production will roll.

An Essay
on Power

THE RESPONSIBILITIES OF LEADERS

few comments on *power,* being or working close to or under a power, which is to say a leader or one who exerts wide primary influence on the affairs of men.

I have written it this way, using two actual people, to give an example of magnitude enough to interest and to furnish some pleasant reading. And I used a military sphere so it could be seen clearly without restimulation of admin problems.

The book referenced is a fantastically able book by the way.

THE MISTAKES OF SIMÓN BOLÍVAR AND MANUELA SÁENZ

> *Reference:* The book entitled: *The Four Seasons of Manuela* by Victor W. von Hagen, a biography.

Simón Bolívar was the Liberator of South America from the yoke of Spain.

Manuela Sáenz was the Liberatress and Consort.

Their acts and fates are well recorded in this moving biography.

But aside from any purely dramatic value, the book lays bare and motivates various actions of great interest to those who lead, who support or are near leaders.

Simón Bolívar was a very strong character. He was one of the richest men in South America. He had real personal ability given to only a handful on the planet. He was a military commander without peer in history. Why he would fail and die an exile to be later deified is thus of great interest. What mistakes did he make?

Manuela Sáenz was a brilliant, beautiful and able woman. She was loyal, devoted, quite comparable to Bolívar, far above the cut of average humanoids. Why then did she live a vilified outcast, receive such violent social rejection and die of poverty and remain unknown to history? What mistakes did she make?

BOLÍVAR'S ERRORS

The freeing of things is the reverse unstated dramatization (the opposite side of the coin) to the slavery enjoined by the mechanisms of the mind. Unless there is something to free men *into,* the act of freeing is simply a protest of slavery. And as no humanoid *is* free while aberrated in the body cycle, it is of course a gesture to free him politically as it frees him only into the anarchy of dramatizing his aberrations with *no* control whatever. And without something to fight exterior and with no exteriorization of his interest, he simply goes mad noisily or quietly.

Once as great a wrong as depraving beings has been done, there is of course no freedom short of freeing one from the depravity itself or *at least* from its most obvious influences in the society. In short, one would have to de-aberrate a man before his whole social structure could be de-aberrated.

If one lacked the whole ability to free Man wholly from his reactive patterns, then one could free Man from their restimulators in the society at least. If one had the whole of the data (but lacked the Scientology Tech), one would simply use reactive patterns to blow the old society apart and then pick up the pieces neatly in a new pattern. If one had no inkling of how reactive one can get (and Bolívar of course had no knowledge whatever in that field), there yet remained a workable formula used "instinctively" by most successful, practical political leaders:

If you free a society from those things you see wrong with it and use force to demand it do what is right, and if you carry forward with decision and thoroughness and without continual temporizing, you can, in the applications of your charm and gifts, bring about a great political reform or improve a failing country.

So Bolívar's first error, most consistent it was, too, was contained in the vital words "you see" in the above paragraph. He didn't look and he didn't even listen to sound intelligence reports. He was so *sure* he could *glow* things right or fight things right or charm things right that he never looked for anything wrong to correct until it was too late. This is the ne plus ultra of personal confidence, amounting to supreme vanity. "When he appeared it would all come right" was not only his belief, but his basic philosophy. So the first time it didn't work, he collapsed. All his skills and charm were channeled into this one test. Only that could he observe.

Not to compare with Bolívar but to show my understanding of this:

I once had a similar one. "I would keep going as long as I could and when I was stopped I would then die." This was a solution mild enough to state and really hard to understand until you had an inkling of what I meant by keeping going. Meteors keep going—very, very fast. And so did I. Then one day, ages back, I finally *was* stopped—after countless little stoppings by social contacts and family to prepare me, culminating in a navy more devoted to braid than dead enemies—and literally I quit. For a while I couldn't get a clue of what was wrong with me. Life went completely unlivable until I found a *new* solution. So I know the frailty of these single solutions. Not to compare myself but just to show it happens to us all, not just Bolívars.

Bolívar had no personal insight at all. He could only "outsight" and even then he did not look or listen. He *glowed* things right. Pitifully, it was his undoing that he could. Until he no longer could. When he couldn't glow he roared and when he couldn't roar he fought a battle. Then civic enemies were not military enemies so he had no solution left at all.

It *never* occurred to him to do more than personally *magnetize* things into being right and victorious.

His downfall was that he made far too heavy a use of a skill simply because it was easy. He was too good at this one thing. So he never looked to any other skill and he never even dreamed there was any other way.

He had no view of any situation and no idea of the organizational or preparatory steps necessary to political and personal victory. He only knew military organization which is where his organizational insight ceased.

He was taught on the high wine of French revolt, notorious in its organizational inability to form cultures, and that fatally by a childhood teacher who was intensely impractical in his own private life (Simón Rodriguez, an unfrocked priest turned tutor).

Bolívar had no personal financial skill. He started wealthy and wound up a pauper, a statistic descending from one of the, if not the, richest man in South America down to a borrowed nightshirt to be buried in as an exile. And *this* while the property of royalists was wide open, the greatest land and mine valuables of South America wide open to his hand, and that's not believable! But true. He never collected his own debt of loans to governments even when the head of those governments.

So it is no wonder we find two more very real errors leading to his downfall: He did not get his troops or officers *rewarded* and he did not aim for any solvency of the states he controlled. It was all right if there were long years of battle ahead for them to be unpaid as no real riches were yet won, but not to *reward* them when the whole place was at his disposal! Well!

The limit of his ability consisted of demanding a bit of cash for current pay from churches—which were not actively against him at first, but which annoyed them no end—and a few household expenses.

He could have (and should have) set aside all royalist property and estates for division amongst his officers, their men and his supporters. It had no owners now. And this failure cost the economy of the country the tax loss of all those productive estates (the whole wealth of the land). So it is no wonder his government, its taxable estates now inoperative or at best hoarded by a profiteer or looted by Indians, was insolvent. Also, by failing to do such an obvious act, he delivered property into the hands of more provident enemies and left his officers and men penniless to finance any support for their own stability in the new society and so for his own.

As for state finance, the great mines of South America, suddenly ownerless, were overlooked and were then grabbed and worked by foreign adventurers who simply came in and took them without payment.

Spain had run the country on the finance of mine tithes and general taxes. Bolívar not only didn't collect the tithes, he let the land become so worthless as to be untaxable. He should have gotten the estates going by any shifts and should have state operated all royalist mines once he had them. To not do these things was complete, but typically humanoid, folly.

In doing this property division, he should have left it all up to officers committees operating as courts of claim without staining his own hands in the natural corruption. He was left doubly open as he not only did not attend to it, he also got the name of corruption when anybody did grab something.

He failed as well to recognize the distant widespread nature of his countries despite all his riding and fighting over them and so sought tightly centralized government, not only centralizing states but also centralizing the various nations into a federal state. And this over a huge landmass full of insurmountable ranges, impassable jungles and deserts and without mail, telegraph, relay stages, roads, railroads, river vessels or even footbridges repaired after a war of attrition.

A step echelon from a pueblo (village) to a state, from a state to a country and a country to a federal state was only possible (in such huge spaces of country where candidates could never be known personally over any wide area and whose opinions could not even be circulated more than a few miles of burro trail) where only the pueblo was democratic and the rest all appointive from pueblo on up, himself the ratifier of titles if he even needed that. With his own officers and armies controlling the land, as owners of all wrested from royalists and the Crown of Spain, he would have had no revolts. There would have been little civil wars, of course, but a court to settle their final claims could have existed at federal level and kept them traveling so much over those vast distances, it would have crippled their enthusiasm for litigation on the one hand and, on the other, by dog-eat-dog settlements, would have given him the strongest rulers—if he took neither side.

He did not step out and abdicate a dictatorial position. He mistook military acclaim and ability for the tool of peace. War only brings anarchy, so he had anarchy. Peace is more than a "command for unity," his favorite phrase. A productive peace is getting men busy and giving them something to make something of that they *want* to make something of and telling them to get on with it.

He never began to recognize a Suppressive and never considered anyone needed killing except on a battlefield. There it was glorious. But somebody destroying his very name and soul, and the security of every supporter and friend, the SP Santander, his vice-president, who could have been arrested and executed by a corporal's guard on one one-hundredth of available evidence, who could suborn the whole treasury and population against him, without Bolívar, continually warned, loaded with evidence, ever even reprimanding him. And this brought about his loss of popularity and his eventual exile.

He also failed in the same way to protect his military family or Manuela Sáenz from other enemies. So he weakened his friends and ignored his enemies just by oversight.

His greatest error lay in that while dismissing Spain he did not dismiss that nation's most powerful minion, the Church, and did not even localize it or reward a South American separate branch to loyalty or do anything at all (except extort money from it) to an organization which continually worked for Spain as only it could work—on every person in the land in a direct anti-Bolívar reign of terror behind the scenes. You either suborn such a group or you take them out when they cease to be universal and become or are an enemy's partner.

As the Church held huge properties and as Bolívar's troops and supporters went *unpaid* even of the penny soldiers' pay, if one was going to overlook the royalist estates, one could at least have seized the Church property and given it to the soldiers. General Vallejo did this in 1835 in California, a nearly contemporary act, with no catastrophe from Rome. Or the penniless countries could have taken them over. You don't leave an enemy financed and solvent while you let your friends starve in a game like South American politics. Oh no.

He wasted his enemies. He exported the "godos" or defeated royalist soldiers. They mostly had no homes but South America. He issued no amnesties they could count on. They were shipped off or left to die in the "ditch"—the best artisans in the country among them.

When one (General Rodil) would not surrender Callao fortress after Peru was *won,* Bolívar, after great gestures of amnesty, failed to obtain surrender and then fought the fort. Four thousand political refugees and four thousand royalist troops died over many months in full sight of Lima, fought heavily by Bolívar only because the *fort* was fighting. But Bolívar had to straighten up Peru urgently, not fight a defeated enemy. The right answer to such a foolish commander as Rodil, as Bolívar did have the troops to do it, was to cover the roads with cannon enfilade potential to discourage any sortie from the fort, put a larger number of his own troops in a distant position of offense but ease and comfort and say, "We're not going to fight. The war's over, silly man. Look at the silly fellows in there, living on rats when they can just walk out and sleep home nights or go to Spain or enlist with me or just go camping," and let anybody walk in and out who pleased, making the fort commander (Rodil) the prey of every pleading wife and mother without and would-be deserter or mutineer within, until he did indeed sheepishly give up the pretense—a man cannot fight alone. But battle was glory to Bolívar. And he became intensely disliked because the incessant cannonade which got nowhere was annoying.

Honors meant a great deal to Bolívar. To be liked was his life. And it probably meant more to him than to see things really right. He never compromised his principles but he lived on admiration, a rather sickening diet since it demands in turn continuous "theater." One is what one is, not what one is admired or hated for. To judge oneself by one's successes is simply to observe that one's postulates worked and breeds confidence in one's ability. To have to be *told* it worked only criticizes one's own eyesight and hands a spear to the enemy to make his wound of vanity at his will. Applause is nice. It's great to be thanked and admired. But to work only for that?

And his craving for that, his addiction to the most unstable drug in history—fame—killed Bolívar. That self-offered spear. He told the world continually how to kill him—reduce its esteem. So as money and land can buy any quantity of cabals, he could be killed by curdling the esteem, the easiest thing you can get a mob to do.

He had all the power. He did not use it for good or evil. One cannot hold power and not use it. It violates the Power Formula. For it then prevents *others* from doing things if *they* had some of the power, so they then see as their only solution the destruction of the holder of the power as he, not using power or delegating it, is the unwitting block to all their plans. So even many of his friends and armies finally agreed he had to go. They were not able men. They were in a mess. But bad or good, they had to do *something*. Things were desperate, broken-down and starving after fourteen years of civil war. Therefore they either had to have *some* of that absolute power or else nothing could be done at all. They were not great minds. He did not need any "great minds," he thought, even though he invited them verbally. He saw their petty, often murderous solutions and he rebuked them. And so held the power and didn't use it.

He could not stand another *personality* threat.

The trouble in Peru came when he bested its real conqueror (from the Argentine), San Martín, in a petty triumph over adding Guayaquil to Colombia. Bolívar wished to look triumphant again and didn't notice it really cost him the support and Peru the support of San Martín—who understandably resigned and went home, leaving Bolívar *Peru to conquer*. Unfortunately, it had already been in his hands. San Martín needed some troops to clean up a small royalist army, that was all. San Martín didn't need Peru's loss of Guayaquil—which never did anybody any real good anyway!

Bolívar would become inactive when faced with two areas' worth of problems. He did not know which way to go. So he did nothing.

Brave beyond any general in history on the battlefield, the Andes or in torrential rivers, he did not really have the bravery needed to trust inferior minds and stand by their often shocking blunders. He feared their blunders. So he did not dare unleash his many willing hounds.

He could lead men, make men feel wonderful, make men fight and lay down their lives after hardships no army elsewhere in the world has ever faced before or since. But he could not *use* men even when they were begging to be used.

It is a frightening level of bravery to use men you know can be cruel, vicious and incompetent. He had no fear of their turning on him ever. When they finally did, only then he was shocked. But he protected "the people" from authority given to questionably competent men. So he really never used but three or four generals of mild disposition and enormously outstanding ability. And to the rest he denied power. Very thoughtful of the nebulous "people" but very bad indeed for the general good. And it really caused his death.

No. Bolívar was theater.

It was all theater. One cannot make such errors and still pretend that one thinks of life as life, red-blooded and factual. Real men and real life are full of dangerous, violent, live situations and wounds *hurt* and starvation is desperation itself, especially when you see it in one you love.

This mighty actor, backed up with fantastic personal potential, made the mistake of thinking the theme of liberty and his own great role upon the stage was enough to interest all the working, suffering hours of men, buy their bread, pay their whores, shoot their wives' lovers and bind their wounds or even put enough drama into very hard-pressed lives to make them want to live it.

No, Bolívar was unfortunately the only actor on the stage and no other man in the world was real to him.

And so he died. They loved him. But they were also on the stage too, where they were dying in his script or Rousseau's script for liberty but no script for living their very real lives.

He was the greatest military general in any history, measured against his obstacles, the people and the land across which he fought.

And he was a complete failure to himself and his friends.

While being one of the greatest *men* alive at that. So we see how truly shabby others in leaders' boots amongst men must be.

MANUELA SÁENZ

The tragedy of Manuela Sáenz as Bolívar's mistress was that she was never *used*, never really had a share and was neither protected nor honored by Bolívar.

Here was a clever, spectacular woman of fantastic fidelity and skill, with an enormous "flair," capable of giving great satisfaction and service. And only her satisfaction ability was taken and that not consistently nor even honestly.

In the first place, Bolívar never married her. He never married anybody. This opened up a fantastic breach in any defense she could ever make against hers or his enemies who were legion. So her first mistake was in not in some way contriving a marriage.

That she had an estranged husband she had been more or less sold to was permitted by her to wreck her life obliquely.

She was too selfless to be real in all her very able plotting.

For this marriage problem she could have engineered any number of actions.

She had the solid friendship of all his trusted advisers, even his old tutor. Yet she arranged nothing for herself.

She was utterly devoted, completely brilliant and utterly incapable of really bringing off an action of any final kind.

She violated the Power Formula in not realizing that she had power.

Manuela was up against a hard man to handle. But she did not know enough to make her own court effective. She organized one. She did not know what to do with it.

Her most fatal mistake was in not bringing down Santander, Bolívar's chief enemy. That cost her everything she had before the end and after Bolívar died. She knew for *years* Santander had to be killed. She said it or wrote it every few days. Yet never did she promise some young officer a nice night or a handful of gold to do it in a day when *dueling was in fashion*. It's like standing around discussing how the plainly visible wolf in the garden that's eating the chickens must be shot, even holding a gun, and never even lifting it while all one's chickens vanish for years.

In a land overridden with priests she never got herself a tame priest to bring about her ends.

She was a fantastic intelligence officer. But she fed her data to a man who could not act to protect himself or friends, who could only fight armies dramatically. She did not see this and also quietly take on the portfolio of secret police chief. Her mistake was waiting to be asked—to be asked to come to him, to act.

She voluntarily was his best political intelligence agent. Therefore she should have also assumed further roles.

She guarded his correspondence, was intimate with his secretaries. And yet she never collected or forged or stole any document to bring down enemies, either through representations to Bolívar or a court circle of her own. And in an area with that low an ethic, that's fatal.

She openly pamphleteered and fought violently as in a battle against her rabble.

She had a great deal of money at her disposal. In a land of for-sale Indians she never used a penny to buy a quick knife or even a solid piece of evidence.

When merely opening her lips she could have had any sequestrated royalist estate, she went to litigation for a legitimate legacy never won and another won but never paid.

They lived on the edge of quicksand. She never bought a plank or a rope.

Carried away by the glory of it all, devoted completely, potentially able and a formidable enemy, she did not *act*.

She waited to be told to come to him even when he lay dying and exiled.

His command over her who never obeyed any other was too absolute for his own or her survival.

Her assigned mistakes (pointed out at the time as her caprice and playacting) were not her errors. They only made her interesting. They were far from fatal.

She was not ruthless enough to make up for his lack of ruthlessness and not provident enough to make up for his lack of providence.

The ways open to her for finance, for action, were completely doorless. The avenue stretched out to the horizon.

She fought bravely but she just didn't take action.

She was an actress for the theater alone.

And she died of it. And she let Bolívar die because of it.

Never once did Manuela look about and say, "See here, things mustn't go this wrong. My lover holds half a continent and even I hold the loyalty of battalions. Yet that woman threw a fish!"

Never did Manuela tell Bolívar's doctor, a rumored lover, "Tell that man he will not live without my becoming a constant part of his entourage, and tell him until he believes it or we'll have a new physician around here."

The world was open. Where Theodora, the wife of Emperor Justinian I of Constantinople, a mere circus girl and a whore, ruled harder than her husband but for her husband behind his back—and made him marry her as well—Manuela never had any bushelbasket of gold brought in to give Bolívar for his unpaid troops with a "Just found it, dear" to his "Where on earth...?" after the royalist captives had been carefully ransomed for jail escapes by her enterprising own entourage and officer friends. She never handed over any daughter of a family clamoring against her to troops and then said, "Which ververbal family is next?"

She even held a colonel's rank but only used it because she wore man's clothing afternoons. It was a brutal, violent, ruthless land, not a game of musical chairs.

And so Manuela, penniless, improvident, died badly and in poverty, exiled by enemies and deserted by her friends.

But why not deserted by her friends? They had all been poverty-stricken to a point quite incapable of helping her even though they wanted to. For she once had the power to make them solvent. And didn't use it. They were in poverty before they won but they did eventually control the land. After that, why make it a bad habit?

––––––––––––

And so we see two pathetic, truly dear but tinsel figures, both on a stage, both *far* removed from the reality of it all.

And one can say, "But if they had not been such idealists they never would have fought so hard and freed half a continent," or "If she had stooped to such intrigue or he had been known for violent political actions they would never have had the strength and never would have been loved."

All very idealistic itself. They died "in the ditch" unloved, hated and despised, two decent, brave people, almost too good for this world.

A true hero, a true heroine. But on a stage and not in life. Impractical and improvident and with no faintest gift either one to use the power they could assemble.

This story of Bolívar and Manuela is a tragedy of the most piteous kind.

They fought a hidden enemy, the Church, they were killed by their friends.

But don't overlook how impractical it is not to give your friends power enough when you have it to give. You can always give some of it to another if the first one collapses through inability. And one can always be brought down like a hare at a hunt who seeks to use the delegated power to kill you—if you have the other friends.

Life is not a stage for posturing and "Look at me!" "Look at me." "Look at me." If one is to lead a life of command or a life near to command, one must handle it as life. Life bleeds. It suffers. It hungers. And it has to have the right to shoot its enemies until such time as comes a golden age.

Aberrated Man is not capable of supporting, in his present state, a golden declared age for three minutes, given all the tools and wealth in the world.

If one would live a life of command or one near to a command, one must then accumulate power as fast as possible and delegate it as quickly as feasible and use every humanoid in long reach to the best and beyond his talents if one is to live *at all.*

If one does not choose to live such a life, then go on the stage and be a real actor. Don't kill men while pretending it isn't real. Or one can become a recluse or a student or a clerk. Or study butterflies or take up tennis.

For one is committed to certain irrevocable natural laws the moment one starts out upon a conquest, either as the man in charge or a person near to him or on his staff or in his army. And the foremost law, if one's ambition is to win, is of course to win. But also to keep on providing things to win and enemies to conquer.

Bolívar let his cycle run to "freedom" and end there. He never had another plan beyond that point. He ran out of territory to free. Then he didn't know what to do with it and didn't know enough, either, to find somewhere else to free. But of course all limited games come to end. And when they do, the players fall over on the field and become rag dolls unless somebody at least tells them the game has ended and they have no more game nor any dressing room or homes but just that field.

And they lie upon the field, not noticing there can be no more game since the other team has fled, and after a bit they have to do *something.* And if the leader and his consort are sitting over on the grass being rag dolls too, of course there isn't any game. And so the players start fighting amongst themselves just to have a game. And if the leader then says, "No, no," and his consort doesn't say, "Honey, you better phone the Baltimore Orioles for Saturday," then of course the poor players, bored stiff, say, "He's out." "She's out." "Now we're going to split the team in half and have a game."

And that's what happened to Bolívar and Manuela. They *had* to be gotten rid of for there was no game and they didn't develop one to play while forbidding the only available game—minor civil wars.

A *whole continent* containing the then major mines of the world, whole populations were left sitting there, "freed." But none owned any of it though the former owners had left. They weren't given it. Nor were they made to manage it. No game.

And if Bolívar had not been smart enough for that, he could at least have said, "Well! You monkeys are going to have quite a time getting the wheels going but that's not my job. You decide on your type of government and what it's to be. Soldiers are my line. Now, I'm taking over those old estates of mine and the royalist ones nearby and the emerald mines just as souvenirs and me and Manuela, we're going home." And he should have said that fifteen minutes after the last royalist army was defeated in Peru.

And his official family with him, and a thousand troops to which he was giving land would have moved right off smartly with him. And the people after a few screams of horror at being deserted would have fallen on each other, sabered a state together here and a town there and gotten busy out of sheer self-protection in a vital new game, "Who's going to be Bolívar now?"

Then when home he should have said, "Say those nice woods look awfully royalist to me, and also those 1,000,000 hectares of grazing land, Manuela. Its owner once threw a royalist fish, remember? So that's yours."

And the rest of the country would have done the same and gotten on with the new game of "You was a royalist."

And Bolívar and Manuela would have had statues built to them by the TON at once as soon as agents could get to Paris with orders from an adoring populace.

"Bolívar, come rule us!" should have gotten an "I don't see any unfree South America. When you see a French or Spanish army coming, come back and tell me."

That would have worked. And this poor couple would have died suitably adored in the sanctity of glory and (perhaps more importantly) in their own beds, not "in a ditch."

And if they had *had* to go on ruling, they could have declared a new game of "pay the soldiers and officers with royalist land."

And when that was a gone game, "Oust the Church and give its land to the poor friendly Indians."

You can't stand bowing back of the footlights forever with no show even if you are quite an actor. Somebody else can make better use of any stage than even the handsomest actor who will not use it.

Man is too aberrated to understand at least seven things about power:

1. Life is lived by lots of people. And if you lead, you must either let them get on with it or lead them on with it actively.

2. When the game or the show is over, there must be a new game or a new show. And if there isn't, somebody else is jolly well going to start one and if you won't let *anyone* do it, the game will become "getting you."

3. If you have power, use it or delegate it or you sure won't have it long.

4. When you have people, use them or they will soon become most unhappy and you won't have them anymore.

5. When you move off a point of power, pay all your obligations on the nail, empower all your friends completely and move off with your pockets full of artillery, potential blackmail on every erstwhile rival, unlimited funds in your private account and the addresses of experienced assassins and go live in Bulgravia and bribe the police. And even then you may not live long if you have retained one scrap of domination in any camp you do not now control or if you even say, "I favor politician Jiggs." Abandoning power *utterly* is dangerous indeed.

   But we can't all be leaders or figures strutting in the limelight and so there's more to know about this:

6. When you're close to power, get some delegated to you, enough to do your job and protect yourself and your interests, for you can be shot, fellow, shot, as the position near power

is delicious but dangerous, dangerous always, open to the taunts of any enemy of the power who dare not really boot the power but can boot you. So to live at all in the shadow or employ of a power, you must yourself gather and *use* enough power to hold your own—without just nattering to the power to "kill Pete," in straightforward or more suppressive veiled ways to him, as these wreck the power that supports yours. He doesn't have to know all the bad news and if he's a power really, he won't ask all the time, "What are all those dead bodies doing at the door?" And if you are clever, you never let it be thought *he* killed them—that weakens you and also hurts the power source. "Well, boss, about all those dead bodies, nobody at all will suppose you did it. *She* over there, those pink legs sticking out, didn't like me." "Well," he'll say if he really is a power, "why are you bothering me with it if it's done and you did it. Where's my blue ink?" Or "Skipper, three shore patrolmen will be along soon with your cook, Dober, and they'll want to tell you he beat up Simson." "Who's Simson?" "He's a clerk in the enemy office downtown." "Good. When they've done it, take Dober down to the dispensary for any treatment he needs. Oh yes. Raise his pay." Or "Sir, could I have the power to sign divisional orders?" "Sure."

7. And lastly and most important, for we all aren't on the stage with our names in lights, always push power in the direction of anyone on whose power you depend. It may be more money for the power, or more ease, or a snarling defense of the power to a critic or even the dull thud of one of his enemies in the dark or the glorious blaze of the whole enemy camp as a birthday surprise.

If you work like that and the power you are near or depend upon is a power that has at least some inkling about how to be one, and if you make others work like that, then the power-factor expands and expands and expands and you too acquire a sphere of power bigger than you would have if you worked alone. Real powers are developed by tight conspiracies of this kind pushing someone up in whose leadership they have faith. And if they are right and also manage their man and keep him from collapsing through overwork, bad temper or bad data, a kind of juggernaut builds up. Don't ever feel weaker because you work for somebody stronger. The only failure lies in taxing or pulling down the strength on which you depend. All failures to remain a power's power are failures to contribute to the strength and longevity of the work, health and power of that power. Devotion requires active contribution outwards from the power as well as in.

If Bolívar and Manuela had known these things, they would have lived an epic, not a tragedy. They would not have died "in the ditch," he bereft of really earned praise for his real accomplishments even to this day. And Manuela would not be unknown even in the archives of her country as the heroine she was.

Brave, brave figures. But if this can happen to such stellar personalities gifted with ability tenfold over the greatest of other mortals, to people who could take a rabble in a vast impossible land and defeat one of Earth's then foremost powers, with no money or arms, on personality alone, what then must be the ignorance and confusion of human leaders in general, much less little men stumbling through their lives of boredom and suffering?

Let us wise them up, huh? You *can't* live in a world where even the great leaders can't lead.

THE BASICS
OF SUPPRESSION

DEFINITIONS

Suppressive Person:

A person who suppresses other people in his vicinity. A Suppressive Person will goof up or vilify any effort to help anybody and particularly knife with violence anything calculated to make human beings more powerful or more intelligent.

The whole rationale of the Suppressive Person (SP) is built on the belief that if anyone got better, the SP would be for it as the others could overcome him then.

He is fighting a battle he once fought and never stopped fighting. He is in an incident. Present time people are mistaken by him for past, long-gone enemies. Therefore he never really knows what he is fighting in present time, so just fights.

"Suppressive Person" is another name for "Anti-Social Personality."

Potential Trouble Source:

Somebody who is connected with a Suppressive Person who is invalidating him, his beingness, his life. The person is a Potential Trouble Source (PTS) because he is connected to the Suppressive Person.

Potential Trouble Source means the person is going to go up and fall down. And he is a trouble source because he is going to get upset and because he is going to make trouble. And he really does make trouble. That's very carefully named.

171

Roller Coaster:

> A case that betters then worsens. The person is doing well or he is not doing well, and then is doing well, and then is not doing well. That is a Roller Coaster. And when he is not doing well, he is sometimes ill.

> A Roller Coaster is *always* connected to a Suppressive Person and will not get steady gain until the Suppressive is found on the case.

Suppress:

> To squash, to sit on, to make smaller, to refuse to let reach, to make uncertain about his reaching, to render or lessen in any way possible by any means possible to the harm of the individual and for the fancied protection of the Suppressor.

Suppression:

> A harmful intention or action against which one cannot fight back. Thus when one can do *anything* about it, it is less suppressive.

> Suppression in its most fundamental sense is knocking out the beingness or location of another or others.

Mistakes, Anatomy Of:

> In the presence of suppression, one makes mistakes.

> People making mistakes or doing stupid things is evidence that a Suppressive Person exists in that vicinity.

TWO TYPES
OF PEOPLE

ou probably have speculated on this many times—are there two kinds of people: good people and bad people? Society is more or less organized on the basis that there are. And certainly one sees that some are successful and some aren't, some are good to know and some aren't.

Even in modern TV fiction, one has the cowboys in the white hats and the cowboys in the black hats. Indeed one probably couldn't have stories at all, to Man's way of thinking, unless there were heroes and ogres. And even fiction is rigged as a moral lesson in good and bad people.

Philosophers, long before Greece, pondered moral conduct in terms of good and bad. And Diogenes was looking for an honest man, implying some weren't.

More recent speculation in the nineteenth century termed all men evil unless forced to be good.

Some schools of thought tried to avoid the point by saying early childhood formed character. Yet other schools maintained Man would always be evil unless personally threatened, which gives us the presence of police in the society. But even police sometimes work on the idea that there are good and bad people.

From all this, one could judge that Man had a problem about whether people are good or bad.

Probably, at this minute, you could think of some examples of good people and bad people. You know those who rave and gnaw the rug at the very thought of Scientology helping anyone, so therefore there must be people of evil intention toward their fellows.

173

And there are.

The research results you would be interested in show clearly that there are two types of behavior—that calculated to be constructive and that calculated to be disastrous.

These are the two dominant behavior patterns. There are people, then, who are trying to build things up and others who are trying to tear things down.

And there are no other types. Actually there aren't even shades of gray.

The disaster type can be repressed into inactivity (and illness) and the constructive type can also be repressed (and made ill).

Thus there are two basic actions, each with many other subsidiary actions.

There is also a cyclic, or combined, type who is alternately constructive and disastrous.

So there are cowboys in white hats and cowboys in black hats. And the cowboys in the gray hats are too sick to be in the game.

One scholarly chap (a very sick fellow) hopefully told me once that there were no true villains, no purely evil people. He was whistling past the graveyard. There may not be evil people, but there are people currently devoted to doing evil actions.

All such conduct is apparent and dominant. We see such people all the time. We just don't want to see them.

The underlying reasons for this are, in the absence of processing, fixed and unchangeable in any one lifetime.

As Man knows a man only in one lifetime, the basic cause or changes have not been observed. Thus to all practical purposes for Man, some are good and some are evil. And if we didn't have Scientology, it would not only not be observed, but couldn't ever be changed.

174

That this condition exists—that half are good and half are bad according to their personalities—oddly enough does not alter basic Scientology concepts. It explains why certain persons *appear* to be evil and some *appear* to be good.

Examining the actual goals of an individual shows us why.

About half the goals of any one individual are constructive, the remainder are destructive.

It takes a being a *very* long time to live completely through the cycle of one goal, much less a *series* of goals.

Therefore any one individual at any given long period of his existence is only fixated on disaster and at a subsequent long period is fixated only on being constructive.

So the same being at different lifetimes is good and evil.

Given a sudden overwhelming experience, a "good person" may be shifted violently in his own goals pattern and become evil. And a "bad person," acted upon powerfully by life, will become good. But they also become sick. Their illness stems from being moved out of present time into past heavy energy patterns. It is no cure to so move them, despite the assertions of nineteenth-century mentalists and their shock "treatment." This shows why shock sometimes works and why changes of character come about. And it also shows why such changes are accompanied by severe illness and early death. The person is thrown violently out of present time into a painful past.

The problem is not a problem of sanity and insanity. It is a problem of disastrous motives and constructive motives and the degree to which either is suppressed.

By suppressing the damaging motives of a being who is currently inclined to disaster, one can make that being "behave." But by suppressing the constructive motives of a being currently inclined to constructiveness (as in the military), one can make that being "behave" also. But both will become physically ill, neurotic or insane in the absence of processing.

So the same being in one long period is constructive and in the next long period disastrous.

As Man measures time in small bits—such as youth, old age or a lifetime—he could conceive of a being as either only constructive or only disastrous.

Fortunately for us, this also solves the ancient riddle that one cannot be granted power without also having good intentions. The only way final and powerful abilities can be returned to an individual is by ridding him of *all* these hidden compulsions.

This gives the Scientologist a useful insight into character. A sick being is one who has been bent upon violence and was suppressed, or one who was bent upon constructiveness and was suppressed.

And it also tells us that no one with obsessive intentions will ever make it to the highest and most powerful levels with disastrous inclinations.

But at the street level, with no processing involved, we have these two basic types—good and evil.

And these subdivide into the good who couldn't be good and became sick, and the evil who couldn't be evil and became sick.

But these facts are more than philosophic observations. They deliver to us understanding and more chance to be right about people. And they give us, as well, the wide-open door to making people well.

One cannot push research into the stratosphere without learning more at sea level also. And this is what has happened here.

The basic travail of Man is that he is divided into those who build and those who demolish and, in this conflict of intentions, his fight (whichever side he is on) is always lost.

Or was lost until the Scientologist came along.

THE ANTI-SOCIAL PERSONALITY, THE ANTI-SCIENTOLOGIST

here are certain characteristics and mental attitudes which cause about 20 percent of a race to oppose violently any betterment activity or group.

Such people are known to have anti-social tendencies.

When the legal or political structure of a country becomes such as to favor such personalities in positions of trust, then all the civilizing organizations of the country become suppressed and a barbarism of criminality and economic duress ensues.

Crime and criminal acts are perpetrated by Anti-Social Personalities. Inmates of institutions commonly trace their state back to contact with such personalities.

Thus, in the fields of government, police activities and mental health, to name a few, we see that it is important to be able to detect and isolate this personality type so as to protect society and individuals from the destructive consequences attendant upon letting such have free rein to injure others.

As they only comprise 20 percent of the population and as only 2½ percent of this 20 percent are truly dangerous, we see that with a very small amount of effort, we could considerably better the state of society.

Well-known, even stellar examples of such a personality are, of course, Napoleon and Hitler. Dillinger, Pretty Boy Floyd,

Christie and other famous criminals were well-known examples of the Anti-Social Personality. But with such a cast of characters in history, we neglect the less stellar examples and do not perceive that such personalities exist in current life, very common, often undetected.

When we trace the cause of a failing business, we will inevitably discover somewhere in its ranks the Anti-Social Personality hard at work.

In families which are breaking up, we commonly find one or the other of the persons involved to have such a personality.

Where life has become rough and is failing, a careful review of the area by a trained observer will detect one or more such personalities at work.

As there are 80 percent of us trying to get along and only 20 percent trying to prevent us, our lives would be much easier to live were we well informed as to the exact manifestations of such a personality. Thus we could detect it and save ourselves much failure and heartbreak.

It is important, then, to examine and list the attributes of the Anti-Social Personality. Influencing as it does the daily lives of so many, it well behooves decent people to become better informed on this subject.

ATTRIBUTES

The Anti-Social Personality has the following attributes:

1. He or she speaks only in very broad generalities. "*They* say..." "Everybody thinks..." "Everyone knows..." and such expressions are in continual use, particularly when imparting rumor. When asked "*Who* is everybody..." it normally turns out to be one source and from this source the Anti-Social Person has manufactured what he or she pretends is the whole opinion of the whole society.

   This is natural to them since to them all society is a large hostile generality, against the Anti-Social in particular.

2. Such a person deals mainly in bad news, critical or hostile remarks, invalidation and general suppression.

"Gossip" or "harbinger of evil tidings" or "rumormonger" once described such persons.

It is notable that there is no good news or complimentary remark passed on by such a person.

3. The Anti-Social Personality alters, to worsen, communication when he or she relays a message or news. Good news is stopped and only bad news, often embellished, is passed along.

Such a person also pretends to pass on "bad news" which is in actual fact invented.

4. A characteristic, and one of the sad things about an Anti-Social Personality, is that it does not respond to treatment or reform or psychotherapy.

5. Surrounding such a personality, we find cowed or ill associates or friends who, when not driven actually insane, are yet behaving in a crippled manner in life, failing, not succeeding.

Such people make trouble for others.

When treated or educated, the near associate of the Anti-Social Personality has no stability of gain, but promptly relapses or loses his advantages of knowledge, being under the suppressive influence of the other.

Physically treated, such associates commonly do not recover in the expected time, but worsen and have poor convalescences.

It is quite useless to treat or help or train such persons so long as they remain under the influence of the anti-social connection.

The largest number of insane are insane because of such anti-social connections and do not recover easily for the same reason.

Unjustly, we seldom see the Anti-Social Personality actually in an institution. Only his "friends" and family are there.

6. The Anti-Social Personality selects habitually the wrong target.

   If a tire is flat from driving over nails, he or she curses a companion or a non-causative source of the trouble. If the radio next door is too loud, he or she kicks the cat.

   If A is the obvious cause, the Anti-Social Personality inevitably blames B or C or D.

7. The Anti-Social cannot finish a cycle-of-action.

   Such become surrounded with incomplete projects.

8. Many Anti-Social Persons will freely confess to the most alarming crimes when forced to do so, but will have no faintest sense of responsibility for them.

   Their actions have little or nothing to do with their own volition. Things "just happened."

   They have no sense of correct causation and particularly cannot feel any sense of remorse or shame therefore.

9. The Anti-Social Personality supports only destructive groups and rages against and attacks any constructive or betterment group.

10. This type of personality approves only of destructive actions and fights against constructive or helpful actions or activities.

   The artist in particular is often found as a magnet for persons with anti-social personalities who see in his art something which must be destroyed and covertly, "as a friend," proceed to try.

11. Helping others is an activity which drives the Anti-Social Personality nearly berserk. Activities, however, which destroy in the name of help are closely supported.

12. The Anti-Social Personality has a bad sense of property and conceives that the idea that anyone owns anything is a pretense, made up to fool people. Nothing is ever really owned.

THE BASIC REASON

The basic reason the Anti-Social Personality behaves as he or she does lies in a hidden terror of others.

To such a person, every other being is an enemy, an enemy to be covertly or overtly destroyed.

The fixation is that survival itself depends on "keeping others down" or "keeping people ignorant."

If anyone were to promise to make others stronger or brighter, the Anti-Social Personality suffers the utmost agony of personal danger.

They reason that if they are in this much trouble with people around them weak or stupid, they would perish should anyone become strong or bright.

Such a person has no trust to a point of terror. This is usually masked and unrevealed.

When such a personality goes insane, the world is full of Martians or the FBI and each person met is really a Martian or FBI agent.

But the bulk of such people exhibit no outward signs of insanity. They appear quite rational. They can be *very* convincing.

However, the list given above consists of things which such a personality cannot detect in himself or herself. This is so true that if you thought you found yourself in one of the above, you most certainly are not anti-social. Self-criticism is a luxury the Anti-Social cannot afford. They must be *right* because they are in continual danger in their own estimation. If you proved one *wrong,* you might even send him or her into a severe illness.

Only the sane, well-balanced person tries to correct his conduct.

RELIEF

If you were to weed out of your past by proper Search and Discovery those Anti-Social Persons you have known and if you then disconnected, you might experience great relief.

Similarly, if society were to recognize this personality type as a sick being as they now isolate people with smallpox, both social and economic recoveries could occur.

Things are not likely to get much better so long as 20 percent of the population is permitted to dominate and injure the lives and enterprise of the remaining 80 percent.

As majority rule is the political manner of the day, so should majority sanity express itself in our daily lives without the interference and destruction of the socially unwell.

The pity of it is, they will not permit themselves to be helped and would not respond to treatment if help were attempted.

An understanding and ability to recognize such personalities could bring a major change in society and our lives.

THE SOCIAL PERSONALITY

Man, in his anxieties, is prone to witch hunts.

All one has to do is designate "people wearing black caps" as the villains and one can start a slaughter of people in black caps.

This characteristic makes it very easy for the Anti-Social Personality to bring about a chaotic or dangerous environment.

Man is not naturally brave or calm in his human state. And he is not necessarily villainous.

Even the Anti-Social Personality, in his warped way, is quite certain that he is acting for the best and commonly sees himself as the only good person around, doing all for the good of everyone—the only flaw in his reasoning being that if one kills everyone else, none are left to be protected from the imagined evils. His *conduct* in his environment and toward his fellows is the only method of detecting either the Anti-Social or the Social Personalities. Their motives for self are similar—self-preservation and survival. They simply go about achieving these in different ways.

Thus, as Man is naturally neither calm nor brave, anyone to some degree tends to be alert to dangerous persons and hence, witch hunts can begin.

It is therefore even more important to identify the Social Personality than the Anti-Social Personality. One then avoids "shooting" the innocent out of mere prejudice or dislike or because of some momentary misconduct.

The Social Personality can be defined most easily by comparison with his opposite, the Anti-Social Personality.

This differentiation is easily done and no test should ever be constructed which isolates only the Anti-Social. On the same test must appear the upper as well as lower ranges of Man's actions.

A test that declares only Anti-Social Personalities without also being able to identify the Social Personality would be itself a suppressive test. It would be like answering "Yes" or "No" to the question "Do you still beat your wife?" Anyone who took it could be found guilty. While this mechanism might have suited the times of the Inquisition, it would not suit modern needs.

As the society runs, prospers and lives *solely* through the efforts of Social Personalities, one must know them as *they,* not the Anti-Social, are the worthwhile people. These are the people who must have rights and freedom. Attention is given to the Anti-Social solely to protect and assist the Social Personalities in the society.

All majority rules, civilizing intentions and even the human race will fail unless one can identify and thwart the Anti-Social Personalities and help and forward the Social Personalities in the society. For the very word "society" implies social conduct and without it there is no society at all, only a barbarism with all men, good or bad, at risk.

The frailty of showing how the harmful people can be known is that these then apply the characteristics to decent people to get them hunted down and eradicated.

The swan song of every great civilization is the tune played by arrows, axes or bullets used by the Anti-Social to slay the last decent men.

Government is only dangerous when it can be employed by and for Anti-Social Personalities. The end result is the eradication of all Social Personalities and the resultant collapse of Egypt, Babylon, Rome, Russia or the West.

You will note in the characteristics of the Anti-Social Personality that intelligence is not a clue to the Anti-Social. They are bright or stupid or average. Thus those who are extremely intelligent can rise to considerable, even head-of-state heights.

Importance and ability or wish to rise above others are likewise not indexes to the Anti-Social. When they do become important or rise, they are, however, rather visible by the broad consequences of their acts. But they are as likely to be unimportant people or hold very lowly stations and wish for nothing better.

Thus it is the twelve given characteristics alone which identify the Anti-Social Personality. And these same twelve, reversed, are the sole criteria of the Social Personality, if one wishes to be truthful about them.

The identification or labeling of an Anti-Social Personality cannot be done honestly and accurately unless one *also,* in the same examination of the person, reviews the positive side of his life.

All persons under stress can react with momentary flashes of anti-social conduct. This does not make them Anti-Social Personalities.

The true Anti-Social Person has a majority of anti-social characteristics.

The Social Personality has a majority of social characteristics.

Thus one must examine the good with the bad before one can truly label the Anti-Social or the Social.

In reviewing such matters, very broad testimony and evidence are best. One or two isolated instances determine nothing. One should search all twelve social and all twelve anti-social characteristics and decide on the basis of actual evidence, not opinion.

The twelve primary characteristics of the Social Personality are as follows:

1. The Social Personality is specific in relating circumstances. "Joe Jones said..." "The *Star* newspaper reported..." and gives sources of data where important or possible.

   He may use the generality of "they" or "people," but seldom in connection with attributing statements or opinions of an alarming nature.

2. The Social Personality is eager to relay good news and reluctant to relay bad.

   He may not even bother to pass along criticism when it doesn't matter.

   He is more interested in making another feel liked or wanted than disliked by others and tends to err toward reassurance rather than toward criticism.

3. A Social Personality passes communication without much alteration and, if deleting anything, tends to delete injurious matters.

   He does not like to hurt people's feelings. He sometimes errs in holding back bad news or orders which seem critical or harsh.

4. Treatment, reform and psychotherapy, particularly of a mild nature, work very well on the Social Personality.

   Whereas Anti-Social People sometimes promise to reform, they do not. Only the Social Personality can change or improve easily.

It is often enough to point out unwanted conduct to a Social Personality to completely alter it for the better.

Criminal codes and violent punishment are not needed to regulate Social Personalities.

5. The friends and associates of a Social Personality tend to be well, happy and of good morale.

   A truly Social Personality quite often produces betterment in health or fortune by his mere presence on the scene.

   At the very least he does not reduce the existing levels of health or morale in his associates.

   When ill, the Social Personality heals or recovers in an expected manner, and is found open to successful treatment.

6. The Social Personality tends to select correct targets for correction.

   He fixes the tire that is flat rather than attack the windscreen.

   In the mechanical arts, he can therefore repair things and make them work.

7. Cycles-of-action begun are ordinarily completed by the Social Personality, if possible.

8. The Social Personality is ashamed of his misdeeds and reluctant to confess them. He takes responsibility for his errors.

9. The Social Personality supports constructive groups and tends to protest or resist destructive groups.

10. Destructive actions are protested by the Social Personality. He assists constructive or helpful actions.

11. The Social Personality helps others and actively resists acts which harm others.

12. Property is property of someone to the Social Personality and its theft or misuse is prevented or frowned upon.

THE BASIC MOTIVATION

The Social Personality naturally operates on the basis of the greatest good.

He is not haunted by imagined enemies, but he does recognize real enemies when they exist.

The Social Personality wants to survive and wants others to survive, whereas the Anti-Social Personality really and covertly wants others to succumb.

Basically the Social Personality wants others to be happy and do well, whereas the Anti-Social Personality is very clever in making others do very badly indeed.

A basic clue to the Social Personality is not really his successes, but his motivations. The Social Personality when successful is often a target for the Anti-Social and by this reason he may fail. But his intentions included others in his success, whereas the Anti-Social only appreciate the doom of others.

Unless we can detect the Social Personality and hold him safe from undue restraint and detect also the Anti-Social and restrain him, our society will go on suffering from insanity, criminality and war, and Man and civilization will not endure.

Of all our technical skills, such differentiation ranks the highest since, failing, no other skill can continue as the base on which it operates, civilization, will not be here to continue it.

Do not smash the Social Personality—and do not fail to render powerless the Anti-Social in their efforts to harm the rest of us.

Just because a man rises above his fellows or takes an important post does not make him an Anti-Social Personality. Just because a man can control or dominate others does not make him an Anti-Social Personality.

It is his motives in doing so and the consequences of his acts which distinguish the Anti-Social from the Social.

Unless we realize and apply the true characteristics of the two types of personality, we will continue to live in a quandary of who our enemies are and, in doing so, victimize our friends.

All men have committed acts of violence or omission for which they could be censured. In all Mankind there is not one single perfect human being.

But there are those who try to do right and those who specialize in wrong and upon these facts and characteristics you can know them.

THE POTENTIAL TROUBLE SOURCE

ne must know what a Suppressive Person (SP) is, what a Potential Trouble Source (PTS) is and the mechanism of how and why a case Roller Coasters and what that is.

PTS AND ROLLER COASTER

A Roller Coaster equals a Suppressive Person in that person's vicinity. If a person Roller Coasters, he is PTS.

A Potential Trouble Source is a connection with a Suppressive. I'll give you the exact mechanics of it:

Postulate–counter-postulate is the anatomy of a problem. Postulate versus postulate. That is the definition and the anatomy of a problem. And there is *no* other definition to a problem.

The guy has had a purpose in life and somebody has suppressed it, or a guy has had a purpose over a twenty-four-hour period and somebody suppressed that purpose. In other words, his purpose was his postulate, the other person saying he couldn't do it was the counter-postulate.

That is simply the anatomy of a problem. And there is *no other reason* for Roller Coaster. There just is no other datum.

A connection with a Suppressive Person is a version of this. It's a version of a problem and is a specialized kind of problem, and that is what causes the Roller Coaster. The individual has run into a postulate–counter-postulate since his last improvement, which makes him a Potential Trouble Source.

189

Potential Trouble Source means the case is going to go up and fall down. And he's a trouble source because he's going to get upset. He's a trouble source because he's going to make trouble. And he's trouble for the auditor and he's trouble for us and he's trouble for himself and so forth. And he really does make trouble. That's very carefully named.

The SP isn't making trouble. He's just poisoning the whole universe. But he isn't making trouble. He's just going *squash!* Anybody says anything to him—*squash!* It's the PTS who makes the trouble.

THE THREE TYPES OF PTS

There are three Types of PTS.

Type I is the easy one. The SP on the case is right in present time, actively suppressing the person.

Type II is harder for the *apparent* Suppressive Person in present time is only a restimulator for the actual Suppressive.

Type III is beyond the facilities of orgs not equipped with hospitals as these are entirely psychotic.

TYPE I

The Type I is normally handled by an Ethics Officer in the course of a hearing.

The person is asked if anyone is invalidating him or his gains or Scientology and if the pc answers with a name and is then told to handle or disconnect from that person, the *good indicators* come in promptly and the person is *quite* satisfied. If, however, there is no success in finding the SP on the case or if the person starts naming org personnel or other unlikely persons as SP, the Ethics Officer must realize that he is handling a Type II PTS and, because the auditing will consume time, sends the person to Tech or Qual for a "Search and Discovery."*

*A Search and Discovery is a process used to find the suppressions the person has had in life. It locates the Suppressives on the case and is used to nullify the influence of Suppressive Persons or things on a case so the person will be able to be processed and will no longer be PTS. Auditors must be trained on the full body of this technology as well as the full body of Ethics Technology before they may use this procedure.

It is easy to tell a Type I PTS from a Type II. The Type I brightens up at once and ceases to Roller Coaster the moment the present time SP is spotted. The pc ceases to Roller Coaster. The pc does not go back on it and begin to beg off. The pc does not begin to worry about the consequences of disconnection. If the pc does any of these things, then the pc is a Type II.

It can be seen that Ethics handles the majority of PTSes in a fast manner. There is no trouble about it. All goes smoothly.

It can also be seen that Ethics cannot afford the time to handle a Type II PTS. Therefore, when Ethics finds its Type I approach does not work quickly, Ethics must send the person to the proper division that is handling Search and Discovery.

TYPE II

The pc who isn't sure, won't disconnect, or still Roller Coasters, or who doesn't brighten up, can't name any SP at all is a Type II.

Only Search and Discovery will help.

The first thing to know is that *case worsening is caused only by a PTS situation.*

There never will be any other reason.

As soon as you doubt this datum and think about "other causes" or try to explain it some other way, you no longer prevent cases from worsening and no longer rescue those who have worsened.

The second thing to know is that *a Suppressive is always a person, a being or a group of beings.*

A Suppressive is *not* a condition, a problem, a postulate. Problems and counter-postulates come into the matter, but the SP as a being or group must always be located as a being or a group, not as merely an idea.

The third thing to know is that *there can be an actual SP and another person or being similar to the actual one who is only an apparent SP.*

An *actual* SP actually suppresses another.

An *apparent* SP only reminds the pc of the actual one and so is restimulated into being a PTS.

The *actual* SP can be in present time (Type I PTS) or is in the past or distant (Type II PTS).

The Type II always has an *apparent* SP who is not *the* SP on the case, is confusing the two and is acting PTS only because of restimulation, not because of suppression.

TYPE III

The Type III PTS is mostly in institutions or would be.

In this case, the Type II's *apparent* SP is spread all over the world and is often more than all the people there are—for the person sometimes has ghosts about him or demons and they are just more apparent SPs but imaginary as beings as well.

All institutional cases are PTSes. The whole of insanity is wrapped up on this one fact.

The insane is not just a bad-off being. The insane is a being who has been overwhelmed by an actual SP until too many persons are apparent SPs. This makes the person Roller Coaster continually in life. The Roller Coaster is even cyclic (repetitive as a cycle).

Handling an insane person as a Type II might work but probably not case for case. One might get enough wins on a few to make one fail completely by so many loses on the many.

Just as you tell a Type II to disconnect from the actual SP (wherever found on the track), you must disconnect the person from the environment.

Putting the person in a current institution puts him in a Bedlam. And when also "treated" it may finish him. *For he will Roller Coaster from any treatment given* until made into a Type II and given a Search and Discovery.

The task with a Type III is *not* treatment as such. It is to provide a relatively safe environment and quiet and rest and no treatment of a mental nature at all. Giving him a quiet court with a motionless object in it might do the trick if he is permitted to sit there unmolested. Medical care of a very unbrutal nature is necessary as intravenous feeding and soporifics (sleeping and quieting drugs) may be necessary. Such persons are sometimes also physically ill from an illness with a known medical cure.

Treatment with drugs, shock, operation is just more suppression. The person will not really get well, will relapse, etc.

Standard auditing on such a person is subject to the Roller Coaster phenomena. They get worse after getting better. "Successes" are sporadic, enough to lead one on, and usually worsen again since these people are PTS.

But, removed from apparent SPs, kept in a quiet surroundings, not pestered or threatened or put in fear, the person comes up to Type II and a Search and Discovery should end the matter. But there will always be some failures as the insane sometimes withdraw into rigid unawareness as a final defense, sometimes can't be kept alive and sometimes are too hectic and distraught to ever become quiet. The extremes of too quiet and never quiet have a number of psychiatric names such as "catatonia" (withdrawn totally) and "manic" (too hectic). Classification is interesting but nonproductive since they are all PTS, all will Roller Coaster and none can be trained or processed with any idea of lasting result no matter the temporary miracle.

(Note: These paragraphs on the Type III make good a promise given in *Dianetics: The Modern Science of Mental Health* to develop "Institutional Dianetics.")

Remove a Type III PTS from the environment, give him or her rest and quiet, do a Search and Discovery when rest and quiet have made the person Type II.

The modern mental hospital with its brutality and suppressive treatments is not the way to give a psychotic quiet and rest.

Before anything effective can be done in this field, a proper institution would have to be provided, offering only rest, quiet and medical assistance for intravenous feedings and sleeping drafts where necessary but not as "treatment" and where *no* treatment is attempted until the person looks recovered and only then a Search and Discovery as above under Type II.

Subsequent to the publication of the findings and technology contained in this chapter, LRH research culminated in the discovery of the full underlying mental and spiritual causes of psychosis and Type III PTS manifestations as well as development of procedures for their resolution. These breakthroughs are available in Hubbard Communications Office Bulletins comprising the Introspection Rundown, which makes it possible to solve this condition solely through address of the spirit with Ethics and Auditing Technology. Therefore, the use or requirement of medical facilities no longer applies to the handling of persons who are Type III PTS. A medical examination may be required by a Case Supervisor before beginning the rundown and acceptance of individuals for participation in the Introspection Rundown is at the discretion of Churches of Scientology.

STABLE DATA FOR HANDLING THE PTS
(PTS = POTENTIAL TROUBLE SOURCE)

here are two stable data which anyone has to have, understand and *know are true* in order to obtain results in handling the person connected to Suppressives.

These data are:

1. That all illness in greater or lesser degree and all foul-ups stem directly and only from a PTS condition.

2. That getting rid of the condition requires three basic actions:

   a. Understanding the tech of the condition.

   b. Discover.

   c. Handle or disconnect.

Persons called upon to handle PTS people can do so very easily, far more easily than they believe. Their basic stumbling block is thinking that there are exceptions or that there is other tech or that the two above data have modifiers or are not sweeping. The moment a person who is trying to handle PTSes gets persuaded there are other conditions or reasons or tech, he is at once lost and will lose the game and not obtain results. And this is very too bad because it is not difficult and the results are there to be obtained.

To turn someone who may be PTS over to an auditor just to have him mechanically audited may not be enough. In the first place this person may not have a clue what is meant by PTS and may be missing all manner of technical data on life and may be so overwhelmed by a Suppressive Person or Group that he is quite incoherent. Thus, just mechanically doing a process may miss the whole show as it misses the person's understanding of why it is being done.

A PTS person is rarely psychotic. But all psychotics are PTS if only to themselves. A PTS person may be in a state of deficiency or pathology which prevents a ready recovery, but at the same time he will not fully recover unless the PTS condition is also handled. For he became prone to deficiency or pathological illness because he was PTS. And unless the condition is relieved, no matter what medication or nutrition he may be given, he might not recover and certainly will not recover permanently. This seems to indicate that there are "other illnesses or reasons for illness besides being PTS." To be sure there are deficiencies and illnesses just as there are accidents and injuries. But strangely enough, the person himself precipitates them because being PTS predisposes him to them. In a more garbled way, the medicos and nutritionists are always talking about "stress" causing illness. Lacking full tech, they yet have an inkling that this is so because they see it is somehow true. They cannot handle it. Yet they recognize it, and they state that it is a senior situation to various illnesses and accidents. Well, we have the tech of this in more ways than one.

What is this thing called "stress"? It is more than the medico defines it—he usually says it comes from operational or physical shock and in this he has too limited a view.

A person under stress is actually under a suppression on one or more dynamics.

If that suppression is located and the person handles or disconnects, the condition diminishes. If he also has all the engrams and ARC breaks, problems, overts and withholds audited out triple flow and if *all* such areas of suppression are thus handled, the person would recover from anything caused by "stress."

Usually the person has insufficient understanding of life or any dynamic to grasp his own situation. He is confused. He believes all his illnesses are true because they occur in such heavy books!

At some time he was predisposed to illness or accidents. When a serious suppression then occurred he suffered a precipitation or occurrence of the accident or illness and then, with repeated similar suppressions on the same chain, the illness or tendency to accidents became prolonged or chronic.

To say then that a person is PTS to his current environment would be very limited as a diagnosis. If he continues to do or be something to which the Suppressive Person or Group objected, he may become or continue to be ill or have accidents.

Actually, the problem of PTS is not very complicated. Once you have grasped the two data first given, the rest of it becomes simply an analysis of how they apply to this particular person.

A PTS person can be markedly helped in three ways:

a. Gaining an understanding of the tech of the condition.

b. Discovering to what or to whom he is PTS.

c. Handling or disconnecting.

Someone with the wish or duty to find and handle PTSes has an additional prior step: He must know how to recognize a PTS and how to handle them when recognized. Thus it is rather a waste of time to engage in this hunt unless one has been checked out on all the material on Suppressives and PTSes and grasps it without misunderstoods. In other words, the first step of the person is to get a grasp of the subject and its tech. This is not difficult to do; it may be a bit more difficult to learn to run an E-Meter and considerably more difficult to learn how to list for items, but there again this is possible and is much easier than trying to grope around guessing.

With this step done, a person has no real trouble recognizing PTS people and can have success in handling them which is very gratifying and rewarding.

Let us consider the easiest level of approach:

i. Give the person the simpler materials on the subject and let him study them so that he knows the elements like "PTS" and "Suppressive." He may just cognite right there and be much better. It has happened.

ii. Have him discuss the illness or accident or condition, without much prodding or probing, that he thinks now may be the result of suppression. He will usually tell you it is right here and now or was a short time ago and will be all set to explain it (without any relief) as stemming from his current environment or a recent one. If you let it go at that, he would simply be a bit unhappy and not get well as he is discussing usually a late lock that has a lot of earlier material below it.

iii. Ask when he recalls first having that illness or having such accidents. He will at once begin to roll this back and realize that it has happened before. You don't have to be auditing him as he is all too willing to talk about this in a most informal manner. He will get back to some early this-lifetime point usually.

iv. Now ask him *who* it was. He will usually tell you promptly. And, as you are not really auditing him and he isn't going backtrack and you are not trying to do more than key him out, you don't probe any further.

v. You will usually find that he has named a person to whom he is still connected! So you ask him whether he wants to handle or disconnect. Now as the sparks will really fly in his life if he dramatically disconnects and if he can't see how he can, you persuade him to begin to handle on a gradient scale. This may consist of imposing some slight discipline on him such as requiring him to actually answer his mail or write the person a pleasant "good roads, good weather" note or to realistically look at how he estranged them. In short, what is required in the handling is a low gradient. All you are trying to do is *move the PTS person from effect over to slight gentle cause.*

vi. Check with the person again, if he is handling, and coach him along, always at a gentle "good roads and good weather" level and no HE&R (Human Emotion and Reaction) if you please.

That is a simple handling. You can get complexities such as a person being PTS to an unknown person in his immediate vicinity that he may have to find before he can handle or disconnect. You can find people who can't remember more than a few years back. You can find anything you can find in a case. But simple handling ends when it looks pretty complex. And that's when you call in the auditor.

But this simple handling will get you quite a few stars in your crown. You will be amazed to find that while some of them don't instantly recover, medication, vitamins, minerals will now work when before they wouldn't. You may also get some instant recovers, but realize that if they don't you have not failed.

The Auditor can do a "Search and Discovery" after this with much more effect as he isn't working with a completely uninformed person.

A being is rather complex. He may have a lot of sources of suppression. And it may take a lot of very light auditing to get him up to where he can do work on Suppressives since these were, after all, the source of his overwhelm. And what he did to *them* might be more important than what they did to *him,* but unless you unburden *him* he may not get around to realizing that.

You can run into a person who can only be handled by Expanded Dianetics.

But you have made an entrance and you have stirred things up and gotten him more aware and just that way you will find he is more at cause.

His illness or proneness to accidents may not be slight. You may succeed only to the point where he now has a chance, by nutrition, vitamins, minerals, medication, treatment and, above all, auditing, of getting well. Unless you jogged this condition, he had no chance at all: for becoming PTS is the first thing that happened to him on the subject of illness or accidents.

Further, if the person has had a lot of auditing and yet isn't progressing too well, your simple handling may all of a sudden cause him to line up his case.

So do not underestimate what you or an auditor can do for a PTS. And don't sell PTS Tech short or neglect it. And don't tolerate PTS conditions in people.

You *can* do something about it.

And so can they.

PTS
HANDLING

er policies on *Physical Healing, Insanity and "Sources of Trouble,"* a PTS (meaning a Potential Trouble Source) is a person "...intimately connected with persons (such as marital or familial ties) of known antagonism to mental or spiritual treatment or Scientology. In practice such persons, even when they approach Scientology in a friendly fashion, have such pressure continually brought to bear upon them by persons with undue influence over them that they make very poor gains in processing, and their interest is solely devoted to proving the antagonistic element wrong."

A SOURCE OF TROUBLE

Such persons with antagonistic family members are a source of trouble to Scientology because their family members are not inactive. In fact, from direct experience with inquiry* after inquiry into Scientology, it has been found that those who have created the conditions which brought about the inquiry in the first place and those who testified before same have been the wives, husbands, mothers, fathers, brothers, sisters or grandparents of some Scientologist. Their testimony has been full of such statements as "My son completely changed after he went into Scientology—he no longer was respectful to me." "My daughter gave up a wonderful career as a hairdresser to go into Scientology." "My sister got these funny staring eyes the way all Scientologists have."

*In reference to various governmental inquiries into Scientology in the mid-1960s. In every instance, Churches of Scientology were exonerated and vindicated.

Their testimony was illogical and their descriptions of what occurred were untrue, but the point of the matter is that such persons *did* cause Scientology, Scientology orgs and fellow Scientologists a great deal of trouble and difficulty.

DON'T CREATE ANTAGONISM

Many Scientologists, in their misunderstanding and misapplication of Scientology, create the conditions that bring about the antagonism in the first place. A few illustrations of how this is done are as follows:

Scientologist to mother: "I now know where you are on the Tone Scale—1.1. Boy, are you sneaky!" (Evaluation and invalidation.)

Father to Scientologist: "Now, I don't want you to borrow the car again without my permission. I have told you time and time..." Scientologist to father: *"Okay! Fine! Okay! Good! Thank you! I got that!"* (Not an acknowledgment but an effort to shut up the father.)

Scientologist to older brother: "You murdered me in a past life, you dirty dog!" (Evaluation and invalidation.)

Mother to Scientologist: "Whatever are you doing?" Scientologist to mother: "I'm trying to confront your dreadful bank." (Invalidation.)

There are so many ways to misuse tech and to invalidate and evaluate for others in a destructive fashion to bring about bypassed charge, ARC breaks and upset that they cannot all be possibly listed. The idea is *not* to do so. Why create trouble for yourself and for your fellow Scientologists, as nothing will have been gained but ill will?

THE WHY

Per *Offenses and Penalties,* it is a *Crime* to be or become a PTS without reporting it or taking action or to receive processing while PTS. Further, as per *Policies on Physical Healing, Insanity and "Sources of Trouble,"* a PTS may not be trained.

This means that a person who is PTS may not receive processing or training while PTS and it also means that they had better do something to handle their condition.

In the original (now reinstated) policy, the PTS individual was required to "handle or disconnect" before he or she could continue with training or processing. Many took the easy course and merely disconnected "temporarily" for the time of their training or processing and so they did not in actual fact *handle* the condition in their lives which was upsetting them as Scientologists. In some cases, there was a misapplication of the tech, as their situations *were* totally handleable with the use of simple Scientology basics.

Now a very workable system for handling PTS situations has been developed, as covered here in *PTS Handling* and in *Outline of Full PTS Handling*.

Following the steps given in these and making full use of *all* bulletins and policies on the subject of PTS handling will ensure situations get terminatedly handled.

Each PTS individual should, as one step of his handling, report to Ethics and, with the assistance of Ethics, find a Why as to his familial antagonism and then set about actually handling the situation. The Why could be that his parents wanted him to be a lawyer and so blame Scientology that he is not one, rather than the fact that he flunked out of law school and couldn't stand the thought of being a lawyer!

Or perhaps the Why is that the Scientologist keeps writing her parents for money or the Why could be that the mother has just read an entheta newspaper article.

In any case, the Why should be found and the PTS individual should then do whatever is necessary to handle.

HANDLING

The person who is PTS should be declared as such by Ethics and should not receive Scientology training or processing until the situation has been handled. (The exception to this is a full PTS Rundown done in the HGC.)

The handling could be as simple as writing to one's father and saying: "I do not complain that you are a janitor, please do not complain that I am a Scientologist. The important thing is that I am your son and that I love and respect you. I know you love me, but please learn to respect me as an adult individual who knows what he wants in life." Or it could be as follows: "I am writing to you, Daddy, because Mother keeps sending me these dreadful newspaper clippings and they are upsetting to me because I know they are not true. You do not do this and so it is easier for me to write to you."

Again, there are as many ways of handling as there are Whys found. Each case is individual. Remember, too, there is always the possibility of a *no* situation. And if the person thinks he's PTS and isn't, he can get sick. Or if he insists he isn't and is, he can also get upset. So find if there *is* a situation first.

It is the purpose of Ethics to ensure that the situation is handled.

PTSNESS AND DISCONNECTION

erhaps the most fundamental right of any being is the right to communicate. Without this freedom, other rights deteriorate.

Communication, however, is a two-way flow. If one has the right to communicate, then one must also have the right to not receive communication from another. It is this latter corollary of the right to communicate that gives us our right to privacy.

These rights are so basic that governments have written them into laws—witness the American Bill of Rights.

However, groups have always regulated these rights to one degree or another. For with the freedom to communicate come certain agreements and responsibilities.

An example of this is a marriage: In a monogamous society, the agreement is that one will be married to only one person at one time. That agreement extends to having Second Dynamic relations with one's spouse and no one else. Thus, should wife Shirley establish a 2D-type of communication line with someone other than her husband Pete, it is a violation of the agreement and postulates of the marriage. Pete has the right to insist that either this communication cease or that the marriage will cease.

HANDLE OR DISCONNECT

In PTS Tech you'll see the phrase "handle or disconnect." It means simply that.

The term *handle* most commonly means, when used in relation to PTS Tech, to smooth out a situation with another person by applying the tech of communication.

The term *disconnection* is defined as a self-determined decision made by an individual that he is not going to be connected to another. It is a severing of a communication line.

The basic principle of "handle or disconnect" exists in any group and ours is no different.

It is much like trying to deal with a criminal. If he will not handle, the society resorts to the only other solution: It "disconnects" the criminal from the society. In other words, they remove the guy from society and put him in a prison because he won't *handle* his problem or otherwise cease to commit criminal acts against others.

It's the same sort of situation that husband Pete is faced with in the example mentioned above. The optimum solution is to handle the situation with wife Shirley and her violations of their group (marriage) agreements. But if Pete cannot handle the situation, he is left with no other choice but to disconnect (sever the marriage communication lines if only by separation). To do otherwise would be disastrous, for he is connected to someone antagonistic to the original agreements, postulates and responsibilities of the group (the marriage).

A Scientologist can become PTS by reason of being connected to someone that is antagonistic to Scientology or its tenets. In order to resolve the PTS condition, he either *handles* the other person's antagonism (as covered here and in full on the PTS/SP Course) or, as a last resort when all attempts to handle have failed, he disconnects from the person. He is simply exercising his right to communicate or not to communicate with a particular person.

With our tech of "handle or disconnect" we are, in actual fact, doing nothing different than any society or group or marriage down through thousands of years.

HISTORY

Earlier, disconnection as a condition was cancelled. It had been abused by a few individuals who'd failed to handle situations which could have been handled and who lazily or irresponsibly disconnected, thereby creating situations even worse than the original because it was the wrong action.

Secondly, there were those who could survive only by living on our lines—they wanted to continue to be connected to Scientologists (see earlier, *The Anti-Social Personality, The Anti-Scientologist*). Thus they screamed to high heaven if anyone dared to apply the tech of "handle or disconnect."

This put Scientologists at a disadvantage.

We cannot afford to deny Scientologists that basic freedom that is granted to everyone else: The right to choose whom one wishes to communicate with or not communicate with. It's bad enough that there are governments trying, through the use of force, to prevent people from disconnecting from them (witness those who want to leave some countries but can't!).

The bare fact is that disconnection is a vital tool in handling PTSness and can be very effective when used correctly.

Therefore, the tech of disconnection was restored to use, in the hands of those persons thoroughly and standardly trained in PTS/SP Tech.

HANDLING ANTAGONISTIC SOURCES

In the great majority of cases, where a person has some family member or close associate who appears antagonistic to his getting better through Scientology, it is *not* really a matter of the antagonistic source wanting the PTS to not *get better*. It is most commonly a lack of correct information about Scientology that causes the problem or upset. In such a case, simply having the PTS disconnect would not help matters and would actually be a nonconfront of the situation. It is quite common that the PTS has a low confront on the terminal and situation. This isn't hard to understand when one looks at these facts:

a. To be PTS in the first place, the PTS must have committed overts against the antagonistic source; and

b. When one has committed overts, his confront and responsibility drop.

When an Ethics Officer finds that a Scientologist is PTS to a family member, he does *not* recommend that the person disconnect from the antagonistic source. The Ethics Officer's advice to the Scientologist is to *handle*.

The handling for such a situation is to educate him in the tech of PTSness and suppression, and then skillfully and firmly guide the PTS through the steps needed to restore good communication with the antagonistic source. This eventually dissolves the situation by bringing about an *understanding* on the part of the antagonistic source as to what Scientology is and why the PTS person is interested and involved in it. Of course, when this is accomplished you no longer have a PTS at all—and you may very well find a new Scientologist on your hands!

The actual steps and procedure of this sort of handling are well covered in Bulletins, Policy Letters and lectures that comprise the full body of PTS/SP technology. (Also see later, *Outline of Full PTS Handling.*)

WHEN DISCONNECTION IS USED

An Ethics Officer can encounter a situation where someone is factually connected to a Suppressive Person, in present time. This is a person whose normal operating basis is one of making others smaller, less able, less powerful. He does not want anyone to get better, at all.

In truth, an SP is absolutely, completely terrified of anyone becoming more powerful.

In such an instance the PTS isn't going to get anywhere trying to "handle" the person. The answer is to sever the connection.

HOW TO DISCONNECT

How a disconnection is done depends on the circumstances.

Example: The pc lives next door to, say, a psychiatric clinic and feels PTS due to this environment. The remedy is simple—the pc can move to another apartment in another location. He need not write any sort of "disconnection letter" to the psychiatric clinic. He simply changes his environment—which is, in effect, a disconnection from the suppressive environment.

Example: A pc is connected to a person or group that has been declared suppressive by HCO in a published Ethics Order. He should disconnect and, if he wants to inform the SP of the fact, he may write a letter of disconnection. Such a letter would be very straightforward. It would state the fact of the disconnection and the reason for it. It would not be mis-emotional or accusative, since this would only serve to stir up further antagonism. The letter would be inspected by the Ethics Officer before it was sent and copies kept for the PTS person's own Ethics File and pc folder. No attempt would be made to establish communication with the declared SP "to clear matters up" or to seek to reform the SP. The SP's reform is strictly in the hands of HCO. The PTS simply disconnects.

Example: One discovers that an employee at his place of business is an SP—he steals money, drives away customers, wipes out other employees and will not correct no matter what you do. The handling is very simple—the PTS fires him and that's the end of it right there!

To fail or refuse to disconnect from a Suppressive Person not only denies the PTS case gain, it is also *supportive* of the Suppressive—in itself a Suppressive Act. And it must be so labeled (see later, *Suppressive Acts, Suppression of Scientology and Scientologists*).

SUPPRESSED PERSON RUNDOWN

There is of course another technical way to handle PTSes and that is to get them through all problems they have had with the terminal involved and the PTSness will disappear (see later, *Outline of Full PTS Handling*). But it still requires that during the handling the person disconnects.

SUMMARY

The technology of Disconnection is essential in the handling of PTSes. It can and has saved lives and untold trouble and upset. It must be preserved and used correctly.

OUTLINE OF FULL PTS HANDLING

PTS situations can arise at any time during a person's Scientology auditing or training and must be handled speedily and well to get the person back on his course of auditing or training. Many preclears new to Scientology require PTS handling as one of their first actions.

Auditing or training must not be continued over an unhandled PTS situation, as processing or study under the duress of suppression will not produce results.

You do not go on hoping or ignore it or call it something else or do any other action except *handle.* Handling PTSness is too easy to allow for any justification or excuse for not doing so, and the steps given below lay out the many handlings which can be used to bring about a full resolution of all PTSness in all pcs.

EDUCATION

A person who is PTS is often the last person to suspect it. He may have become temporarily or momentarily so. And he may have become so very slightly. Or he may be *very* PTS and have been so for a long time. But he is nevertheless PTS and we must educate him on the subject.

PTS C/S-1

The PTS C/S-1, given in various bulletins, must be done before any other PTS handling is begun.

This action sets a person up to understand his PTS situation and the mechanics of it. A thorough PTS C/S-1 is the basis of all successful PTS handling.

PTS INTERVIEW

A metered PTS interview, as covered in various bulletins, will, in most cases, assist the person to spot the antagonistic or SP element. Once spotted, the Potential Trouble Source must be assisted in working out a handling for that terminal (or more rarely, the PTS may need to disconnect from that person).

(If *any* difficulty is encountered on this step or if the SP cannot easily be found, the preclear or student is probably not PTS Type I and should be turned over to an auditor qualified to handle Type II PTS situations with more advanced PTS Tech.)

HANDLING

Once the antagonistic terminal has been located, a handling is done to move the PTS person from *effect* to *slight gentle cause* over his situation. This handling is done per a program which will include whatever is needed to accomplish the result and will, of course, vary depending on the person and his circumstances.

When the antagonistic person exists in present time, in the physical universe, a "good-roads, good-weather" approach to the antagonistic terminal is usually what is needed. The handling must be agreed upon by the Potential Trouble Source and the person assisting him and must be tailored to put the person at cause over his particular situation.

Handling may include coaching him along to see how he himself actually precipitated the PTS condition in the first place by not applying or by misapplying Scientology basics to his life and relationship with the now antagonistic terminal.

BOOKS, LECTURES AND FILMS

It quite often happens that the persons antagonistic to the preclear have no real concept of what Scientology is. This can also be true of a very new Scientologist who then misinforms others.

The book *What Is Scientology?* is a very useful tool. The preclear can send a copy of it to persons antagonistic to him and it will give them hope that the person will respond better to life or, if they are antagonistic to Scientology, can show them what they're being antagonistic to.

Recommendations that the PTS person obtain and use this book (or anyone else who wants to inform his friends or get them on the right road, as the book was not written for the purpose of de-PTSing people) should be made by the interviewing officer. The book was specially priced so it would be more generally available despite the high cost of publishing. It is a large and imposing book and contains the true answers to all the questions people might ask and so saves the PTS person or any other person a great deal of explanation time.

Scientology: The Fundamentals of Thought and other basic books, lectures and films (particularly the film *Introduction to Scientology*) are very useful tools. The preclear can send a copy of a book, lecture or film to the antagonistic person. Or he can bring the person in to the local org to listen to a lecture or see a film.

HOW TO HANDLE FALSE DATA AND LIES

In some cases antagonism stems from false data or outright lies that the antagonistic person has heard or read.

The handling for this is based on the datum that truth must exist before lies, and truth blows the lie away as it is later on the chain.

The handling for a person who has false data on Scientology is to fill in any vacuum of missing data with factual data about Scientology and to prove any lies, rumors and false data encountered to be false.

Any lies are disproven by documenting the truth. Packs documenting the falsity of common lies can be obtained through one's local org.

Extraordinary successes in handling PTS situations with the *Can We Ever Be Friends?* recording and booklet occur when these are used. Many parents, friends, relatives of Scientologists, who, due to misunderstoods or misinformation, thought they were opposed to Scientology and its aims have discovered, after listening to this recording, that they are in full agreement with it and now give Scientology their support. The results available with this recording cannot be underestimated. It can be used by itself when communication has really broken down between the two persons or in conjunction with other PTS handlings.

DISCONNECTION

In the rare cases where disconnection is validly indicated in order to handle the person's PTSness, it should be done exactly per *PTSness and Disconnection.*

PTS/SP COURSE

A full and complete PTS handling would consist of getting the person through the PTS/SP Course. This *must* be included as part of the handling, as otherwise the person will never learn the full mechanics of Suppressive Persons and why one becomes PTS.

With the knowledge of PTS/SP technical data under his belt, a person can be at cause over Suppressive Persons and is far less likely to become PTS to anyone in the future.

FURTHER HANDLINGS

There are further handlings that can be done on PTSes which utilize Scientology processing. These are the *PTS Rundown* and the *Suppressed Person Rundown.*

The PTS Rundown is done when preclears who have had standard, successful PTS handlings Roller Coaster at a later date, become ill, slump after making gains or continue to find additional terminals they are PTS to. Or it is done when the person doesn't brighten up with standard PTS handling, or when he isn't sure of the SP or can't name any SP at all.

If after the PTS Rundown, the person feels fine but the persons suppressing him are still making trouble, then the PTS person must have a Suppressed Person Rundown.

The Suppressed Person Rundown can produce the wondrous result of changing the disposition of an antagonistic terminal at a distance, by auditing the PTS preclear. Where this terminal was antagonistic, invalidative, hostile or downright suppressive, he can suddenly have a change of heart and seek to make peace with the PTS preclear.

SUMMARY OF HANDLING

Thus, any full and complete PTS handling consists of:

1. Education,

2. PTS interview (discovering to what or whom he is PTS),

3. Handling (or in rare cases disconnection, if warranted),

4. PTS/SP Course (can be started earlier),

5. PTS Rundown (if needed),

6. Suppressed Person Rundown (if needed).

POLICIES ON PHYSICAL HEALING
INSANITY AND "SOURCES OF TROUBLE"

t has been the longstanding policy of Central Organizations to handle physical illness and insanity in the following manner.

HEALING

Any process labeled "healing," old or new, refers to healing by mental and spiritual means and should therefore be looked upon as the relief of difficulties arising from mental and spiritual causes.

The proper procedure in being requested to heal some complained-of physical disability is as follows:

1. Require a physical examination from whatever practitioners of the physical healing arts may be competent and available;

2. Clearly establish that the disability does not stem from immediately physical causes;

3. If the disability is pronounced to be curable within the skill of the physical practitioner and is in actual fact a disease or illness which surrenders to contemporary physical treatment, to require the person to be so treated before Scientology processing may be undertaken;

4. If, however, the physical practitioner's recommendation includes surgery or treatment of an unproven nature or the illness or disease cannot be accurately diagnosed as a specific physical illness or disease with a known cure, the person may be accepted for processing on the reasonable assumption that no purely physical illness is proven to exist, and that it is probably mental or spiritual in origin.

POLICIES REGARDING THE INSANE

With insane persons or persons with a proven record of insanity, do the following:

1. Establish to the best of your ability within reasonable administrative limits and known tests that any HGC pc accepted for processing does not have a history of deserved institutionalization in an insane asylum or similar place;

2. Process only those persons who have no such history;

3. Do not recommend any other treatment by practitioners in the field of insanity where there exists any evidence that such practitioners injure, disable or maltreat patients by violently-reacting drugs, by painful shocks, surgery or other barbaric and outdated means of "mental treatment";

4. If no recommendation is possible under (3) above, recommend only rest and a change of environment, but not in a professional capacity.

SOURCES OF TROUBLE

Policies similar to those regarding physical illness and insanity exist for types of persons who have caused us considerable trouble.

These persons can be grouped under "Sources of Trouble." They include:

a. Persons intimately connected with persons (such as marital or familial ties) of known antagonism to mental or spiritual treatment or Scientology. In practice such persons, even when they approach Scientology in a friendly fashion, have such pressure continually brought to bear upon them by persons with undue influence over them that they make very poor gains in processing and their interest is solely devoted to proving the antagonistic element wrong.

They, by experience, produce a great deal of trouble in the long run as their own condition does not improve adequately under such stresses to effectively combat the antagonism.

Their present time problem cannot be reached as it is continuous and, so long as it remains so, they should not be accepted for auditing by any organization or auditor.

b. Criminals with proven criminal records often continue to commit so many undetected harmful acts between sessions that they do not make adequate case gains and therefore should not be accepted for processing by organizations or auditors.

c. Persons who have ever threatened to sue or embarrass or attack or who have publicly attacked Scientology or been a party to an attack and all their immediate families should never be accepted for processing by a Central Organization or an auditor. They have a history of only serving other ends than case gain and commonly again turn on the organization or auditor. They have already barred themselves out by their own overts against Scientology and are thereafter too difficult to help, since they cannot openly accept help from those they have tried to injure.

d. "Responsible-for-condition" cases have been traced back to other causes for their condition too often to be acceptable. By responsible-for-condition cases is meant the person who insists a book or some auditor is "wholly responsible for the terrible condition I am in." Such cases demand unusual favors, free auditing, tremendous effort on the part of auditors. Review of these cases show that they were in the same or worse condition long before auditing, that they are using a planned campaign to obtain auditing for nothing, that they are not as bad off as they claim, and that their antagonism extends to anyone who seeks to help them, even their own families. Establish the rights of the matter and decide accordingly.

e. Persons who are not being audited on their own determinism are a liability as they are forced into being processed by some other person and have no personal desire to become better. Quite on the contrary, they usually want only to prove the person who wants them audited wrong and so do not get better. Until a personally determined goal to be processed occurs, the person will not benefit.

f. Persons who "want to be processed to see if Scientology works" as their only reason for being audited have never been known to make gains as they do not participate. News reporters fall into this category. They should not be audited.

g. Persons who claim that "if you help such and such a case" (at great and *your* expense) because somebody is rich or influential or the neighbors would be electrified should be ignored. Processing is designed for bettering individuals, not progressing by stunts or giving cases undue importance. Process only at convenience and usual arrangements. Make no extraordinary effort at the expense of other persons who do want processing for normal reasons. Not one of these arrangements has ever come off successfully as it has the unworthy goal of notoriety, not betterment.

h. Persons who "have an open mind" but no personal hopes or desires for auditing or knowingness should be ignored, as they really don't have an open mind at all, but a lack of ability to decide about things, and are seldom found to be very responsible and waste anyone's efforts "to convince them."

i. Persons who do not believe anything or anyone can get better. They have a purpose for being audited entirely contrary to the auditor's and so, in this conflict, do not benefit. When such persons are trained, they use their training to degrade others. Thus they should not be accepted for training or auditing.

j. Persons attempting to sit in judgment on Scientology in hearings or attempting to investigate Scientology should be given no undue importance. One should not seek to instruct or assist them in any way. This includes judges, boards, newspaper reporters, magazine writers, etc. All efforts to be helpful or instructive have done nothing beneficial, as their first idea is a firm "I don't know" and this usually ends with an equally firm "I don't know." If a person can't see for himself or judge from the obvious, then he does not have sufficient powers of observation even to sort out actual evidence. In legal matters, only take the obvious effective steps—carry on no crusades in court. In the matter of reporters, etc., it is not worthwhile to give them any time, contrary to popular belief. They are given their story before they leave their editorial rooms and you only strengthen what they have to say by saying anything. They are no public communication line that sways much. Policy is very definite. Ignore.

To summarize Sources of Trouble, the policy in general is to cut communication as the longer it is extended the more trouble they are. I know of no case where the types of persons listed above were handled by auditing or instruction. I know of many cases where they were handled by firm legal stands, by ignoring them until they changed their minds, or just turning one's back.

In applying such a policy of cut-communication, one must also use judgment as there are exceptions in all things and to fail to handle a person's momentary upset in life or with us can be quite fatal. So these policies refer to non-Scientology persons in the main or persons who appear on the outer fringes and push toward us. When such a person bears any of the above designations, we and the many are better off to ignore them.

Scientology works. You don't have to prove it to everyone. People don't deserve to have Scientology as a divine right, you know. They have to earn it. This has been true in every philosophy that sought to better Man.

And the less enturbulence you put on your lines, the better and the more people you will eventually help.

THE STRESS OF POLICY

All the above "Sources of Trouble" are also forbidden training and when a person being trained or audited is detected to belong under the above headings (a) to (j), he or she should be advised to terminate and accept refund, which must be paid at once, and the full explanation should be given them at that time.

Thus the few may not, in their own turmoil, impede service to and the advance of the many.

Scientology is an applied religious philosophy designed and developed to make the able more able. In this sphere it is tremendously successful.

Efforts to involve philosophy with medical imperialism, psychiatric sadism, the bigoted churchman, bring about a slowing of our progress.

These people are sick spiritually because of their own continuous harmful actions against patients and the society and are beyond our normal means to help.

These policies will continue in existence until such time as those interested care to invest the time and treasure necessary to build the institutions and reeducate the professions which now practice medical and physical mental healing—and this is definitely not within our time, but would belong to some remote future when more men are sane.

However, such a program would depend upon the continued existence of the medical imperialist and the psychiatrist and as their more reprehensible activities are rather new and very radical, they may be abandoned by public and government long before Scientology could help them. This is probably the more likely occurrence as even in Russia the communist has now forsworn all violent treatments of the insane, according to their delegates to the London Medical Conference of this year,* and Russian practitioners look with contempt and scorn upon the Western psychiatrist. The medical doctor of England, taken over by socialism, has lost his ambition for medical imperialism and has no contest with Scientology. In the United States the American Medical Association has become locked in mortal combat with the government and probably will be socialized entirely in a few years due to fee abuses and lack of gains. The medical doctor remains strong only in more backward small nations such as Australia where world trends are late in arriving.

*The year being referred to is 1964.

Even the Church in Rome is considering a surrender of principles and amalgamation with other faiths in an effort to save a dwindling religious membership.

Thus there may be no medical practitioner, as we know him, left in a few decades. Membership in the psychiatric profession is declining.

In the place of these institutions, if we ever get around to them, we may find ourselves dealing with completely different practices in the fields of physical healing and the treatment of the insane. All we ask of them is that they are competent in their treatments and less greedy for monopoly than their predecessors. And if this is so, then our policies will then remain fully in force, but in a spirit of cooperation, not with the desire to protect ourselves and the public from them and the products of their bungling.

Ours are the powerful communication lines. They are powerful because they are theta lines. Entheta (enturbulated theta) obtains all its apparent power by being parasitic on theta lines. Only when you add the power of our lines to the weakness of entheta lines can they then have strength.

Example: It was the FCDC communication to its own field about that government raid* that (a) cost the most in cash and (b) did the most damage. You can actually ignore an entheta line in almost all cases without the faintest consequence. It only has power when we let it have power by answering it.

---

*government raid: refers to a 1963 raid by the United States Food and Drug Administration in which E-Meters and literature from the Founding Church of Scientology in Washington, DC, were seized under the bogus allegation that these were being presented to the public as "medical cures." Ultimately, however, the Church not only emerged victorious with sweeping recognition of religious bona fides, but the court ordered the return of all seized materials.

ETHICS IN
SCIENTOLOGY
ORGANIZATIONS

Scientology Makes A Safe Environment

e're working to provide a safe environment for Scientology and Scientologists in orgs everywhere.

The dangerous environment of the world, of injustice, sudden dismissals, war, atomic bombs, will only persist and trouble us if we fail to spread our safe environment across the world.

It starts with our own orgs. They must be safe environments.

Only good tech and justice can make the org environment safe. Like an auditing room, we must be able to work undisturbed by the madness at our doors.

We can make every org a safe island and then, by expanding and joining those orgs, bring peace and a safe environment to all the world.

It not only *can* be done. It is happening this moment. Push it along. Support policy, good tech and justice.

WHY ETHICS?

ou can't run preclears without Ethics to hand. Technical fact. Particularly on lower-level processes and also on higher-level processes, the Potential Trouble Source (connected to a Suppressive) will go to pieces under auditing—not improve.

Current statistic on this is 20 percent PTS or mild SP and, of this, 2½ percent is very vicious Suppressive Person.

Your Director of Training (D of T) *can't* train a class that has a PTS or SP in it.

Your Director of Processing (D of P) can't audit people if he can't handle this PTS and SP factor efficiently.

Your Director of Review will go round the bend if he can't shunt PTSes or SPs to Ethics. He'll have to become the Ethics Officer.

This is not policy I am talking about. It is *technical* fact. It just *can't* be done and never will be possible on lower technology and requires fantastic skill to get a real gain even with higher-level processes. So accept this *technical* fact and you'll understand both ethics and all your case failures.

With no available Ethics Officer to take PTSes or SPs off the lines and handle (by spotting and using standard policy actions), your traffic will thin, your jobs will be a burden and the org will fail.

The whole staff has to know the ethics drill and follow it.

Ethics is for the public far more than staff. You must use the drill.

A Supervisor to whom a student is impolite must send the student to Ethics. If the student is slow, the Supervisor *must* send to Review for special attention at the student's expense.

Staff Auditors, finding a pc savage or unchanging, must send to Review which probably sends to Ethics. Staff Auditors, finding a case failing, *must* send to Review which again may send to Ethics.

The ultimate in dumbness is the person who thinks "Ethics is to make pcs answer questions." Or the person who thinks it is for espionage on staff members.

Ethics is a long-arm part of technology. And, incidentally, spots PTSes and SPs who get onto staffs, as they sometimes do.

Ethics is a fine-edged tool, a vital part of an org if one wishes to train people in Scientology or process them successfully.

If tech is out, ethics will get tech in. If ethics is out, tech won't ever go in. It's like that. I learned this the hard way. Let's hope others learn it on easier channels. The "ARC broke pc" or "ARC broke student" is 95 percent ethics-type. That's the discovery. Use it.

If you have ethics *in,* the 80 percent will flow through the organization in a mad torrent.

INDICATORS OF ORGS

ust as pcs have indicators, so do orgs.

There is a probable long list of good indicators. When these are present, Ethics is quiet and hangs on to an interrogation, etc., only long enough to get policy and technology in.

There is a probable long list of bad indicators. When these are present, Ethics becomes industrious in ratio to the number of bad indicators.

The first indicators, good or bad, are statistics—the Organization Information Center (OIC) graphs for units, sections, departments, divisions and the org. When these are rising, the rise is a *good indicator.* When these are falling, the fall is a *bad indicator.*

The second of these indicators, good or bad, are *technical gains.* When technology is *in,* cases are gaining. This is a good indicator. When technology is *out,* cases are losing. This is a bad indicator.

Ethics only exists to hold the fort long enough and settle things down enough to get technology in. Ethics is never carried on for its own sake. It is pushed home only until technology is functioning and then technology resolves matters and Ethics prowls off looking for other targets.

We don't "hang" people because we started to "hang" them and so must do so. We start to "hang" people and keep right on "tying the noose" in a workmanlike fashion right up to the instant we can get tech in—which of course makes the "noose" unnecessary.

But if tech never does get in then we complete the "hanging."

You will find if you *label* a Suppressive you will someday get him back and get tech in on him. If you don't ever label, they wander off and get lost.

Labeling as a Suppressive is our "hanging."

When things are bad (bad indicators heavily visible), putting a "body on the gallows" is very salutary. We call it "putting a head on a pike." Too many *bad* indicators and too goofed up a situation and we *must* put a head on a pike. Then things simmer down and we can begin to get tech in.

That's the whole purpose of ethics—to *get tech in.* And we use enough to do so, to get correct standard tech in and being done.

When there are lots of bad indicators about—low and falling statistics, goofed cases—we get very handy with our interrogatories and put the place very nearly under martial law. We call this a State of Emergency. Once Emergency is declared, you usually have to put a head or two on a pike to convince people that you mean it. After that, necessity level rises and the place straightens up. If an Emergency is *continued* beyond a reasonable time, we resort to very heavy discipline and Comm Ev the executives who wouldn't get off it.

Ethics, then, is applied to the *degree* required to produce the result of getting tech in. Once tech is really in on a person (with a case gain), or a Tech Division, let us say, and auditors actually audit standard processes by the book, we *know* it will resolve and we ease off with ethics.

Ethics, then, is the tool by which you get good indicators in by getting tech in. Ethics is the steamroller which smooths the highway.

Once the road is open, we are quite likely to skip remaining investigation and let it all be.

But somebody *promising* to be good is never good enough. We want statistics. Bettered statistics.

SYMPTOMS OF ORGANIZATIONS

Orgs have various symptoms which tell us how things really are ethicwise.

One of these is dilettantism.

DILETTANTE-ISM

Dilettante = One who interests himself in an art or science merely as a pastime and without serious study.

In an org, this manifests itself with: "People should live a little." "One needs a rest from Scientology." "One should do something else too." All that kind of jazz.

It also manifests itself in nonconsecutive scheduling, part-time students, "because things are different in this town and people can come only two nights...." Ask what they do with other nights. Bowling. Horse racing.

Boy, you better maul the case folders of staff. You have a Suppressive aboard. Maybe six.

Scientology, that saves lives, is a modern miracle, is being compared to bowling. Get it?

That org or portion just isn't serious. Scientology is an idle club to it, an old lady's sewing circle. And to somebody, signing people up for training and auditing are just con games they put over on the public.

SUPPRESSIVES!

Root them out.

Wild Rumors—This symptom is caused by Potential Trouble Sources. Find whose case Roller Coasters (gets better, gets worse). Investigate. You'll find a Suppressive or two outside the org.

Put a head on a pike with an HCO Ethics Order and publish it widely.

ARC Broken Field—Appoint a Comm Ev Chairman to inquire into matters and form a list of Interested Parties based on reports he will now receive.

Bad Tech—When results just don't happen in the Academy, HGC or Review, one or another, look for the Potential Trouble Sources and Suppressives. Only they can keep tech out. Put a big head on a pike and then begin to interrogate every slip in the place. Suddenly tech is in again.

There are many such symptoms.

At the root of every bad condition will be found a Suppressive Person.

Locate your Potential Trouble Sources by locating passers of rumors, etc. Then locate the Suppressive and "shoot."

Calm reigns. Tech is in.

And that's all one means to accomplish.

Today, *technology works on every case.* If the local org can't handle a case, higher orgs can.

If you get tech in well enough in an org, tech handles all. Beautifully. But if it is out, only ethics can bat down the reasons it can't be gotten in.

OPTIMUM STATE

The optimum state of an org is so high that there is no easy way to describe it. All cases getting cracked, Releases and Clears by the hundreds, command of the environment. Big. That's an optimum state for *any* org.

If it isn't rising *toward* optimum today, it is locally being held down.

The viewpoint of Ethics is there is no adequate reason why an org is stumbling except ethics reasons. Let others take care of any other lacks. Ethics *never* gets reasonable about lack of expansion.

If Ethics shoves hard enough, others will get a high enough necessity level to act.

So when an org is low: Find out where its statistics are down and who is a PTS or an SP and *act*.

That's the job of Ethics. Thus little by little we take off the brakes for a cleared Earth.

ETHICS OFFICER HAT

his is a quick outline of the activities of the Ethics Officer.

The purpose of the Ethics Officer is:

To help Ron clear orgs and the public if need be of entheta and enturbulation so that Scientology can be done.

The activities of the Ethics Officer consist of isolating individuals who are stopping proper flows by pulling withholds with Ethics Technology and by removing as necessary Potential Trouble Sources and suppressive individuals off org comm lines and by generally enforcing Ethics Codes.

The technology of how this is done is quite precise.

In a nutshell, (a) one finds an imperfect functioning of some portion of the org and then (b) finds something that one doesn't understand about it and then (c) interrogates by despatch the individuals in that portion connected with the imperfect functioning.

Just those three steps done over and over are usually quite enough to keep an org running quite smoothly.

On first taking over post in an enturbulated org, or in viewing a portion of the org in an enturbulated condition, the actions of the Ethics Officer consist of:

1. Run back entheta by asking for names of who said it to the person who is now saying it;

2. Locate those persons and find out who told *them,* and then;

233

3. Look amongst *those* names for no-case-change or for Potential Trouble Sources. Bill voices a rumor (usually with a "they" say...). The Ethics Officer asks Bill what "they's" name is. Bill thinks and finally says it was Pete. The Ethics Officer locates Pete and asks Pete who told him, and when Pete says "they" the Ethics Officer finds out what "they's" name is. Pete says it was Agnes. Ethics Officer locates Agnes. Agnes maintains it is true and can't say who said it. Ethics Officer looks up Agnes' case folder or puts Agnes on a meter and sees by high or very low TA that he has a Suppressive. Or he finds Agnes has a Suppressive husband and that she is a Potential Trouble Source.

The Ethics Officer then handles it as per Ethics Policy Letters.

In short, rumor comes from *somewhere.* The somewhere is a Potential Trouble Source or a Suppressive. One runs it down and applies the remedies contained in Ethics HCO Policy Letters to that person.

An Ethics Officer's first job is usually cleaning up the org of its Potential Trouble Sources and requesting a Comm Ev for the Suppressives. That gets things in focus quickly and smooths an org down so it will function.

Then one looks for *down* statistics in the Organization Information Center (OIC) charts. These aren't understandable, of course, so one interrogates by sending interrogatories to the people concerned. In their answers, there will be something that doesn't make sense at all to the Ethics Officer. Example: "We can't pay the bills because Josie has been on course." The Ethics Officer is only looking for something he himself can't reconcile. So he sends interrogatories to the person who wrote it *and* to Josie. Sooner or later some wild withhold or even a crime shows up when one does this.

The trick of this "Org Auditing" is to find a piece of string sticking out—something one can't understand and, by interrogatories, pull on it. A small cat shows up. Pull with some more interrogatories.

A baby gorilla shows up. Pull some more. A tiger appears. Pull again and wow! You've got a General Sherman tank!

It *isn't* reasonable for people to be lazy or stupid. At the bottom you find the *real* cause of no action in a portion of an org or continuous upset.

When you have your General Sherman, call a Court of Ethics on it. Or take action. But in actual fact you have probably already fixed it up.

There's always a *reason* behind a bad statistic. Send out interrogatories until you *have the real reason* in view. It will never be "Agnes isn't bright." It is more likely, Agnes is on a typing post but never knew how to type. Or worse, the Director of Processing (D of P) audits org pcs for his own profit. Or the Director of Training (D of T) simply never comes to work.

The real explanation of a down statistic is always a very easily understood thing. If you interrogate enough, you'll get the real explanation and then you can act.

Never use conduct for anything but an indicator of what you should interrogate.

Never buy rumors as generalities. *Somebody* said them and that somebody has a *name.* Get the name.

FILING

Filing is the real trick of Ethics work. The files do all the work, really.

Executive Ethics Reports patiently filed in folders, one for each staff member, eventually makes one file fat. There's your boy.

Call up a Court of Ethics on him and his area gets smooth.

Whatever report you get, file it with a *name.* Don't file by departments or divisions. File by *names.*

The files do 90 percent of the work. When one file gets fat, call the person up for ethics action.

TIME MACHINE

Run a Time Machine and let it accumulate data for you.

The orders that fall off of it that weren't complied with should be reported to the senior issuing them.

But file those noncompliances. Soon, a file gets fat and we know why the org isn't running in one of its portions.

POLICY

All Ethics Policy applies to the actions of an Ethics Officer.

But the above is his workaday world, auditor to the org, filing his replies, watching for the fat file and then calling a Court on it.

That way an org soon begins to run like a well-greased river, doing its job in a happy atmosphere.

Be as sudden and swift and unreasonable as you like. You aren't there to win a popularity contest.

Make Executives report all those Ethics items they should. Make them write their orders and send you a copy. Make your Comm Center give you the responses for pairing with the copies. File carefully and call the lightning down on the person who gets a fat Ethics File.

It's an easy job. Mostly admin. But so is all intelligence work. The files do the job if you make people report and if you file well yourself.

And when you feel exasperated and balked and feel like taking it out on somebody, do so by all means.

Who ever heard of a tame Ethics Officer?

The sanity of the planet is all that is at stake.

ETHICS
PROTECTION

thics actions must parallel the purposes of Scientology and its organizations.

Ethics exists primarily to get technology in. Tech can't work unless ethics is already in. When tech goes out, Ethics can (and is expected to) get it in. For the purpose of Scientology, amongst others, is to apply Scientology. Therefore when tech is in, Ethics actions tend to be dropped. Ethics continues its actions until tech is in and as soon as it is, backs off and only acts if tech goes out again.

The purpose of the org is to get the show on the road and keep it going. This means production. Every division is a production unit. It makes or does something that can have a *statistic* to see if it goes up or down. Example: a typist gets out 500 letters in one week. That's a statistic. If the next week the same typist gets out 600 letters, that's an *up* statistic. If the typist gets out 300 letters, that's a *down* statistic. Every post in an org can have a statistic. So does every portion of the org. The purpose is to keep production (statistics) up. This is the only thing that gives a good income for the staff member personally. When statistics go down or when things are so organized you can't get one for a post, the staff members' pay goes down as the org goes down in its overall production. The production of an organization is only the total of its individual staff members. When these have down statistics so does the org.

Ethics actions are often used to handle down individual statistics. A person who is not doing his job becomes an Ethics target.

Conversely, if a person *is* doing his job (and his statistic will show that) ethics is considered to be *in* and the person is *protected* by Ethics.

As an example of the proper application of ethics to the production of an org, let us say the Letter Registrar has a high statistic (gets out lots of effective mail). Somebody reports the Letter Registrar for rudeness, somebody else reports the Letter Registrar for irregular conduct with a student. Somebody else reports the Letter Registrar for leaving all the lights on. Proper Ethics Officer action = look up the general statistics of the Letter Registrar and, seeing that they average quite high, file the complaints with a yawn.

As the second example of ethics application to the production of an org, let us say a Course Supervisor has a low statistic (very few students moved out of his course, course number growing, hardly anyone graduating, a bad Academy statistic). Somebody reports this Course Supervisor for being late for work, somebody else reports him for no weekly Ad Comm report and bang! Ethics looks up the person, calls for an Ethics Hearing with trimmings.

We are not in the business of being good boys and girls. We're in the business of going free and getting the org production roaring. Nothing else is of any interest then to Ethics but (a) getting tech in, getting it run and getting it run right and (b) getting production up and the org roaring along.

Therefore if a staff member *is* getting production up by having his own statistic excellent, Ethics sure isn't interested. But if a staff member isn't producing, shown by his bad statistic for his post, Ethics is fascinated with his smallest Misdemeanor.

In short, a staff member can "get away with murder" so long as his statistic is up and can't "sneeze" without a chop if it's down.

To do otherwise is to permit some Suppressive Person to simply ethics chit every producer in the org out of existence.

When people do start reporting a staff member with a high statistic, what you investigate is the person who turned in the report.

In an ancient army a particularly brave deed was recognized by an award of the title of Kha-Khan. It was not a rank. The person remained what he was, *but* he was entitled to be forgiven the death penalty ten times in case in the future he did anything wrong. That was a Kha-Khan.

That's what producing, high statistic staff members are—Kha-Khans. They can "get away with murder" without a blink from Ethics.

The average fair-to-poor statistic staff member of course gets just routine ethics with Hearings or Courts for too many misdeeds. The low statistic fellow gets a Court if he sneezes.

Ethics *must* use all org discipline only in view of the production statistic of the staff member involved.

And Ethics must recognize a Kha-Khan when it sees one—and tear up the bad report chits on the person with a yawn.

To the staff member this means—if you do your job you are protected by Ethics.

REWARDS AND PENALTIES
HOW TO HANDLE PERSONNEL AND ETHICS MATTERS

he whole decay of Western government is explained in this seemingly obvious law:

WHEN YOU REWARD DOWN STATISTICS AND PENALIZE UP STATISTICS YOU GET DOWN STATISTICS.

If you reward nonproduction you get nonproduction.

When you penalize production you get nonproduction.

The welfare state can be defined as that state which rewards nonproduction at the expense of production. Let us not then be surprised that we all turn up at last slaves in a starved society.

The Soviet Union could not even feed herself but depended on conquest to eke out an existence—and don't think they didn't strip the conquered! They had to.

Oddly enough, one of the best ways to detect a Suppressive Person is that he or she stamps on up statistics and condones or rewards down statistics. It makes an SP very happy for everyone to starve to death, for the good worker to be shattered and the bad worker patted on the back.

Draw your own conclusions as to whether or not Western governments (or welfare states) became at last Suppressives. For they used the law used by Suppressives: If you reward nonproduction you get nonproduction.

Although all this is very obvious to us, it seems to have been unknown, overlooked or ignored by twentieth-century governments.

In the conduct of our own affairs in all matters of rewards and penalties, we pay sharp heed to the basic laws as above and use this policy:

We award production and up statistics and penalize nonproduction and down statistics. Always.

Also we do it *all* by statistics—not rumor or personality or who knows who. And we make sure everyone has a statistic of some sort.

We promote by statistic only.

We penalize down statistics only.

The whole of government as government was only a small bit of a real organization—it was an ethics function plus a tax function plus a disbursement function. This is about 3/100ths of an organization. A twentieth-century government was just these three functions gone mad. Yet they made the whole population wear the hat of government.

We must learn and profit from what they did wrong. And what they mainly did wrong was reward the down statistic and penalize the up statistic.

The hard worker-earner was heavily taxed and the money was used to support the indigent. This was *not* humanitarian. It was only given "humanitarian" reasons.

The robbed person was investigated exclusively, rarely the robber.

The head of government who got into the most debt became a hero.

War rulers were deified and peacetime rulers forgotten no matter how many wars they prevented.

Thus went ancient Greece, Rome, France, the British Empire and the US. *This* was the decline and fall of every great civilization on this planet: they eventually rewarded the down statistic and penalized the up statistic. That's *all* that caused their decline. They came at last into the hands of Suppressives and had *no* technology to detect them or escape their inevitable disasters.

Thus, when you think of "processing Joe to make a good D of P out of him and get him over his mistakes," forget it. That rewards a down statistic. Instead, find an auditor with an up statistic, reward it with processing and make *him* the D of P.

Never promote a down statistic or demote an up statistic.

Never even hold a Hearing on someone with an up statistic. Never accept an Ethics Chit on one—just stamp it "Sorry, Up Statistic" and send it back.

But someone with a steadily down statistic, investigate. Accept and convert any Ethics Chit to a Hearing. Look for an early replacement.

Gruesomely, in my experience, I have only seldom raised a chronically down statistic with orders or persuasion or new plans. I have only raised them with changes of personnel.

So don't even consider someone with a steadily down statistic as part of the team. Investigate, yes. Try, yes. But if it stays down, don't fool about. The person is drawing pay and position and privilege for not doing his job and that's too much reward even there.

Don't get reasonable about down statistics. They are down because they are down. If someone were on the post, they would be up. And act on that basis.

Any duress leveled by Ethics should be reserved for down statistics.

We even investigate social areas of down statistic. Psychiatry's cures are zero. The negative statistic of more insane is all that is "up." So investigate and "hang."

If we reverse the conduct of declining governments and businesses, we will of course grow. And that makes for coffee and cakes, promotion, higher pay, better working quarters and tools for all those who earned them. And who else should have them?

If you do it any other way, everyone starves. We are peculiar in believing there is a virtue in prosperity.

You cannot give more to the indigent than the society produces. When the society, by penalizing production, at last produces very little and yet has to feed very many, revolutions, confusion, political unrest and Dark Ages ensue.

In a very prosperous society where production is amply rewarded, there is always more left over than is needed. I well recall in prosperous farm communities that charity was ample and people didn't die in the ditch. That only happens where production is already low and commodity or commerce already scarce (scarcity of *commercial* means of distribution is also a factor in depressions).

The cause of the Great Depression of the 1920s and 1930s in the US and England has never been pointed out by welfare "statesmen." The cause was income tax and government interference with companies and, all during the 1800s, a gradual rise of nationalism and size of governments and their budgets, and no commercial development to distribute goods to the common people, catering to royal governments or only a leisure class still being the focus of production.

Income tax so penalized management, making it unrewarded, and company law so hampered financing that it ceased to be really worthwhile to run companies and management quit. In Russia, management went into politics in desperation. Kings were always decreeing the commoner couldn't have this or that (it put the commoner's statistic up!) and not until 1930 did anyone really begin to sell to the people with heavy advertising. It was Madison Avenue, radio, TV and Bing Crosby, not the Gre-e-eat Roosevelt who got the US out of the Depression. England, not permitting wide radio coverage, did not come out of it and her empire is dust. England still too firmly held the "aristocratic" tradition that the commoner mustn't possess to truly use her population as a market.

But the *reason* they let it go this way and the *reason* the Great Depression occurred and the *reason* for the decline of the West is this one simple truth:

If you reward nonproduction, you get it.

It is *not* humanitarian to let a *whole* population go to pieces just because a few refuse to work. And some people just won't. And when work no longer has reward, none will.

It is far more humane to have enough so everyone can eat.

So specialize in production and everybody wins. Reward it.

There is nothing really wrong with socialism helping the needy. Sometimes it is vital. But the reasons for that are more or less over. It is a temporary solution, easily overdone and like communism is simply old-fashioned today. If carried to extremes, like drinking coffee or absinthe or even eating, it becomes quite uncomfortable and oppressive. And today, socialism and communism have been carried far too far and now only oppress up statistics and reward down ones.

By the way, the natural law given here is the reason Scientology goes poorly when credit is extended by orgs and when auditors won't require proper donations. With credit and no donation, we are rewarding down statistics with attention and betterment as much as we reward up statistics in the society. A preclear who can work and produces as a member of society deserves, of course, priority. He naturally is the one who can pay. When we give the one who can't pay just as much attention, we are rewarding a down social statistic with Scientology and, of course, we don't expand because we don't expand the ability of the able. In proof, the most expensive thing you can do is process the insane and these have the lowest statistic in the society.

The more you help those in the society with low statistics, the more tangled affairs will get. The orgs require fantastic attention to keep them there at all when we reward low society statistics with training and processing. The worker pays his way. He has a high statistic. So give him the best in training and processing—not competition with people who don't work and don't have any money.

Always give the best service to the person in society who does his job. By not extending credit you tend to guarantee the best service to those with the best statistics and so everyone wins again. None are *owed* processing or training. We are not an earthwide amends project.

No good worker *owes* his work. That's slavery.

We don't *owe* because we do *better.* One would owe only if one did worse.

Not everyone realizes how socialism penalizes an up statistic. Take health taxes. If an average man adds up what he pays the government, he will find *his* visits to medicos are *very* expensive. The one who benefits is only the chronically ill, whose way is paid by the healthy. So the chronically ill (down statistic) are rewarded with care paid for by penalties on the healthy (up statistic).

In income tax, the more a worker makes, the more hours of his workweek are taxed away from him. Eventually he is no longer working for his reward. He is working for no pay. Therefore people tend to refuse higher pay (up statistics). It has a penalty that is too great. On the other hand, a totally indigent nonworking person is paid well just to loaf. The up statistic person cannot hire any small services to help his own prosperity as he is already paying it *via* the government to somebody who doesn't work.

Socialisms pay people *not* to grow crops no matter how many are starving. Get it?

So the law holds.

Charity is charity. It benefits the donor, giving him a sense of superiority and status. It is a liability to the receiver but he accepts it as he must and vows (if he has any pride) to cease being poor and get to work.

Charity cannot be enforced by law and arrest, for then it is extortion and not charity.

And get no idea that I beat any drum for capitalism. That too is old-old-*old* hat.

Capitalism is the economics of living by nonproduction. It by exact definition is the economics of living off interest from loans, which is an extreme of rewarding nonproduction.

Imperialism and colonialism are also bad as they exist by enslaving the population of less strong countries. And that too is getting a reward for nonproduction like they did in Victorian England from all the colonies.

Parasitism is parasitism. Whether high or low it is unlovely.

All these isms are almost equally nutty and their inheritors, if not their originators, were all of a stamp—suppressive.

All I beat the drum for is that the working worker deserves a break and the working manager deserves his pay and the successful company deserves the fruits of its success.

Only when success is bought by enslavement or rewards are given to bums or thieves will you find me objecting.

This is a new look. It is an honest look.

Reward the up statistic and damn the down and we'll all make out.

DISCIPLINE
SPS AND ADMIN
HOW STATISTICS CRASH

ne of the ways an SP works to stop an activity or to halt an Affluence is to pick out key personnel and spread wild, false and alarming stories about them.

Another way, often used in conjunction with the above, is to pound a key executive with alarming entheta about staff, divisions or activities. This urges the key executive to take uncalled-for action which upsets things and which may lead to the dismissal of valuable staff.

Also, it is a symptom of an org under external pressure to come down on its own personnel rather than on the public or on real SPs.

SPs tend to vanish in memory since they speak in generalities. "Always" "everyone" salt their language so that when you say, "Who told you?" in tracing a rumor, it is hard to remember since "everyone" seems to have said it. Actually, the SP who did say it used "everyone" in his comm so often as to become in memory "everyone."

A GOOD MANAGER IGNORES RUMOR AND ONLY ACTS ON STATISTICS.

Had I heeded over the years any rumormonger, we would have no orgs. I generally don't listen and, if I do, only go so far as inspecting stats.

It is easy to discipline staff and hard to discipline the public. A *lazy* executive only disciplines staff. It takes more confront to tackle the public.

When an executive listens to rumor and bad things about his fellow staff members without looking at the actual production statistics, that executive can harm the org badly.

I have never tried to make staff members "be good." I have only tried to make them produce and wear their hats.

Our whole statistic system exists to end excessive discipline of valuable staff members.

To me a staff member whose stats are up can do no wrong.

I am not interested in wog morality. I am only interested in getting the show on the road and keeping it there.

Also, I detest having to discipline anyone for anything, particularly a Scientologist. And the only discipline I use is to hold the fort until people are Clear enough to see the light. They always do. All misconduct comes from aberration.

However, if anyone is getting industrious trying to enturbulate or stop Scientology or its activities, I can make Captain Bligh look like a Sunday school teacher. There is probably no limit on what I would do to safeguard Man's only road to freedom against persons who, disdaining processing, seek to stop Scientology or hurt Scientologists.

I well know Man's fixation on trying to make "everybody good." Which means, really, inactive. The best men I have had in wars routinely have been continually arrested and generally frowned on by "shore patrols," "military police," etc. To the body politic, a *quiet* person is the ideal. When the guns begin to go, these quiet ones are all hiding and only the active ones are there to fight. I often wonder what would happen to a state if it *did* achieve its apparent goal of making one and all inactive little sheep.

So I don't care what men or women do if they just wear their hats and keep their stats up. Only when Scientology is being slowed or stopped do you find me rigging up the tools of discipline.

In actual fact, I rather hold the person who is inactive because he is afraid of punishment in contempt. I respect only those who are strong enough to be decent without the "self-protection" of evil.

I use discipline to hold the edges of a channel, not to stop the flow.

SPs *love* to coax those with power to slay. As the basic ambition of any SP is *"Everybody dead so I can be safe,"* he or she will use all manner of lies and mechanisms to excite a thirst for discipline in those in power.

If I ever heed any "Kill everybody" advice, it is to put the adviser up against a brick wall.

————————

All evil stems from aberration. And it can be pretty evil. And awfully aberrated. The only road out from evil is processing. Therefore, one must protect the road to freedom as the answer to evil and must protect as well all those who are working to keep the road in.

The world will never become good because of discipline or oppression of evil. All discipline presupposes that the person being disciplined wants to survive. The truly evil only want to succumb. So discipline threat is no answer. The truly evil *love* pain and suffering and deprivation. So it coerces nothing and improves nothing when you seek to solve all evil with discipline. Only the already decent can be disciplined. It only obliges the evil ones. So all you can do really is to get the evil ones parked off the lines.

The executive in disciplining is concerned with those who would stop or hinder the flow and those who are just plain idle or stupid. So he severely leaves alone all upstats and only acts to move the Suppressives off the lines and not let the idle and stupid slow the flow. An executive could never make the world reform by discipline alone. He can by processing. So his only use of discipline is to continue to make processing possible. It's as simple as that.

ETHICS, THE DESIGN OF

I t is very easy for a staff member and even an Ethics Officer to completely misunderstand ethics and its functions. In a society run by SPs and controlled by incompetent police, the citizen almost engramically identifies any justice action or symbol with oppression.

Yet in the absence of true ethics, no one can live with others and stats go down inevitably. So a justice function must exist to protect producers and decent people.

To give you an example: When a little boy this life, the neighborhood a block around and the road from home to school were unusable. A bully about five years older than I, named Leon Brown, exerted a very bad influence over other children. With extortion by violence and blackmail and with corruption, he made the area very dangerous. The road to school was blocked by the five O'Connell kids, ranging from seven to fifteen, who stopped and beat up any smaller child. One couldn't go to school safely and was hounded by the truant officer, a hulking brute complete with star, if one *didn't* go to school.

When I was about six, I got very tired of a bloody nose and spankings because my clothes were torn and avidly learned "lumberjack fighting," a crude form of judo, from my grandfather.

With this "superior tech" under my belt, I searched out and found alone the youngest O'Connell kid, a year older than I, and pulverized him. Then I found alone and took on the next in size and pulverized *him*. After that, the O'Connell kids, all five, fled each time I showed up and the road to school was open and I convoyed other little kids so it was safe.

Then one day I got up on a nine-foot-high board fence and waited until the twelve-year-old bully passed by and leaped off on him, boots and all, and after the dust settled that neighborhood was safe for every kid in it.

So I learned about justice. Kids would come from blocks away to get help in *their* neighborhood. Finally, for a mile around, it was a safe environment for kids.

From this I learned two lessons:

1. Strength is nothing without skill and tech and, reversely, without skill and tech the strength of brutes is a matter of contempt.

2. Strength has two sides, one for good and one for evil. It is the intention that makes the difference.

On further living I found that only those who sought only peace were ever butchered. The thousands of years of Jewish passivity earned them nothing but slaughter.

So things do not run right because one is holy or good. Things run right because one makes them run right.

Justice is a necessary action to any successful society. Without it, the brute attacks the weak, the decent and the productive.

There are people who suppress. They are few. They often rise up to being in charge and then all things decay. They are essentially psychopathic personalities. Such want position in order to kill. Such as Genghis Khan, Hitler, psychiatrists, psychopathic criminals, want power only to destroy. Covertly or overtly they pay only with death. They arrived where they arrived, in charge of things, because nobody when they were on their way up said "No." They are monuments to the cowards, the reasonable people who didn't put period to them while they were still only small bullies and still vulnerable.

Ethics has to get there before tech can occur. So when it doesn't exist or goes out, then tech doesn't occur and suppression sets in and death follows.

So if someone doesn't hold the line, all become victims of oppression.

TWO SECTIONS

The Ethics Section is in Department 3. This department is called Inspection and Reports.

In small orgs there is only one person in that department.

Primarily his duties consist of inspecting and reporting to his divisional head and the Executive Council (EC).

That is the first section's function.

When inspection reveals outness and reports (such as graphs or direct info to the EC) do not result in correction, *then* it is a matter for the second section.

The second section of Department 3 is Ethics.

Now it is an Ethics matter. If correctly reported outnesses that threaten the org are *not* corrected, then one assumes that suppression exists.

Because he has files of Damage Reports and chits and because he can see and investigate, the Ethics Officer locates *who* is causing outnesses and suppressing the org. By condition assignments, publication and Comm Evs he gets in ethics.

It occasionally happens that it is someone high up in the org. It sometimes happens his seniors or the EC scold him for daring to report on things or to them. Then he knows the suppression is high up and he is delinquent in duty if he does not report it to the next highest org, and if no action there, right on up to the top. Anyone removing him for daring to report the factual results of his inspections can be severely handled by upper organizations. The Ethics Officer can only be in trouble if he fails to do his job and keep in ethics.

Hitting people with conditions is such a small part of Ethics that it is almost an abandonment of post. Letting people be hit with wrong conditions is a Comm Ev offense.

Letting an SP collapse stats or an org is a "shooting offense."

An Ethics Officer uses ethics to protect Ethics Upstats and keep the stats up and to smoke out crimes that push people and stats down. It is a simple function.

The basic duties of Dept 3 are what it says. Inspection and Reports. These alone usually work. When they don't and stats fall or people fall off the org board, one goes into Ethics actions.

You don't let incompetent and suppressive people on staff in the first place and you crowd Ethics in on them if they're found to be there.

You *don't* confuse an executive's effort to get the stats up with suppression.

The Ethics Officer is making the environment safe so that production can occur and service can be given. He is making it unsafe for those who by neglect or continual errors or suppression push stats down and get good staff members to leave.

If none of this is well understood and yet someone is making it impossible to work, find a nine-foot-high board fence...

The Ethics Officer must know his Ethics Policy. He must understand why he is there.

And the rest of the people in the org should understand it too.

THE ETHICS OFFICER
HIS CHARACTER

f a staff has no confidence in their Ethics Officer (E/O), their morale is difficult to sustain.

A staff member has his head down, doing his job. Suddenly he finds out that nobody has mailed any letters or magazines for a month. This is a shock, an ARC break. He was doing *his* job. So he natters a bit and resolves to keep his eye open after this. He may even do some investigation on his own. In other words, he's distracted from his post and duties. The environment is not safe.

Where was the E/O? Who didn't notice there was nothing going out?

A few weeks later the staff member hears that the address plates are full of duplicates, wrong addresses and half missing. This is a shock. It means the magazine never reached anyone really despite all the work. The staff member says to hell with it. There couldn't be an Ethics Officer worth anything and the org must be full of SPs.

So the staff member goes out and has a cigarette and sneers.

So do I.

A safe environment is a productive environment. An unsafe environment is an empty hall.

ETHICS FUNCTIONS

Now this would appear that the E/O runs the org. Or that he gets in everyone's way. Or that he is a whip that forces people to work.

Or any other silly idea borrowed from a wog world where the police make things about as safe as a snake pit full of assorted reptiles.

The *tech* fact is the data we have about SPs. There are very few of these in proportion to decent people. That one fact is something this society's police don't know. According to extant social tech, *all* people are basically bad and are only made "good" through punishment. So everyone everywhere has to be threatened. That's extant wog tech. It doesn't work. The crime rate soars, so obviously the know-how isn't to be found out "there." People are all animals, "they" say, and must be herded. Well that's the "modern social scientist's" nutty idea. Society does not know that all they'd have to do is round up their few SPs and they'd have no crime. Instead, whenever they arrest criminals they prove to these that society is brutal and crime justified and just let them loose again. They don't straighten SPs up because the "social scientists," the psychologist and psychiatrist, are at this writing at least mainly SPs themselves and haven't any tech but the club.

So the E/O must understand at once that he is dealing with a new, highly precise tech. It is the tech of Ethics. A meter, a case folder, a course study record, a knowledge of the HCOBs on SPs and case types and PTS phenomena, and you can identify an SP promptly. He makes things go wrong, hurts people, oppresses. Around him all the right actions vanish and the wrong actions appear.

Now because he or she can make others go PTS, then *they* make mistakes.

So you get a whole group making things go wrong.

The E/O, knowing his Ethics Tech, can sort out the group, find the real SP, remove him or depower him and zingo the group will rebound and do great.

If an E/O finds himself having to assign lots of conditions, finds as he inspects the org that the HCO PL on Promotional Actions of the Org or the old Org Rudiments List, when checked against the org, demonstrates too many outnesses, he knows that he is dealing with one or more SPs in the org or around its area.

Careful investigation by the E/O (and he has very exact procedures all to be found in the Org Exec Course Ethics Pack) discloses the source or sources of the trouble. He verifies all against the person's stats, study and case record and his meter, and then he acts.

If he is right, the org straightens right out. If the E/O is wrong in his investigation and action, things will get worse—i.e., stats will go down. So he can do it all over again, "exhume the body" he incorrectly "shot," apologize and now find the real SP!

So Ethics has its own tech, very superior tech indeed.

Ethics could clean up a whole nation and make it boom, using its tech correctly.

As Ethics is a powerful tech, an uninformed E/O who thinks he is a sort of Local Cop-KGB-FBI-Scotland Yard sure has missed the point. They are (or are at this writing) total failures, as witness the condemnation of crime stats in their areas. They are simply oppressive terror symbols. They take psychiatric advice and get psychiatric results. The end product is mutiny and revolution by the population.

When you threaten the whole population, you get riot and civil commotion. When you have riot and civil commotion, the police are threatening (because of lack of Ethics Tech) the whole population whereas less than 10 percent, even as little as 1 percent, are bad hats.

SUPPRESSIVE REASONABLENESS

The greatest enemy of the E/O is the reasonable person. There are no good reasons for any outness except:

a. Natural catastrophes (such as earthquakes, lightning, etc.)

b. Suppressive Persons

c. Persons who are PTS to Suppressive Persons.

When an exec starts to explain the "reasons" for low stats instead of working to get high stats, he is being reasonable.

When Joe Blow has just smashed his fifth typewriter and the Dissem Sec starts to explain how he's just a good boy gone a bit ARC breaky, she is being "reasonable." He's either an SP or he's PTS to someone.

The explanation is the answer to the E/O's *who*, not the Dissem Sec's *why*.

The ECs of three orgs are at violent war with each other. Somebody explains how reasonable this is. Their E/Os had better meet quietly and find out *who* is an SP and *who* is PTS in that battle royal and *act*.

Reasonableness is suppressive since it lets oppression continue without action being taken.

Suppressive reasonableness is a common trait. It comes from *the inability to confront evil*.

Evil takes a bit of confronting.

People who want desperately to "have no trouble" often won't confront and handle trouble.

Murder is murder. It occurs. A murder is not a frightened wish it had not occurred. It occurred. Somebody did it. There's the body.

Psychiatrists, for instance, have two major types in their ranks, both psychopathic. One is a theetie-weetie who thinks all criminals are poor abused things and the other is himself a criminal psychopath who turns criminals loose on the society just to get even with people for his own fancied wrongs. Tracing several major crimes, it can be found that the violent criminal was in the hands of a psychiatrist earlier and told him his intentions, yet was let loose on society.

Such a criminal—a rapist, a murderer—can't be helped by psychiatry. But that isn't the point. Decent people died and some died horribly. That doesn't make a very safe environment, does it?

It is true that we could straighten this criminal out if we could keep him out of circulation for a while. It is true the criminal is in trouble, *but it is also true that he commits crimes*.

So an E/O doesn't want somebody in circulation in a group or a society who commits crimes.

The job of the E/O is to disconnect and depower the criminal and so protect the group.

The criminal, the SP (same thing) is *trying to get even with people*. That's his common denominator. He does it by covert omissions or overt violence. It all amounts to the same thing.

The E/O works for from 90 percent to 99 percent of the group, not for the 1 percent.

When the E/O has done his duty to the group, he can then take up the individual. I always handle things in that order:

1. Safeguard the group.

2. Rehab the individual.

You will have a mess if you only do one or the other or try to rehab the individual criminal without safeguarding the group.

In actual practice, you safeguard the group by removing or isolating the individual. Then you see what can be done for the individual to rehab him *without* endangering the group in any way.

An E/O can be used by an SP (with false reports or stupid orders) to needle and hurt a group. The duty of the E/O is plain. Follow policy.

An E/O can be paralyzed when seniors will not let him do his job, either because they don't understand it or because they are suppressive. The stats tell which one.

But the E/O has an action in this case.

I recall that the first two E/Os ever appointed did their job, tried to clean up the org where two criminals and a spy were in full bloom and were clobbered by the OES (Organization Exec Sec) and removed. The same executive carried the org over Niagara Falls within a year. He was having homosexual relations with the spy! The fault here was a lack of investigation or investigatory skill and Ethics Tech not yet developed fully. If these two E/Os had found that they couldn't work and couldn't function despite crashing org stats, they should have located who was blocking any action by simple investigation and they would have found the crime. And with that in hand they could have said, "See here…"

E/O CONDUCT

An E/O should never discuss staff members who are merely under investigation or act in a way to Third Party people. An E/O gets the *facts* and then acts.

An E/O should himself be an Ethics Upstat. E/Os who aren't don't last long.

An E/O should act like a shepherd, not a wolf. When the facts are in plain view, he or she should act like a panther with one straight pounce.

An E/O who is an efficient E/O is *very* popular with a staff. If he or she knows his business and carries it out effectively, the E/O easily becomes a local hero.

An E/O shouldn't permit a staff to be nagged, threatened or given floods of conditions. When he sees these things occurring, he knows it's time to investigate for *who* has got people PTS and handle without other orders.

An E/O's rehab actions should be limited to reinvestigation on request, correcting actions based on false reports, and seeing that Qual does any case handling that comes up.

When an E/O sees big efforts being spent on trying to get ex-wolves back into the fold, he investigates for the source of the effort and, having found it, finds out *who* and *why*. One E/O never could get an org going but sure worked to get ex-wolves painted white. One head of an org had a staff in virtual mutiny but worked continuously to get reinstated to grace three people who over the years had done nothing (on clear evidence) but shoot upstats for outside pay—yet the E/O of that org didn't even try to find out why the head of that org was so constantly PTS as to worry only about rehabbing and reinstating SPs. And the E/O of that org also sent no report or appeal to a higher org!

An E/O can get so irresponsible as to assign his whole function to just ethics conditions assignments. Never enforced, no sort-out of staff ever attempted, no real confront at all, just a weary round of conditions and threats of conditions. That E/O was removed of course. Lots of threats and conditions mean only somebody is SP and a lot of others are PTS.

An E/O trying to handle a long org history of down stats and trouble should look first only at those who have been in the org throughout the trouble period. One or more will be SP or PTS but good.

An E/O who has had an area all calm but suddenly sees it roughed up should look only at those who came into it since it went bad.

An E/O is only trying to make a safe environment in which staff members can work happily and good service is being given to the public.

An E/O in the final analysis is answerable to me that all is well and secure with his area.

JOKERS AND DEGRADERS

 t is an old principle that people who do not understand something occasionally make fun of it.

A recent investigation, however, into the backgrounds and case condition of a small handful of people who were joking about their posts and those around them showed a somewhat more sinister scene.

Each of these persons fell into one or more of the following categories:

1. Were Rock Slammers. (Some List One.)

2. Were institutional-type cases.

3. Were "NCG" (meaning No Case Gain). (The only cause of which is continuous present time overts.)

4. Were severely PTS (Potential Trouble Source). (Connected to Rock Slammers.)

It might be supposed that misunderstood word phenomena could also be part of this. The rebellious student in universities is usually handled by clearing up his misunderstoods or curing his hopelessness for his future. However, the investigation did not find that any of these jokers or degraders were acting that way solely because of misunderstood words, but the possibility cannot be ruled out.

The four categories above were, however, fully verified.

All the persons investigated were found to be the subject of declining statistics, both having them and causing them. Their areas were enturbulated. At least one of the jokers was physically driving basic course students out of an org.

In some cultural areas, wit and humor are looked upon as a healthy release. However, in the case of orgs, this was not found to be the case. Intentional destruction of the org or fellow staff members was the direct purpose.

Therefore all Executives, HCO personnel and Case Supervisors as well as Qual personnel and Staff Section Officers have a valuable indicator. Where they have a joker or degrader on their hands, they also have one or more of the above four conditions in that person.

This opens the door to handling such people.

Properly assigned and then fully done conditions are the correct ethics handlings.

Correctly done Expanded Dianetics, which includes Confessionals and fully done PTS handlings are the case remedies.

Where Ethics Tech itself is not known or neglected and where there are no HCOs one can, of course, not expect the matter to be handled. And this would be too bad because the case gain and life improvement available in proper ethics handlings, when fully followed through, can be quite miraculous.

Where Rock Slammers have been undermining the tech and it is not fully known or used or is altered into unworkability, one cannot expect Confessionals to be properly done or Expanded Dianetics to be known and properly applied.

The joker is advertising his symptoms. He is also advertising an area of the org where there is enturbulation and down statistics as well as staff members being victimized.

Therefore this is an administrative and technical indicator which cannot be overlooked and should be followed up.

Spotted, investigated and handled, this can be the beginning of an upward spiral for an organization.

Where someone is driving ethics out, tech is not likely to go in. You have to get in ethics and tech before you can begin to get in admin.

The next time you, as an executive, wonder why you are working so hard, look for the Joker in the deck.

Humor is one thing. Destroyed orgs and human beings are quite something else.

It is our business to get the show on the road and get the job done.

OT LEVELS

Psychotics deal with doing people in. Their whole mission in life is destruction.

They inveigh against lower-level gains and seek to discredit them since these run contrary to their aberrated purpose.

But when it gets to Clears and OT levels, psychos go berserk!

They are, it happens, terrified of punishment for their own crimes.

The thought of someone being sensible or powerful enough to punish them (the way *they* would do) is more than they can stand.

You can, with the utmost certainty, identify a criminal psychotic by the way he vilifies or degrades or seeks to stop Clears and OTs from coming into existence.

It is lost on him that immorality and crime in others stem from the very things he is doing to them.

So look well at psychs and anti-religious campaigners. They are speaking from their own blackened souls, and they speak from terror.

That people when they grow saner are less inclined to vengeance is an argument they cannot assimilate. They know if *they* had the power to torture and kill everyone, they would do so.

Thus the psychs with their rantings and electric shocks wear their own brand clearly marked on them by their own conduct in life.

Recognize them for what they are—psychotic criminals—and handle them accordingly.

Don't let them stop Man from going free.

ETHICS
REPORTS

KNOWLEDGE REPORTS

e live in an era of "civilization" where it has become general not to care what is going on.

The First Dynamic "nothing to do with me" attitude is the product of drugs, TV and the psychiatrists and psychologists who have perverted education and produced a criminal society wherein the individual is supposed to be the effect of everything, incapable of handling his environment.

Although we are changing this society, it is nevertheless a constant challenge to one's own ability to keep things going right.

Factually, to succeed in this "civilization" or *any* society, crude or sophisticated, one has to act continually to keep one's own environment under some control. To do otherwise results in a lingering or sudden and always painful death. It *does* matter what goes on around one. The only thing which does not care is a corpse.

It is a rather simple thing—not heroic. If one can't control a coffee cup, he is likely to get scalded! If one can't control a car, he is a statistic.

Extend this to one's fellows slightly and it is plain to see that total permissiveness (as loudly advocated by the psychs) is suicide. Standing with a bland look while Joe sticks pins in someone or something is not good manners, it's idiocy!

To live at all, one has to exert some control over his equals as well as his juniors and (believe it or not) his superiors.

When misconduct and out-ethics is occurring in a group, it is almost impossible for other members of the group not to know of it. At least some of them are aware of the outness.

When a group has down stats, it is not true that *all* of them are trying to fail. Only a few are dedicated to not doing their jobs.

The question one can ask of any group that is not doing well is this: Why did the *other* group members tolerate and ignore the loafers or out-ethics cats in it?

In analyzing countless numbers of groups with whom it has been my good fortune—or misfortune—to be associated, I finally isolated *one* factor which made an upstat group upstat and a downstat group downstat and a horror to be around.

The single most notable difference between an upstat, easy to live and work with group and a downstat, hard to live and work with group is that the individual group members themselves enforce the action and mores of the group.

That is the difference—no other.

In an upstat group, at the first pinprick, Joe would probably have a black eye!

In a downstat group, Joe could go on and on with his pins, each group member watching and shrugging.

In a group where members have some concept of controlling their environment and their fellows, you don't have loafers or out-ethics cats. *Because* the rest of the group, on an individual basis, just won't tolerate it.

Those who would have a tendency to wreak havoc or loaf don't dare. And the group becomes easy to live with and work with.

It is not whether the group individuals should be preselected or carefully made ethical by some process or inspired leadership or a separate police force. It is whether the group members themselves exert any control on each other.

One can say, "Oh well! If I reported the Registrar violating policy, the Executive Director would fire me—she is his wife!" One can say, "If I complain they won't let me wear my hat, they'll Comm Ev me for Third Party actions." If such conditions prevail, the group has already lost the group ability to control the environment—and they will be downstat. Their pay will be low—their working conditions rotten.

Do we have a mechanism to prevent this?

Yes, we do.

It is called Knowledge Reports. (See *Staff Member Reports* and other types of chits given in this chapter.)

Knowledge Reports are enforced as follows:

1. Anyone who knew of a loafing or destructive or off-policy or out-ethics action and *who did not file a Knowledge Report* becomes an *accessory* in any justice action taken thereafter.

2. Forbidding anyone to write a Knowledge Report makes the person forbidding it *and* the person accepting this illegal order both accessories to any later action taken.

3. Failing to write down a disclosed crime in a worksheet or a report makes the person failing to do so an *accessory* to the crime.

4. Failing to file a Knowledge Report written by another makes one an accessory to the contents.

5. Removing Knowledge Reports from files makes one an accessory to the contents.

6. Failing to advise the International Justice Chief of serious charges in Knowledge Reports makes one an accessory to the reported outness.

7. Knowingly false statements made in Knowledge Reports, when proven false beyond any reasonable doubt with intent to cause trouble, may become the subject of a Chaplain's Court with damages awarded. (See *Chaplain's Court, Civil Hearings.*)

8. Any person who knew of an outness or Crime and failed to report it and thus became an accessory receives the same penalty as the person disciplined as the actual offender.

With these policies, a person with knowledge of nonoptimum conduct by other group members cannot be stopped from writing and filing the report in the person's Ethics File and cannot even be stopped from going outside the org and informing, by whatever comm line, the International Justice Chief. And that does not mean this is to be used to withhold from anyone that he is writing a report.

BOARDS OF REVIEW

It shall be part of *every* Board of Review action (see *Board of Review*) at any level to examine the status of Knowledge Reports as they relate to any case reviewed and to take any action indicated by these policies.

SUMMARY

This makes it a pretty rough group for a loafer or criminal to be around. *Unless* he or she decides to rise above the aberrations and get busy and go straight.

IT IS A FAILURE OF THE INDIVIDUAL GROUP MEMBERS TO CONTROL THEIR FELLOWS THAT MAKES A GROUP HARD FOR ALL TO LIVE AND WORK WITH.

If it is present, when that is cured, the group will become a joy to be with and work will become a breeze.

If the stats of a group, large or small, are down, try it.

And get a *real* group in return that, collectively, can control the environment and prosper because its group members individually help control each other.

STAFF MEMBER REPORTS

Staff members must personally make certain reports in writing.

Failure to make these reports involves the executive or staff member not making a report in any offense committed by a junior under him or, in case of job endangerment, by a senior over him.

These reports are made to the Ethics Section of the Department of Inspection and Reports.

The report form is simple. One uses a clipboard with a packet of his division's color-flash paper on it. This includes a piece of pencil carbon paper. This is the same clipboard and carbon one uses for his routine orders.

It is a despatch form addressed simply to the Ethics Section. It is dated. It has under the address and in the center of the page the person or portion of the org's name. It then states what kind of a report it is (see below).

The original goes to Ethics by drawing an arrow pointing to "Ethics" and the carbon goes to the person or portion of the org being reported on *by channels* (B routing).

The following are the reports required:

1. *Damage Report.* Any damage to anything noted with the name of the person in charge of it or in charge of cleaning it.

2. *Misuse Report.* The misuse or abuse of any equipment, materiel or quarters, meaning using it wrongly or for a purpose not intended.

3. *Waste Report.* The waste of org materiel.

4. *Idle Report.* The idleness of equipment or personnel which should be in action.

5. *Alter-is Report.* The alteration of design, policy, technology or errors being made in construction.

6. *Loss or Theft Report.* The disappearance of anything that should be there giving anything known about its disappearance such as when it was seen last.

7. *A Found Report.* Anything found, sending the article with the despatch or saying where it is.

8. *Noncompliance Report.* Noncompliance with legal orders.

9. *Dev-T Report.* Stating whether off-line, off-policy or off-origin and from whom to whom and subject.

10. *Error Report.* Any Error made.

11. *Misdemeanor Report.* Any Misdemeanor noted.

12. *A Crime Report.* Any Crime noted or suspected, but if suspicion only it must be so stated.

13. *A High Crime Report.* Any High Crime noted or suspected, but if only suspected it must be so stated.

14. *A No-Report Report.* Any failure to receive a report or an illegible report or folder.

15. *A False Report Report.* Any report received that turned out to be false.

16. *A False Attestation Report.* Any false attestation noted, but in this case the document is attached to the report.

17. *An Annoyance Report.* Anything about which one is annoyed, giving the person or portion of an org or org one is annoyed with, but the Department of Inspection and Reports and a senior org are exempt and may not be reported on.

18. *A Job Endangerment Report.* Reporting any order received from a superior that endangered one's job by demanding one alter or depart from known policy, the orders of a person senior to one's immediate superior altered or countermanded by one's immediate superior, or advice from one's immediate superior not to comply with orders or policy.

19. *Technical Alter-is Report.* Any ordered alteration of technology not given in an HCOB, book or LRH tape.

20. *Technical Noncompliance Report.* Any failure to apply the correct technical procedure.

21. *Knowledge Report.* On noting some investigation is in progress and having data on it of value to Ethics.

These reports are simply written and sent. One does *not* expect an executive to front up to personnel who err. One *does* expect an executive to make a report routinely on the matter, no matter what the executive also does.

Only in this way can bad spots in the organization be recognized and corrected. For reports other than one's own collect and point out bad conditions before those can harm the org.

These reports are filed by Ethics in the Ethics Files in the staff member's folder or in the folder of the portion of the org. A folder is only made if Ethics receives an Ethics Report.

Unless the staff member is part of a portion of an org or an org that is under a State of Emergency, *five* such reports *can* accumulate before Ethics takes any action. But if the report is deemed very serious, Ethics may take action at once by investigating.

If a State of Emergency exists in that portion of the org or org, *one* report can bring about a Court of Ethics as there is no leeway in an Emergency Condition.

The most serious reports, which are the only ones taken up at once, are Technical Alter-is, Noncompliance, any False Reports,

False Attestations, No Reports, Misdemeanors, Crimes and High Crimes. The others are left to accumulate (except in Emergency when *all* reports on that portion or org are taken up at once).

THINGS THAT SHOULDN'T BE

If you see something going on in the org or incorrect that you don't like, and yet do not wish to turn in an Ethics Chit, or indeed don't know who to report, *write a despatch to the Inspection Officer.*

Tell him what you have noticed and give him what data you can.

The Inspection Officer will then investigate it and make a report to the right executives or turn in an Ethics Chit on the offending persons himself.

Don't just natter if there's something you don't like.

Tell the Inspection Officer. Then something can be done about it.

TECH AND QUAL ETHICS CHITS

his is a *very* important policy. When it is neglected the org will soon experience a technical dropped statistic and lose income and personnel.

The most attacked area of an org is its Tech and Qual personnel as these produce the effective results which make Scientology seem deadly to Suppressives.

The Suppressive is *terrified* of anyone getting better or more powerful as he is dramatizing some long-gone (but to him it is right now) combat or vengeance. He or she confuses the old enemies with anyone about and looks on anyone who tries to help as an insidious villain who will strengthen these "enemies."

Thus Tech and Qual personnel are peculiarly liable to covert, off-line, off-policy annoyances which in time turn them into PTSes. Their cases will Roller Coaster and they begin to go off-line, off-policy and off-origin (see Dev-T Policy Letters) themselves.

This results in a technical breakdown and an apparency of busyness in those divisions which does not in fact produce anything, being Dev-T.

The policy then is:

No Tech or Qual personnel may omit giving Ethics Chits to Ethics on any incident or action covered in the Dev-T Policy Letters or which indicate SP or PTS activity.

This means they may not "be decent about it" or "reasonable" and so refrain.

This means they must know their Ethics and Dev-T Policy Letters.

This means they may not themselves act like Ethics Officers or steal the Ethics hat.

It means that they must chit students who bring a body and ask for unusual solutions; they must chit *all* discourteous conduct; they must chit all Roller Coaster cases; they must chit all suppressive actions observed; they must chit snide comments; they must chit alter-is and entheta; they must chit derogatory remarks; they must chit all Dev-T. Anything in violation of Ethics or Dev-T Policy Letters must be reported.

Ethics will find then that only two or three people in those areas are causing all the upset. This fact routinely stuns Tech and Qual personnel when it is called to their attention—that only two or three are making their lives miserable.

Ethics, seeing tech statistics drop, *must* investigate all this and *when Ethics finds* the Qual and Tech personnel have not been handing in Ethics Chits, the Ethics Officer must report them to the HCO Exec Sec for disciplinary action.

NON-ENTURBULATION ORDER

What to do with the two or three students or pcs causing trouble?

Ethics issues a Non-Enturbulation Order. This states that those named in it (the SPs and PTSes who are students or preclears) are forbidden to enturbulate others and if *one* more report is received of their enturbulating anyone, an SP Order will be issued forthwith.

This will hold them in line until tech can be gotten in on them and takes them off the back of Tech and Qual personnel.

NOT THEORETICAL

This is *not* a theoretical situation or policy. It is issued directly after seeing tech results go down, Tech and Qual cases Roller Coaster and results drop.

Ethics found that the entire situation came about through no chits from Tech and Qual personnel about troublesome people which resulted in no restraint and a *collapse* of Divisions 4 and 5 comm lines and results.

When Tech and Qual personnel try to take the law into their own hands or ignores issuing Ethics Chits, chaos results, not case gains.

Keep Tech Results *up*.

DISPUTED ETHICS CHITS

hen anyone receives an Ethics Chit which the recipient feels is incorrect, the answer is not to issue another chit naming the person that issued the first chit. Such action merely sets up a vicious circle of Ethics Chits going between two persons.

The purpose of Ethics is to get technology and policy in and get the org going, not to start slanging matches. Therefore, if anyone receives an Ethics Chit, he or she should first take a good look at his or her actions and see what needs to be done in order to avoid a repetition of the offense.

If, however, after careful consideration they consider the chit really unjustified, they should politely despatch the Ethics Officer, stating briefly their reasons, supported where possible with data, and ask for the chit to be withdrawn.

If, in light of the data received, Ethics is satisfied that the chit was incorrectly issued, he/she can return the chit and explanation to the originator asking for the chit to be withdrawn. If the originator decides now to withdraw the chit after seeing the explanation, he returns it to Ethics requesting cancellation and Ethics removes the chit from the file.

If the originator is dissatisfied with the explanation, the chit should not be withdrawn. The originator sends the despatch and chit back to the Ethics Officer with "To Ethics—File" written on it. Ethics infos the receiver and files. In this case, the receiver can, if he wishes, appeal by despatch to the Ethics Officer and ask for a Hearing. Thereupon, the Ethics Officer calls both the originator and the receiver (unless the originator is a Secretary or above) to his office and, taking only the facts set out in the receiver's despatch to Ethics, makes a quick investigation.

The Ethics Officer then makes one of the following adjudications:

1. Have the Ethics Chit destroyed.

2. Have the Ethics Chit destroyed. And if he finds that the chit was carelessly or incorrectly issued (bearing in mind what information was available to the originator at the time of issue), indicate the incorrectness to the originator and order any necessary checkouts on the relevant Policy Letter(s) violated to correct the originator into future on-policy handling.

3. If he discovers the chit to have been a willful and knowing false report, convene an Ethics Hearing on the originator (not for the fact of filing, only for the willful and knowing false report). Or if the originator is a Director or above, request an Executive Ethics Hearing be convened by the Office of LRH via the HCO Area Secretary.

4. Order the Ethics Chit to remain on the file.

5. Take up all the receiver's Ethics Chits and hold the Hearing accordingly.

If the originator is a Secretary or above, the Ethics Officer and the receiver visit the Secretary in his office for the Hearing on appointment. But a Secretary or above need not grant the appointment at all, if so inclined. In such a case, the Hearing is held, without the originator, in the Ethics Office.

No person may be penalized for issuing an Ethics Chit.

CLEANING OF ETHICS FILES

n amnesty for a portion of an org or an org or a general amnesty can be declared by the Office of LRH.* An amnesty will be effective up to a date three months before it is issued. The Ethics Files are therefore nullified previous to the date declared in the amnesty.

An amnesty signalizes a feat of considerable moment by a portion of an org or an org or Scientology.

An HCO Executive Letter can compliment a portion of an org or an org and wipe out the Ethics Files of the portion of an org or the org complimented. An award is usually added for the persons responsible.

Maintenance of a State of Normal Operation or Affluence for three weeks after an Emergency cleans the portion of an org or the org's Ethics Files.

An *individual* may clean his own file by approaching Ethics and offering *to make amends*.

The person may be shown but may not touch his Ethics Files which are always kept locked when the office is empty. The person should present a written and signed *Amends Project Petition* to Ethics. Ethics attaches the person's file to it and sends it safely to the Office of LRH Ethics Authority Section. If accepted as adequate amends by the Office of LRH, it is authorized by the Ethics Authority Section and returned to Ethics which places it on its Projects Time Machine.

*See Amnesty Policy for more information on who may declare an amnesty, its purpose and use.

When accomplished, the Amends Project is taken off the Time Machine and forwarded to the Inspection Section which inspects and verifies it is done and sends all to the Office of LRH Ethics Authority Section which then authorizes the retirement of the reports on the person.

If the project comes off the Time Machine without being done, the matter goes at once to a Court of Ethics.

Any Amends Project must benefit the org and be beyond routine duties. It may not only benefit the individual. Offers to "get audited at own expense in Review" are acceptable as auditing will benefit everyone. "To get trained at own expense up to _____ and serve the org two years afterwards" is acceptable amends. But the person's staff pay is also suspended entirely during any auditing or training undertaken as amends. "To get another department's files in order on my own time" would be acceptable amends. No work one would normally do himself on post is acceptable amends. A donation or fine would not be acceptable amends. Doing what one should do anyway is not amends, it is the expected. No org funds may be employed in an Amends Project.

No amends are thereafter accepted if the person has failed to complete an Amends Project since the effective date of the last amnesty applying to the person's portion or org.

Any bonus *specifically given by the person's name* also cleans the person's Ethics Files without comment.

The responsibility for handling the cleaning of files is that of the Ethics Section of the Department of Inspection and Reports, which notes amnesties, compliments and specific bonus awards and handles its Ethics Files accordingly.

No Amends Projects may be accepted except through the Office of LRH and a superior may not bring a junior, who wishes his files cleaned by *amends,* into Ethics and assist him to make the proper project applications. It must be voluntarily done by the junior.

No amnesties, compliments or bonuses may be made or declared except by the Office of LRH and as authorized by policy.

THE
THIRD PARTY

THE THIRD PARTY LAW

I have for a very long time studied the causes of violence and conflict amongst individuals and nations.

If Chaldea could vanish, if Babylon could turn to dust, if Egypt could become a badlands, if Sicily could have 160 prosperous cities and be a looted ruin before the year zero and a near desert ever since—and all this in *spite* of all the work and wisdom and good wishes and intent of human beings, then it must follow as the dark follows sunset that something must be unknown to Man concerning all his works and ways. And that this something must be so deadly and so pervasive as to destroy all his ambitions and his chances long before their time.

Such a thing would have to be some natural law unguessed at by himself.

And there *is* such a law, apparently, that answers these conditions of being deadly, unknown and embracing all activities.

The law would seem to be:

A THIRD PARTY MUST BE PRESENT AND UNKNOWN IN EVERY QUARREL FOR A CONFLICT TO EXIST.

Or

FOR A QUARREL TO OCCUR, AN UNKNOWN THIRD PARTY MUST BE ACTIVE IN PRODUCING IT BETWEEN TWO POTENTIAL OPPONENTS.

Or

WHILE IT IS COMMONLY BELIEVED TO TAKE TWO TO MAKE A FIGHT, A THIRD PARTY MUST EXIST AND MUST DEVELOP IT FOR ACTUAL CONFLICT TO OCCUR.

It is very easy to see that two in conflict are fighting. They are very visible. What is harder to see or suspect is that a Third Party existed and actively promoted the quarrel.

The usually unsuspected and "reasonable" Third Party, the bystander who denies any part of it, *is* the one that brought the conflict into existence in the first place.

The hidden Third Party, seeming at times to be a supporter of only one side, is to be found as the instigator.

This is a useful law on many dynamics.

It *is* the cause of war.

One sees two fellows shouting bad names at each other, sees them come to blows. No one else is around. So *they,* of course, "caused the fight." But there *was* a Third Party.

Tracing these down, one comes upon incredible data. That is the trouble. The incredible is too easily rejected. One way to hide things is to make them incredible.

Clerk A and Messenger B have been arguing. They blaze into direct conflict. Each blames the other. *Neither one is correct and so the quarrel does not resolve since its true cause is not established.*

One looks into such a case *thoroughly.* He finds the incredible. The wife of Clerk A has been sleeping with Messenger B and complaining alike to both about the other.

Farmer J and Rancher K have been tearing each other to pieces for years in continual conflict. There are obvious, logical reasons for the fight. Yet it continues and does not resolve. A close search finds Banker L who, due to their losses in the fighting, is able to loan each side money, while keeping the quarrel going, and who will get their lands completely if both lose.

It goes larger. The revolutionary forces and the Russian government were in conflict in 1917. The reasons are so many the attention easily sticks on them. But only when Germany's official state papers were captured in World War II was it revealed that *Germany* had promoted the revolt and financed Lenin to spark it off, even sending him into Russia in a blacked-out train!

One looks over "personal" quarrels, group conflicts, national battles and one finds, if he searches, the Third Party, unsuspected by both combatants or, if suspected at all, brushed off as "fantastic." Yet careful documentation finally affirms it.

––––––––––

This datum is fabulously useful.

In marital quarrels, the *correct* approach of anyone counseling is to get both parties to carefully search out the *Third* Party. They may come to many *reasons* at first. These *reasons* are not *beings.* One is looking for a Third *Party,* an actual *being.* When both find the Third Party and establish proof, that will be the end of the quarrel.

Sometimes two parties, quarreling, suddenly decide to elect a being to blame. This stops the quarrel. Sometimes it is not the right being and more quarrels thereafter occur.

Two nations at each other's throats should each seek conference with the other to sift out and locate the actual Third Party. They will always find one if they look, and they *can* find the right one. As it will be found to exist in fact.

––––––––––

There are probably many technical approaches one could develop and outline in this matter.

There are many odd phenomena connected with it. An accurately spotted Third Party is usually not fought at all by either party, but only shunned.

Marital conflicts are common. Marriages can be saved by both parties really sorting out *who* caused the conflicts. There may have been (in the whole history of the marriage) several, but only one at a time.

Quarrels between an individual and an organization are nearly always caused by an individual Third Party or a third group. The organization and the individual should get together and isolate the Third Party by displaying to each other all the data they each have been fed.

Rioters and governments alike could be brought back to agreement could one get representatives of both to give each other what they have been told by *whom.*

Such conferences have tended to deal only in recriminations or conditions or abuses. They must deal in beings only, in order to succeed.

This theory might be thought to assert also that there are no bad conditions that cause conflict. There are. But these are usually *remedial by conference unless a Third Party is promoting conflict.*

In history we have a very foul opinion of the past because it is related by recriminations of two opponents and has not spotted the Third Party.

"Underlying causes" of war should read "hidden promoters."

There are no conflicts which cannot be resolved unless the true promoters of them remain hidden.

———————

This is the natural law the ancients and moderns alike did not know.

And not knowing it, being led off into "reasons," whole civilizations have died.

It is worth knowing.

It is worth working with in any situation where one is trying to bring peace.

THIRD PARTY, HOW TO FIND ONE

he way *not* to find a Third Party is to compile a questionnaire that asks one and all in various ways, "Have you been a *victim*?" "Do you feel ARC broken about ethics?"

Any officer, Board of Investigation or Committee of Evidence that uses this approach (1) does not find any Third Party and (2) caves in people.

A *Third Party* is one who by false reports creates trouble between two people, a person and a group, or a group and another group.

To find a Third Party one has to ask:

1. a. Have you been told you were in bad?

   b. What was said?

   c. *Who* said it?

2. a. Have you been told someone was bad?

   b. What was said?

   c. *Who* said it?

3. a. Have you been told someone was doing wrong?

   b. What was said?

   c. *Who* said it?

4. a. Have you been told a group was bad?

   b. What was said?

   c. *Who* said it?

———————

This is quite capable of running a couple light-years of track, so a questionnaire should have a limiter such as "In this organization _____?"

This is also a considerable process! And it may have a lot of answers. So a lot of space should be left for each question.

By then combining names given, you have one name appearing far more often than the rest. This is done by counting names. You then investigate this person.

Usual action, if they are not an enemy, is to issue a Non-Enturbulation Order and say why.

———————

The *victim*-type questionnaire will only give you your most valuable executives! Who have been trying to get people to do their jobs!

We have had experience with this so *it is a Comm Ev Offense* to use a *victim*-type approach and say one is "looking for a Third Party."

This policy is *vital* to HCO Executive Secretaries, HCO Area Secretaries, Ethics Officers and Missionaires.

THE
SCIENTOLOGY
JUSTICE CODES
AND THEIR
APPLICATION

THE JUSTICE OF SCIENTOLOGY
ITS USE AND PURPOSE
BEING A SCIENTOLOGIST

he reason we have Justice Codes is to have justice. We don't want or need injustice.

When we have no codes, "justice" can be anything any authority cares to make it.

We have had too much caprice passing for justice. It is time we had justice.

Committees of Evidence work. I recall one Tech Director accused of tampering with a student. I was told he was about to be disciplined and sacked. I stopped that action and had a Committee of Evidence convened. Accurate testimony revealed the story false and the Tech Dir innocent. Without that Committee, he would have been ruined. I know of other instances where a Committee found the facts completely contrary to rumor. Some are guilty, most are innocent. But thereby we have justice and our necks aren't out. If a person is to keep the law, he or she must know what the law is. And must be protected from viciousness and caprice in the *name* of law. If a person doesn't keep the law, knowing well what it is, he or she hurts all of us and should be handled.

The enturbulence of the society around us is fantastic. There is no just civil law left, really. It is that lawless and disorderly condition in the society about us which makes it hard for us to work. Shortly we will be even more powerful. That power must not be lawless or we will have anarchy and dismay, enough to stop our growth.

If we have a superior law code and legal system which gives real justice to people, we will simply flow easily over the society and everybody will win.

Where we fail to apply our own admin, tech and justice procedures to the society around us (let alone Scientology), we will fail.

There is too much truth in our lines not to cause a social upheaval. Therefore, let us have justice and expand into higher order, not plunge the world into darkness because our power as a group struck innocent and guilty alike.

A Scientologist must understand his own justice system. Without understanding, again there will be no justice.

Already the following points need correction in the uninformed person concerning our justice.

A Committee of Evidence is not a court. It is simply a fact-finding body with legal powers, convened to get at the facts and clean up the ARC breaks caused by rumor. When it has the truth of it, then a Convening Authority acts—but only in exact accordance with a Justice Code.

Our justice really rehabilitates in the long run. It only disciplines those who are hurting others and gives them a way to change so they can eventually win too—but not by hurting us.

A SCIENTOLOGIST WHO FAILS TO USE SCIENTOLOGY TECHNOLOGY AND ITS ADMINISTRATIVE AND JUSTICE PROCEDURES ON THE WORLD AROUND HIM WILL CONTINUE TO BE TOO ENTURBULATED TO DO HIS JOB.

That sounds extreme to anyone.

But if you look it over, you will find that the "power" of the "society" and "state" is pretended and is made from an effort to be powerful where they actually lack power. Our situation is quite the reverse. Ours is the power of truth and we *are* capable of power as a group, having power as individuals due to processing and power of wisdom due to superior technology.

Therefore, when we grant too much beingness to *their* "power," we are granting validity to a falsehood and so it recoils on us.

We are, in short, knocking our own heads off by failing to use our knowledge and authority when we administer or handle our fellow man or society. It's like refusing auditing to somebody or not making it possible. It's also investing a lie with power. Society is losing ground because its "power" is based on a pack of falsehoods. *We* will lose ground if we empower those lies.

There's real magic to be seen here. For instance, every upset we have is traceable to *our* not knowing or failing to apply *our* technology and admin and justice procedures to the society around us and its individuals, firms and groups.

This is worse than you think. A Scientology executive not handling Dev-T (Developed and unnecessary Traffic) from a government in accordance with our Dev-T Policies, when it was off-line and off-policy, recently caused an upset. A government official was off-policy (his own bureau's) and the Scientology executive did not follow *our* procedure of (a) send it back to source, (b) correct the policy error and (c) inform his superiors when results were not obtained. You say, "But that's wild! Run a government by Scientology admin?" Well, all I know is that it caused trouble when we didn't.

Evidently it's not "them" and "us." It's just "us" and a false "them."

So all we have to do is to get their hats on and they're *us.*

Failure to take our usual justice actions on offenders against us will result in eventual chaos. What matter if they don't appear before the Committee of Evidence we convene on them?

How do we know they won't? How could the Victoria Parliament* ever come right if we failed to (a) convene a Committee of Evidence, (b) follow our legal procedures?

No, they just stay "them."

Has anybody informed the FDA** of our amnesty? Well, did you know the FDA was looking for a way out of their mess for fear we'd sue for a million? They'd drop the E-Meter case if they thought we wouldn't sue.

How do we know if we don't try?

_____

So therefore we *must* use Scientology tech, admin and justice in all our affairs. No matter how mad it sounds, we only fail when we don't.

_____

And therefore every Scientologist should understand his own tech, codes and procedures.

Some Scientologists believe when a Comm Ev is convened that they are at once suspended.

Nobody *can* be suspended or punished by the *convening* of a Committee of Evidence. It's there to find the truth. *Only* when its Findings are submitted to its Convening Authority and where the Convening Authority acts can anyone be suspended or transferred or demoted.

*A reference to the Parliament of Victoria, Australia, who, in the mid-1960s, conducted an "inquiry" into Scientology. This "inquiry," conducted by a one-man board, resulted in discriminatory anti-Scientology legislation. The Church appealed this matter resulting in a decision that not only exonerated the Church and vindicated its practices, but which resulted in full legal recognition. The Church continued pursuing the matter of Australian discrimination to that nation's highest court, resulting in full religious recognition in a decision that stands today as the foremost legal decision on the subject of religion in all Commonwealth countries.

**FDA: United States Food and Drug Administration. Refers to a 1963 FDA raid and seizure of E-Meters and literature from the Founding Church of Scientology in Washington, DC, under the bogus allegation that these were being presented to the public as "medical cures." Ultimately, however, the Church not only emerged victorious with sweeping recognition of religious bona fides, but the court ordered the return of all seized materials.

Don't react to Scientology justice as though it were wog law. In society's "courts," one is given the works and truth has little bearing on the findings. A mean judge or clever attorney and small legal errors decide a lot of their cases. Wog courts are like throwing dice. There is huge cost and publicity and punishment galore, even for the innocent.

So we must preserve our justice.

And use it.

That's the main lesson. If we don't use it in all questions where the truth of the matter is in doubt, we'll just go on being wogs.

If we don't exhibit our science as a *group* and show a good example, what can we achieve?

So let's grow up to our own technology and take responsibility for it.

And wear our hats as Scientologists to the world.

OFFENSES
AND PENALTIES

These are the penalties we have always more or less used, and these are the offenses which have been usually considered offenses in Scientology.

Formerly, they were never written down or routinely enforced, there was no recourse and these lacks made staff members uncertain of their fate. They knew something happened, but not why. They knew certain things were frowned on, but not how much or little. The penalties were suddenly administered without warning as to what they would be or for what offense.

This, then, is a Code of Discipline which we have almost always more or less used, made plain for everyone to see, with limits against overpunishment and recourse for those who are wronged.

Accordingly, this code of offenses and their penalties becomes firm and expressed policy.

Lack of specified offenses, penalties and recourse bring everyone to uncertainty and risk at the whim of those in command.

There are four general classes of crimes and offenses in Scientology. These are Errors, Misdemeanors, Crimes and High Crimes.

ERRORS

Errors are minor unintentional omissions or mistakes. These are:

> *Auditing "goofs."*
>
> *Minor alter-is of tech or policy.*

Small instructional mistakes.

Minor errors or omissions in performing duties.

Admin errors or omissions not resulting in financial loss or loss of status or repute for a senior.

Errors are dealt with by corrections of the person, reprimand or warnings by seniors.

Certificates, classifications and awards may not be cancelled or suspended or reduced for an Error. The offender may not be transferred or demoted or fined or suspended for committing an Error. No Committee of Evidence may be convened because of an Error.

Repeated corrections, warnings or reprimands by a senior can, however, bring the repeated Error offenses into the category of Misdemeanor.

MISDEMEANORS

These are:

Noncompliance.

Discourtesy and insubordination.

Mistakes resulting in financial or traffic loss.

Commissions or omissions resulting in loss of status or the punishment of a senior.

Neglect or gross errors resulting in the need to apply the Emergency Formula to their person, section, unit, department, organization, zone or division.

Knowing and repeated departures from Standard Technology, instructional procedures or policy.

Continued association with squirrels.

Abuse or loss or damage of org materiel.

Waste of org materiel.

Waste of funds.

Alteration of senior policy or continued ignorance of it.

Consistent and repeated failures to wear their hat regarding Dev-T.

Refusing an E-Meter check.

Refusing auditing when ordered by a higher authority.

Disturbing a course or class.

Disrupting a meeting.

The discovery of their having an undisclosed criminal background in this lifetime.

The discovery of an undisclosed tenure in a mental hospital.

Processing a known Trouble Source or the family or adherents of a Suppressive Person or Group.

Omissions resulting in disrepute or financial loss.

Inadequate or declining income or traffic in a section, unit, department, org, zone or division.

Assisting the inadequacy or decline of income or traffic in a section, unit, department, org, zone or division.

Failure to acknowledge, relay or comply with a direct and legal order from an executive staff member.

Auditor's Code breaks resulting in a disturbance of the preclear.

Failure to follow the Supervisor's Code resulting in disturbed students.

Contributing to a Crime.

Failure to appear before a Committee of Evidence as a witness or Interested Party when personally given summons or receiving summons by registered post.

Refusing to testify before a Committee of Evidence.

Showing contempt or disrespect to a Committee of Evidence when before it.

Destroying documents required by a Committee of Evidence or refusing to produce them.

Withholding evidence.

False swearing on a signed statement or form.

Impeding justice.

Refusing to serve on a Committee of Evidence.

Refusing to vote while a member of a Committee of Evidence.

Misconduct.

Issuing data or information to wrong grades or unauthorized persons or groups or issuing data or information broadly without authority.

Invoicing and/or depositing checks obtained in confidence.

Giving org services on the basis of confidence checks received without having had the confidence check made good and correctly invoiced and banked first. (Definition of *confidence check:* a check known by the person accepting it as *not* valid and covered by funds at time of acceptance, but accepted nevertheless on basis of promise by the drawer to make it good at a later date.)

Such offenses are subject to direct punishment by order and, for a staff member, the punishment is the assignment of a personal Condition of Emergency for up to three weeks and, for an executive staff member, the assignment of up to a three-month personal Condition of Emergency.

Personal Conditions of Emergency reduce pay or units one-third for the period assigned.

Recourse may be had by requesting a Committee of Evidence for return of pay, but not damages.

The same offenses may be cause for convening a Committee of Evidence, but may not be used for both a Committee and punishment by direct order—one or the other.

However, if any of these offenses become the subject of a Committee of Evidence, the penalty for a Misdemeanor may be increased to include suspension of a single certificate and/or classification (but no more) or a minor demotion or transfer, but not dismissal. None of these offenses may be made the subject of dismissal by direct order or Committee of Evidence.

Persons may not be dismissed for Misdemeanors. Nor may any certificates, classifications or awards be cancelled.

Nonstaff or field or mission Scientologists committing those of the above (except org) offenses applicable may have a Committee of Evidence convened on them.

Where serious, repeated or of magnitude harmful to many, the same offenses can be reclassed as Crimes by a Convening Authority.

CRIMES

These cover offenses normally considered criminal. Offenses which are treated in Scientology as Crimes are:

Theft.

Mayhem.

Harmful, flagrant and continued Code Breaks resulting in important upsets.

Noncompliance with urgent and vital orders resulting in public disrepute.

Placing Scientology or Scientologists at risk.

Omissions or noncompliance requiring heavy intervention by seniors consuming time and money.

Failure or refusal to acknowledge, relay or execute a direct legal order from an International Board Member or an Assistant Board Member.

Being or becoming a Potential Trouble Source without reporting it or taking action.

Receiving auditing while a Potential Trouble Source.

Withholding from local Scientology executives that he or she is a Potential Trouble Source.

Failing to report a Potential Trouble Source to local HCO.

Organizing or allowing a gathering or meeting of staff members or field auditors or the public to protest the orders of a senior.

Being a knowing accessory to a Suppressive Act.

Using a local Scientology title to set aside the orders or policies from the International Board.

Following illegal orders or illegal local policies or alter-is, knowing them to be different or contradictory to those issued by the International Board.

Not directly reporting flagrant departures from International Board policy in a section, unit, department, org, zone or division.

Being long absent from post while a senior executive without advising the Board Member of his or her division.

Permitting a section, unit, department, org, zone or division to collapse.

Not taking over as a deputy in a crisis not otherwise being handled.

Passing org students or preclears to outside auditors for private commission.

Using an org position to build up a private practice.

Taking private donations while on staff to audit outside pcs, run private courses, coach or audit students or org pcs.

Embezzlement.

Taking commissions from merchants.

Reselling org materiel for private gain.

Using an org position to procure personal or non-Scientology funds or unusual favors from the public, a firm, student or pc.

Impersonating a Scientologist or staff member when not authorized.

Inciting to insubordination.

Instigating a local power push against a senior.

Spreading destructive rumors about senior Scientologists.

Pretending to express a multiple opinion (use of "everybody") in vital reports, which could influence Assistant Board or Board decisions.

Not reporting the discovery of a Crime or High Crime to HCO of the nearest Scientology organization while in authority or as a member of a Committee of Evidence or as a witness before a Committee of Evidence.

Refusal to accept penalties assigned in a recourse action.

Refusal to uphold discipline.

Getting another staff member disciplined by giving false reports about him or her.

Overworking an executive by ignoring one's duties.

Falsifying a communication from higher authority.

Falsifying a telex message or cable.

Causing a staff member to lose prestige or be disciplined by giving false reports.

Seeking to shift the blame to an innocent staff member for the consequences of one's own offenses.

Protecting a staff member guilty of a Crime or High Crime listed in this code.

Stealing or seducing another's wife or husband.

Committing offenses or omissions that bring one's senior staff member, unit, department, org or zone official to personal risk and/or a Committee of Evidence, civil or criminal court.

Willful loss or destruction of Scientology property.

Making out or submitting or accepting false purchase orders.

Juggling accounts.

Illegally taking or possessing org property.

Causing severe and disreputable disturbances resulting in disrepute.

Obtaining loans or money under false pretenses.

Condoning circumstances or offenses capable of bringing a course, section, unit, department, org, zone or division to a state of collapse.

Holding Scientology materials or policies up to ridicule, contempt or scorn.

Heckling a Scientology Supervisor or Lecturer.

Falsely degrading an auditor's technical reputation.

Impersonating an executive staff member.

Pretending Scientology certificates, classifications or awards not actually held to obtain money or credit.

Accepting donations for auditing hours or training courses for advance which are not then delivered as to hours and time in training (but not results or subject matter).

Using Scientology harmfully.

Not bringing a preclear up through the grades but overwhelming the preclear with high levels.

Processing or giving aid or comfort to a Suppressive Person or Group.

Knowingly using Scientology to obtain sexual relations or restimulation.

Seducing a minor.

Neglect or omission in safeguarding the copyrights, registered marks, trademarks, registered names of Scientology.

Issuing the data or information or instructional or admin procedures of Scientology without credit or falsely assigning credit for them to another.

Issuing any Scientology data under another name.

Condoning the suppression of the word "Scientology" in Scientology use or practice.

Allying Scientology to a disrelated practice.

Neglect of responsibilities resulting in a catastrophe even when another manages to avert the final consequences.

Creating problems in the implementation of orders.

Using policy to create problems.

Committing a problem.

Committing a solution which becomes a problem.

Case on post.

Crimes are punished by convening Committees of Evidence and may not be handled by direct discipline. Crimes may result in suspension of certificates, classifications or awards, reduction of post, or even dismissal or arrest when the Crime clearly warrants it. But such penalties must be assigned as Findings of a Committee of Evidence for Crimes and may not be assigned by direct discipline. Certificates, classifications or awards may not be cancelled for a Crime.

HIGH CRIMES

These consist of publicly departing Scientology or committing Suppressive Acts.

Cancellation of certificates, classifications and awards are amongst the penalties which can be leveled for this type of offense as well as those recommended by Committees of Evidence.

A reward system for merit and good performance also exists.

SUPPRESSIVE ACTS
SUPPRESSION OF SCIENTOLOGY AND SCIENTOLOGISTS

ue to the extreme urgency of our mission, I have worked to remove some of the fundamental barriers from our progress.

The chief stumbling block, huge above all others, is the upset we have with Potential Trouble Sources and their relationship to Suppressive Persons or Groups.

A *Potential Trouble Source* is defined as a person who while active in Scientology or a pc yet remains connected to a person or group that is a Suppressive Person or Group.

A *Suppressive Person* or *Group* is one that actively seeks to suppress or damage Scientology or a Scientologist by Suppressive Acts.

Suppressive Acts are acts calculated to impede or destroy Scientology or a Scientologist and which are listed at length below.

A Scientologist caught in the situation of being in Scientology while still connected with a Suppressive Person or Group is given a present time problem of sufficient magnitude to prevent case gain, as only a PTP can halt progress of a case. Only ARC breaks worsen it. To the PTP is added ARC breaks with the Suppressive Person or Group. The result is no-gain or deterioration of a case by reason of the suppressive connection in the environment.

Any Scientologist, in his own experience, can probably recall some such cases and their subsequent upset.

Until the environment is handled, nothing beneficial can happen. Quite the contrary. In the most flagrant of such cases, the Scientologist's case worsened and the Suppressive Person or Group sent endless distorted or false reports to press, police, authorities and the public in general.

Unless the Potential Trouble Source, the preclear caught up in this, can be made to take action of an environmental nature to end the situation, one has a pc or Scientologist who may cave in or squirrel because of no case gain and also a hostile environment for Scientology.

This material gives the means and provides the policy for getting the above situation handled.

A Potential Trouble Source may receive no processing until the situation is handled.

Suppressive Persons or Groups relinquish their rights as Scientologists by their very actions and may not receive the benefits of the Codes of the Church.

The families and adherents of Suppressive Persons or Groups may not receive processing. It does not matter whether they are or are not Scientologists. If the families or adherents of Suppressive Persons or Groups are processed, any auditor doing so is guilty of a Misdemeanor. (See *Offenses and Penalties.*)

A Potential Trouble Source knowingly permitting himself or herself or the Suppressive Person to be processed without advising the auditor or Scientology authorities is guilty of a Crime.

SUPPRESSIVE ACTS

Suppressive Acts are defined as actions or omissions undertaken to knowingly suppress, reduce or impede Scientology or Scientologists.

Such Suppressive Acts include:

Any felony (such as murder, arson, etc.) against person or property.

Sexual or sexually perverted conduct contrary to the well-being or good state of mind of a Scientologist in good standing or under the charge of Scientology, such as a student or a preclear.

Blackmail of Scientologists or Scientology organizations threatened or accomplished—in which case the crime being used for blackmail purposes becomes fully outside the reach of Ethics and is absolved by the fact of blackmail unless repeated.

Using the trademarks and service marks of Dianetics and Scientology without express permission or license from the owner of the marks or its authorized licensee.

Falsifying records that then imperil the liberty or safety of a Scientologist.

Testifying or giving data against Scientology falsely or in generalities or without personal knowledge of the matters to which one testifies.

Organizing splinter groups to diverge from Scientology practices, still calling it Scientology or calling it something else.

Organizing a splinter group to use Scientology data or any part of it to distract people from standard Scientology.

Using Scientology (or perverted and alter-ised tech and calling it Scientology) harmfully so as to bring about disrepute to an org, group or Scientology itself.

Issuing alter-ised Scientology technical data or information or instructional or admin procedures, calling it Scientology or calling it something else to confuse or deceive people as to the true source, beliefs and practices of Scientology.

Unauthorized use of the materials of Dianetics and Scientology.

Holding, using, copying, printing or publishing confidential materials of Dianetics and Scientology without express permission or license from the author of the materials or his authorized licensee.

Falsely attributing or falsely representing oneself or others as Source of Scientology or Dianetics Technology; or using any position gained with staff and/or public to falsely attribute non-Source material to Source or to falsely represent non-Source material as authorized Scientology or Dianetics Technology.

Acts calculated to misuse, invalidate or alter-is legally, or in any other way, the trademarks and service marks of Dianetics and Scientology.

Intentional and unauthorized alteration of LRH Technology, Policy, Issues or Checksheets.

Developing and/or using squirrel processes and checksheets.

Knowingly giving testimony which is false, a generality or not based on personal knowledge to imperil a Scientologist.

Public disavowal of Scientology or Scientologists in good standing with Scientology organizations.

Public statements against Scientology or Scientologists but not to Committees of Evidence duly convened.

Proposing, advising or voting for legislation or ordinances, rules or laws directed toward the suppression of Scientology.

Pronouncing Scientologists guilty of the practice of standard Scientology.

Testifying hostilely before state or public inquiries into Scientology to suppress it.

Reporting or threatening to report Scientology or Scientologists to civil authorities in an effort to suppress Scientology or Scientologists from practicing or receiving standard Scientology.

Bringing civil suit against any Scientology organization or Scientologist, including the nonpayment of bills or failure to refund, without first calling the matter to the attention of the International Justice Chief and receiving a reply.

Demanding the return of any or all donations made for standard training or processing actually received or received in part and still available but undelivered only because of departure of the person demanding (the donations must be refunded but this policy applies).

Writing anti-Scientology letters to the press or giving anti-Scientology or anti-Scientologist data to the press.

Continued membership in a divergent group.

Continued adherence to a person or group pronounced a Suppressive Person or Group by HCO.

Failure to handle or disavow and disconnect from a person demonstrably guilty of Suppressive Acts.

Being at the hire of anti-Scientology groups or persons.

Calling meetings of staffs or field auditors or the public to deliver Scientology into the hands of unauthorized persons or persons who will suppress it or alter it or who have no reputation for following standard lines and procedures.

Infiltrating a Scientology group or organization or staff to stir up discontent or protest at the instigation of hostile forces.

Mutiny.

Seeking to splinter off an area of Scientology and deny it to properly constituted authority for personal profit, personal power or "to save the organization from the higher officers of Scientology."

Engaging in malicious rumormongering to destroy the authority or repute of higher officers or the leading names of Scientology or to "safeguard" a position.

Delivering up the person of a Scientologist without justifiable defense or lawful protest to the demands of civil or criminal law.

Receiving money, favors or encouragement to suppress Scientology or Scientologists.

Using an org position or comm line to build up a private practice which reroutes org students, pcs and/or staff off org lines.

Severe breach of ecclesiastical and/or fiduciary duty as an executive or corporate official of any Scientology or Dianetics organization which has resulted in severe harm, loss or disrepute for Scientology or the organization.

Using Scientology lines for personal profit in such a way as to cause disruption in the organization or to block the flow of public up the Bridge.

Using the mailing lists of Scientology or Dianetics organizations for personal profit or gain.

Employing org staff members to the detriment of the production or the establishment of the organization.

Providing an organization's pc folders, Ethics Files, student files, accounts files, Central Files folders or Central Files lists or partial lists, or Addresso lists or partial lists to any individual, group, organization, mission or other unit or agency for any reason or purpose, except those covered explicitly in existing Church policy; or to provide such files or lists to any individual, group, organization, mission or other unit or agency which is unauthorized by or in bad standing with the Mother Church.

Calculated efforts to disrupt Church services or the flow of public up the Bridge through the Churches.

Refusal to allow staff or public to progress up the Bridge or creating blocks on the Bridge preventing such progression.

Blatant and willful obstruction of Church operations or interference with Church contractual and other obligations to the detriment of Church expansion or activities.

Neglect or violation of any of the ten points of Keeping Scientology Working:

One: Having the correct technology.

Two: Knowing the technology.

Three: Knowing it is correct.

Four: Teaching correctly the correct technology.

Five: Applying the technology.

Six: Seeing that the technology is correctly applied.

Seven: Hammering out of existence incorrect technology.

Eight: Knocking out incorrect applications.

Nine: Closing the door on any possibility of incorrect technology.

Ten: Closing the door on incorrect application.

Tolerating the absence of or not insisting upon star-rated checkouts on all processes and their immediate technology and on relevant Policy Letters on HGC interns or Staff Auditors in the Tech Div or Staff Auditors or interns in the Qual Div, for the levels and actions they will use, before permitting them to audit org pcs, and on Supervisors in Tech and Qual who instruct or examine, or failing to insist upon this policy or preventing this policy from going into effect or minimizing the checkouts or lists.

Technical Degrades:

1. *Abbreviating an official course in Dianetics and Scientology so as to lose the full theory, processes and effectiveness of the subjects.*

2. *Adding comments to checksheets or instructions labeling any material "background" or "not used now" or "old" or any similar action, which will result in the student not knowing, using and applying the data in which he is being trained.*

3. *Employing any checksheet for any course not authorized by myself or the Authority, Verification and Correction Unit International (AVC Int).*

   (Hat checksheets may be authorized locally per policy on checksheet format.)

4. *Failing to strike from any checksheet remaining in use any such comments as "historical," "background," "not used," "old," etc.,* or verbally stating it to students.

5. *Permitting a pc to attest to more than one grade at a time on the pc's own determinism without hint or evaluation.*

6. *Running only one process for a lower grade between 0 to IV, where the grade End Phenomena has not been attained.*

7. *Failing to use all processes for a level where the End Phenomena has not been attained.*

8. *Boasting as to speed of delivery in a session, such as "I put in Grade 0 in three minutes." Etc.*

9. *Shortening time of application of auditing for financial or labor-saving considerations.*

10. *Acting in any way calculated to lose the technology of Dianetics and Scientology to use or impede its use or shorten its materials or its application.*

STEPS TO HANDLE THE SUPPRESSIVE PERSON

Suppressive Acts are clearly those covert or overt acts knowingly calculated to reduce or destroy the influence or activities of Scientology or prevent case gains or continued Scientology success and activity on the part of a Scientologist. As persons or groups that would do such a thing act out of self-interest only to the detriment of all others, they cannot be granted the rights and beingness ordinarily accorded rational beings.

If a person or a group that has committed a Suppressive Act comes to his, her or their senses and recants, his, her or their only terminal is the International Justice Chief, via the Continental Justice Chief, who:

A. Tells the person or group to stop committing present time overts and to cease all attacks and suppressions so he, she or they can get a case gain.

B. Requires a public announcement to the effect that they realize their actions were ignorant and unfounded and stating, where possible, the influences or motivations which caused them to attempt to suppress or attack Scientology; gets it signed before witnesses and published broadly, particularly to persons directly influenced or formerly associated with the former offender or offenders. The letter should be calculated to expose any conspiracy to suppress Scientology or the preclear or Scientologist if such existed.

B1. Requires that all debts owed to Scientology organizations or missions are paid off.

B2. May require that, subject to the approval of the International Justice Chief, an Amends Project suitable and commensurate with the severity and extent of the Suppressive Acts committed be completed before further A to E Steps are undertaken.

Before any such Amends Project is begun, the person must submit an Amends Project Petition to the International Justice Chief, using full CSW and stating what he proposes to do as amends, and this must be approved by the International Justice Chief to be considered valid. Evidence of genuine ethics change may be required before approval of the Amends Project is given. (Examples of such evidence might be, depending upon the High Crimes committed: the person has obtained an honest job; has paid off all debts owed to others; valid contributions have been made to the community; the person has totally ceased those actions for which he was declared, etc.)

It is also within the power of the International Justice Chief, when approving an Amends Project Petition, to require, as a protector of the Church and its tenets and membership, that such Amends Project be carried out entirely off any Scientology organization, mission or network lines, and to require, before the Amends Project may be considered complete, extensive evidence over a protracted period of time that the person has, beyond any doubt, ceased his or her suppressive actions, has created no problems for the Church or any member of the Church in any way on any line, and has undertaken and completed an action which is clearly and undeniably of benefit to Mankind.

C. Requires training beginning at the lowest level of the Bridge at their expense if executives in charge of training will have the person or the group members.

D. Makes a note of all of the above matters with copies of the statement and files in the Ethics Files of those concerned.

E. Informs the International Justice Chief and forwards a duplicate of the original statements which show signatures.

Any Potential Trouble Source owing money to any Scientology organization is handled the same as any other Scientologist. Failure to discharge a financial obligation becomes a civil matter after normal, within-org avenues of collection have been exhausted.

Any PTS who fails to either handle or disconnect from the SP who is making him or her a PTS is, by failing to do so, guilty of a Suppressive Act.

Civil court action against SPs to effect collection of monies owed may be resorted to, as they are not entitled to Scientology justice procedures.

Until a Suppressive Person or Group is absolved or until permitted to actively engage in the training required in point C, as duly authorized and published, his, her or their only Scientology terminal is the International Justice Chief via the Continental Justice Chief, or members of a duly authorized and convened Committee of Evidence.

A Suppressive Declare Order upon a person or group and all of the conditions inherent within it remain in force until the order has been officially cancelled by an authorized and published Church issue.

Also, until a Suppressive Person or Group is absolved, but not during the period when the person requests and has a Committee of Evidence, or an amnesty occurs, no Scientology justice other than the material herein applies to such persons, no Committee of Evidence may be called on any Scientologist or person for any offenses of any kind against the Suppressive Person except for offenses which violate the laws of the land or except to establish in cases of real dispute whether or not the person was suppressing either Scientology or the Scientologist.

Such persons are in the same category as those whose certificates have been cancelled, and persons whose certificates, classifications and awards have been cancelled are also in this category.

The imagination must not be stretched to place this label on a person. Errors, Misdemeanors and Crimes do not label a person as a Suppressive Person or Group. Only High Crimes do so.

A Committee of Evidence may be called by any Convening Authority who wishes more concrete evidence of efforts to suppress Scientology or Scientologists, but if such a Committee's Findings, passed on, establish beyond reasonable doubt Suppressive Acts, the policy here applies.

Outright or covert acts knowingly designed to impede or destroy Scientology or Scientologists is what is meant by Acts Suppressive of Scientology or Scientologists.

The greatest good for the greatest number of dynamics requires that actions destructive of the advance of the many by Scientology means, overtly or covertly undertaken with the direct target of destroying Scientology as a whole, or a Scientologist in particular, be summarily handled due to the character of the reactive mind and the consequent impulses of the insane or near insane to ruin every chance of Mankind via Scientology.

POTENTIAL TROUBLE SOURCE

A Scientologist connected by familial or other ties to a person who is guilty of Suppressive Acts is known as a Potential Trouble Source or Trouble Source. The history of Dianetics and Scientology is strewn with these. Confused by emotional ties, dogged in refusing to give up Scientology, yet invalidated by a Suppressive Person at every turn, they cannot, having a PTP, make case gains. If they would act with determination one way or the other—reform the Suppressive Person or otherwise standardly handle the situation—they could then make gains and recover their potential. If they make no determined move, they eventually succumb.

Therefore the policy herein extends to suppressive non-Scientology wives and husbands and parents or other family members or hostile groups or even close friends. So long as a wife or husband, father or mother or other family connection or hostile group, who is attempting to suppress the Scientology spouse or child, remains continuingly acknowledged or in communication with the Scientology spouse or child or member, then that Scientologist or preclear comes under the *family* or *adherent* clause and may not be processed or further trained until he or she has taken appropriate action to cease to be a Potential Trouble Source.

The validity of this policy is borne out by the fact that the US government raids and other troubles were instigated by wives, husbands or parents who were actively suppressing a Scientologist or Scientology or who were acting under the influences of persons or agencies who had deliberately misinformed them regarding Scientology. The suppressed Scientologist did not act in good time to avert the trouble by handling the antagonistic family member.

Any processing of the Potential Trouble Source is denied or illegal while the connection exists and a person not actively seeking to settle the matter may be subjected to a Committee of Evidence if processed meanwhile.

POTENTIAL TROUBLE SOURCES AND DISCONNECTION

The subject and technology of "disconnection" is thoroughly covered in *PTSness and Disconnection* and in the basic technical materials referenced therein.

Unwarranted or threatened disconnection has the recourse of the person or group being disconnected from requesting a Committee of Evidence from the nearest Convening Authority (or HCO) and producing to the Committee any evidence of actual material assistance to Scientology without reservation or bad intent. The Committee must be convened if requested.

The real motives of Suppressive Persons have been traced to quite sordid hidden desires—in one case the wife wanted her husband's death so she could get his money and fought Scientology because it was making the husband spiritually well. Without handling the wife or the connection with the woman, the Scientologist, as family, drifted on with the situation and the wife was able to cause a near destruction of Scientology in that area by false testimony to the police and government and press. Therefore this is a serious thing—to tolerate or remain connected to a source of active suppression of a Scientologist or Scientology without standardly handling or acting to expose the true motives behind the hostility and reform the person. No money, particularly, may be accepted as donation or loan from a person who is "family" to a Suppressive Person and therefore a Potential Trouble Source. There is no source of trouble in Scientology's history greater than this one for frequency and lack of attention.

Anyone absolved of Suppressive Acts by an amnesty or a Committee of Evidence ceases to be declared Suppressive. Anyone found guilty of Suppressive Acts by a Committee of Evidence and its Convening Authorities remains declared unless saved by an amnesty.

The policy herein is calculated to prevent future distractions of this nature as time goes on.

RIGHTS OF A SUPPRESSIVE PERSON OR GROUP

A truly Suppressive Person or Group has no rights of any kind *as Scientologists.*

However, a person or group may be falsely labeled a Suppressive Person or Group. Should the person or group claim the label to be false, he, she or they may request a Committee of Evidence via their nearest Continental Justice Chief. The executive with the power to convene a Committee of Evidence must do so if one is requested for recourse or redress of wrongs.

The person or representative of the group labeled Suppressive is named as an Interested Party to the Committee. They attend it where it convenes.

The Committee must pay attention to any actual evidences that the person or group that is accused of being suppressive may produce, particularly to the effect of having helped Scientology or Scientologists or a Scientologist, and if this is seen to outweigh the accusations, proof or lack of it, the person is absolved.

Any knowingly false testimony, forgeries or false witnesses introduced by the person or group accused of being suppressive can result in an immediate finding against the person or group.

Any effort to use copies of the testimony or Findings of a Committee of Evidence called for this purpose or holding it to scorn in a civil court immediately reverses any favorable finding and automatically labels the person or group Suppressive.

If the Findings, as passed upon by the Convening Authority and the International Justice Chief, demonstrate guilt, the person or group is so labeled as a Suppressive Person or Group.

Failing to prove guilt of Suppressive Acts, the Committee must recommend to absolve the person or group publicly.

When a person, by some circumstance, has been incorrectly declared, then *after* he has had a Committee of Evidence and the Suppressive Person Declare Order has been cancelled, he may, if he wishes, request a Board of Review who, upon full review of the matter, may, if warranted, ask for the return of lost pay or status the person may have experienced while incorrectly declared a Suppressive Person. (See *Board of Review.*)

RECOURSE OF A POTENTIAL TROUBLE SOURCE

A person labeled a Potential Trouble Source and so barred from receiving auditing, may request a Committee of Evidence of the nearest Continental Justice Chief via HCO as recourse if he or she contests the allegation.

The Committee of Evidence requested must be convened by the nearest Convening Authority.

If evidences of disconnection are given, the Committee of Evidence Findings and Recommendations and the Convening Authority, once the Findings are duly approved, must remove the label of Potential Trouble Source from the Scientologist. If the alleged Suppressive Person or Group is clearly and beyond reasonable doubt shown not to be guilty of Suppressive Acts or is shown clearly to have reformed, the Committee of Evidence must recommend removal of the label Suppressive Person or Group from the suspected person or group. However, once a person or group has been declared Suppressive by an authorized, published order, the removal or lifting of the Declare Order or label must be approved by the International Justice Chief.

But should the former Potential Trouble Source's state of case show no gain after reasonable time in processing, any executive of Division 4 (Training and Processing) may order a new Committee of Evidence in the matter and if it and its Convening Authority recommend to reverse the former Findings, and if such Findings are approved on International Justice lines, the labels are applied. But no auditor may be disciplined for auditing either during the period between the two Findings.

RECOURSE OF AN AUDITOR

An auditor disciplined for processing a Potential Trouble Source or a Suppressive Person or a member of a Suppressive Group, may request a Committee of Evidence if he can persuade the Potential Trouble Source and the Suppressive Person or a representative of the Suppressive Group to appear before it.

The auditor so requesting may also have named as an Interested Party or Parties, with himself, the person or persons who supplied the information or misinformation concerning his actions.

No damages or costs may be borne by or ordered by a Committee of Evidence in cases involving Potential Trouble Sources or Suppressive Persons or Groups.

When the Potential Trouble Source or Suppressive Person or Group representative fails to appear before a Committee of Evidence on a Bill of Particulars labeling persons as Potential Trouble Sources or Suppressive Persons or Groups at the published time of its convening, the Bill of Particulars stands as proven and the Convening Authority is bound so to declare.

EVIDENCE OF DISCONNECTION

Any HCO Secretary may receive evidences of disconnection or disavowal and, on finding them to be bona fide, must place copies of such evidences in the Ethics File and in the CF (Central Files) folders of all persons named in them.

The disconnecting person then ceases to be a Potential Trouble Source (once any additional PTS handling of a technical nature required by the Case Supervisor has been successfully completed).

The procedure for a recanting Suppressive Person or Group is outlined above.

EVIDENCES OF SUPPRESSION

It is wise for any Scientologist, HCO Secretary or Committee of Evidence, in matters concerning Suppressive Acts, to obtain valid documents, letters, testimonies duly signed and witnessed, affidavits duly sworn to and other matters and evidences which would have weight in a court of law. Momentary spite, slander suits, charges of Scientology separating families, etc., are then guarded against.

———

If matters concerning Suppressive Acts are given good and alert attention, properly enforced, they will greatly accelerate the growth of Scientology and bring a new calmness to its people and organizations and far better case gains where they have not heretofore been easy to achieve.

Preclears with present time problems, ARC broken with associated but Suppressive Persons will not obtain case gains but, on the contrary, may experience great difficulty.

Observance of these facts and disciplines can help us all.

Nothing in the policy herein shall ever or under any circumstances justify any violation of the laws of the land or intentional legal wrongs. Any such offense shall subject the offender to penalties prescribed by law as well as to ethics and justice actions.

TRAINING AND PROCESSING REGULATIONS
TECHNICAL DISCIPLINE

STUDENTS' QUESTIONS

1. The only answers permitted to a student's demand for verbal technical data or unusual solutions are:

   "The material is in (HCOB, Policy Letter or tape)."

   "What does your material state?"

   "What word did you miss in the (Bulletin, Policy Letter or tape)?"

   And for requests for unusual auditing solutions:

   "What did you actually do?"

   Any other answer by Technical Secretaries, Ds of T, Instructors or course personnel is a Misdemeanor.

2. Any Instructor teaching or advising any method not contained in HCOBs or on tapes, or slighting existing HCOBs, Policy Letters or tapes may be charged with a Crime.

3. Any Instructor in any way obscuring the source of technology by wrongly attributing it may be found guilty of a false report.

STAFF AUDITORS' ACTIONS

4. Any Staff Auditor who runs any process on any org pc that is not given in grade and level HCOBs may be charged by the Tech Sec or D of P with a Misdemeanor.

5. Any alteration or nonstandard rendition of a process is a Misdemeanor.

6. Any Staff Auditor running a pc above the pc's grade instead of for the next grade, or running processes out of sequence in a grade may be charged with a Misdemeanor.

7. Any Staff Auditor reporting falsely, verbally or in writing, on an Auditor's Report may be charged with a Crime.

8. Any Staff Auditor turning in an illegible report may be charged with a no report which is a Misdemeanor.

9. Any Staff Auditor attesting falsely to TA or falsely reporting the flattening of a process may be charged with a Misdemeanor.

10. Any Staff Auditor who receives orders to run an illegal process must report the matter at once to HCO Ethics, requesting that the person so advising be charged with endangering the Staff Auditor's job and repute.

STUDENT REGULATIONS

11. Former regulations [prior to April 1965] for students are abolished.

12. Students are covered as Scientologists by the HCO Ethics Codes and may request recourse from injustice and have the same privileges as any field Scientologist.

13. Tech Secs, Ds of T, Supervisors and Instructors as well as Qualifications Division personnel may request a Court of Ethics from the Department of Inspection and Reports for any student they find it necessary to discipline under the HCO Justice Codes, such discipline being in lieu of a Committee of Evidence. However the student may request a Committee of Evidence instead if he or she feels a wrong is being done.

14. Any student knowingly altering technology, applying processes improperly or using technology illegally on HGC pcs, on lower-unit students or the public, while a student, may be charged with a Misdemeanor.

15. A student damaging another by willful application of incorrect technology may be charged by his Supervisors with a Crime and a Court of Ethics action must be requested by his Supervisors.

16. A student falsely enrolling may be charged by the org with a Crime.

17. Blowing a course is handled under Suppressive Acts. If so charged, the student may have recourse if applied for before 60 days to the Department of Inspection and Reports Ethics Section.

PRECLEAR REGULATIONS

18. Preclears are covered by HCO Justice Codes.

19. A preclear may have recourse when feeling unjustly wronged by applying to the Ethics Section of the Department of Inspection and Reports of the org.

20. A preclear refusing to answer an auditing question may be charged by the Staff Auditor with a "no report" and taken before a Court of Ethics at once.

21. An HGC or staff preclear must report flagrant breaches of the Auditor's Code to the Ethics Section of the org, but if the report is false beyond reasonable doubt the preclear may be charged with a Suppressive Act.

22. A student preclear or HGC preclear blowing an org without reporting to the Tech Sec, D of P or the Ethics Section first, and who will not permit *any* auditor to handle the matter at the org *where* the auditing occurred, must be fully investigated at any cost by HCO in the pc's own area. The auditing session must be fully investigated by the Ethics Section and if any Auditor's Code breaks are found to have occurred in that auditing, the auditor may be brought before a Court of Ethics. The entire matter and its final results must be reported to the Office of LRH and higher authorities as called for in policy.

23. Charges against HGC or student preclears may also be made by the Tech Sec, the Qualifications Sec, Ds of T, Ds of P, Supervisors and Staff Auditors.

QUALIFICATIONS DIVISION

24. Any person undergoing Review is subject to the same actions as in the HGC or Academy and any personnel of the Qualifications Division may charge students and pcs under the Justice Codes and bring them before a Court of Ethics.

25. Persons charged by Qualifications Division personnel may request recourse if wronged.

26. The Qualifications Division may request a Court of Ethics on Technical Division personnel, preclears and students for false reports, false attestations and no reports as well as other justice matters. And the Technical Division personnel may, on their part, request a Court of Ethics on Qualifications Division personnel, students or preclears.

———————

This policy does not change any HCO Codes of Justice but only augments them for the purposes of assisting peaceful and effective training and processing with the exact technology issued.

ETHICS AND STUDY TECH

he basic Why of the majority of cases of post nonperformance of a staff member and *out-tech* in an org stems from misunderstood words.

The primary point that has to be gotten in is Study Tech.

This is also our bridge to society.

Yet Study Tech is the tech that includes misunderstood word tech.

Thus if Study Tech is not in, people on staffs see nothing wrong with hearing or reading orders containing words they do not understand and have no urge to look them up. Further, they often feel they do know words that they in fact do not know.

When this situation exists, it is next to impossible to get Study Tech and Word Clearing Tech in. For the orders seeking to get in Study Tech may contain words the person does not understand. Thus he doesn't really comply with the orders and Study Tech does not get *in*. Thus the ability to hear or read and understand continues to be missing.

Therefore, these ethics actions become part of standard ethics:

1. *A person may be summoned to a Court of Ethics or Executive Court of Ethics if it be found that he has gone past a word he does not understand when receiving, hearing or reading an order, HCOB, Policy Letter or tape, any and all LRH written or printed materials including books, PABs, despatches, telexes and mimeo issues, which resulted in a failure to do duties of his post, without his at once making an effective effort to clear the words on himself, whether he knew he*

was missing them or not as the source of his inaction or damaging actions.

The charge is *neglecting to clarify words not understood.*

2. *A staff member who does not use Study Tech or get it known while studying or instructing may be summoned to a Court of Ethics or an Executive Court of Ethics.*

The charge is *failure to employ Study Tech.*

3. *A student alter-ising or misadvising others on the use of Study Tech may be summoned before a Court of Ethics.*

The charge is *advocating a misuse or neglect of proper Study Tech.*

4. *An auditor failing to clear each and every word of every command or list used may be summoned before a Court of Ethics.*

The charge is *out-tech.*

5. *Any Public Division person, staff member or Scientologist found using terms, circumstances or data on raw public in public lectures or promotion or in PR beyond the public ability to grasp without stressing Study Tech or at once taking effective measures to clarify, or releasing materials broadly to a wrong public, may be summoned to a Court of Ethics if any flap or upset results.*

The charge is *failure to apply Study Tech in dissemination.*

SUPPRESSIVE

Furthermore, as Study Tech is our primary bridge to society and the basic prevention of out-tech and out-admin, if any offense (as above) found guilty in a Court of Ethics is *repeated* and the person has had two such Courts on this offense, the person may be summoned before a Committee of Evidence on a charge of *committing an act or omission undertaken to knowingly suppress, reduce or impede Scientology or Scientologists.* And if found guilty beyond reasonable doubt, may be declared a Suppressive Person and expelled with full penalties.

AXIOM 28

Failures to teach or use Study Tech or alterations of Study Tech are actually offenses against Axiom 28 as it is applied internally in an org on admin and tech and from the org to society.

Study Tech including its technology of Word Clearing is in fact the technology of Axiom 28.

The Axiom (amended) follows:

AXIOM 28:

COMMUNICATION IS THE CONSIDERATION AND ACTION OF IMPELLING AN IMPULSE OR PARTICLE FROM SOURCE-POINT ACROSS A DISTANCE TO RECEIPT-POINT, WITH THE INTENTION OF BRINGING INTO BEING AT THE RECEIPT-POINT A DUPLICATION AND UNDERSTANDING OF THAT WHICH EMANATED FROM THE SOURCE-POINT.

The Formula of Communication is:

Cause, Distance, Effect, with Intention, Attention and Duplication *with Understanding*.

The component parts of Communication are:

Consideration, Intention, Attention, Cause, Source-point, Distance, Effect, Receipt-point, Duplication, Understanding, the Velocity of the impulse or particle, Nothingness or Somethingness. A non-Communication consists of Barriers. Barriers consist of Space, Interpositions (such as walls and screens of fast-moving particles) and Time. A communication, by definition, does not need to be two-way. When a communication is returned, the Formula is repeated, with the Receipt-point now becoming a Source-point and the former Source-point now becoming a Receipt-point.

———

STUDY TECH AND POST

It has been found that certain staff could not perform their duties because they knowingly went by misunderstood words in despatches and telexes.

331

By this willful failure they had dumped their hats on seniors for two years.

They were wiped out on post, could not evaluate or find out what was going on. And spent a bulk of their time sleeping.

Therefore:

6. *Any person who goes by misunderstood words or abbreviations in telexes or despatches or materials he handles on post without clarifying them shall be summonsed to a Court of Ethics.*

The charge is *neglect of duty* and the minimum sentence is Treason.

7. *Any auditor failing to write clearly on worksheets or put down enough text to make the worksheet understandable shall be summonsed to a Court of Ethics.*

The charge is *no report.*

8. *Any Case Supervisor who permits an auditor to write incomprehensibly or omit data shall be summonsed to a Court of Ethics.*

The charge is *condoning neglect of duty.*

ADDITIONAL PENALTY

Whenever these points are found to be out in an area and not enforced, there can be no plea of ignorance and the seniors of the area are themselves liable to Comm Ev.

Violations of Study Tech and failures to use this technology are responsible for great losses and out-tech, out-admin and overwork of seniors.

The matter has been regarded too lightly and has caused great losses, blows and has impeded progress on this planet.

SCIENTOLOGY
JUSTICE
PROCEDURES

ADMINISTERING JUSTICE

here are some things to firmly keep in mind when you have to use HCO's Justice function:

1. Only the criminally inclined desire a society in which the criminal is free to do as he pleases.

2. Only the criminally inclined are frightened enough of justice to protest and complain that it exists.

3. Without order nothing can grow or expand.

4. Justice is one of the guards that keeps the channel of progress a channel and not a stopped flow.

5. All reactive minds can exert pain and discomfort on a being. They demand the suppression of the good and the production of the bad. Therefore, in administering justice, restrain just a trifle more than a bank can compel a bad action. The external threat need be just enough to make the internal pressure to do wrong the lesser of two discomforts. Judgment lies in how much external restraint to apply.

6. Decent people are in favor of justice. Don't confuse the opinion of the majority who wish it with the snarls of the few who fear it.

7. A person who is dramatizing his criminal intent can become very angry if he is not prevented from hurting others.

8. A thetan is good. He invented a bank to keep others good. That mechanism went wrong. And that's why we're here.

9. In a session you would keep a burglar from bursting in the room and disturbing the preclear. In Scientology you keep offenders out so we can get on with our session with society.

10. Look up the person who rails against justice most and you will have the one you have been looking for.

11. The only overt in handling justice is not to work for the greatest good of the greatest number.

COMMITTEES OF EVIDENCE
SCIENTOLOGY JURISPRUDENCE, ADMINISTRATION OF

 his system is for use in all matters of justice in Scientology.

There can be no personal security without easily accessible, swift and fair justice within a group.

The jurisprudence employed must be competent, acceptable to the members of the group and effective in accomplishing good order for the group and personal rights and security for its individual members.

Justice used for revenge, securing advantages for a clique, increases disorder.

Justice should serve as a means of establishing guilt or innocence and awarding damages to the injured. The fact of its use should not preestablish guilt or award. Justice which by its employment alone establishes an atmosphere of guilt or greed is harmful and creates disorder.

Justice should clarify. Good justice in effect runs out group engrams. Bad justice runs them in.

I have been working for some time on a system of justice acceptable to Scientologists and have evolved one in *Committees of Evidence.* These work excellently by actual test and satisfy the requirements of justice.

I require that full use be made of these Committees in all matters relating to Scientology organizations, groups and concerns.

I do not recommend that individuals in authority act in disciplinary measures or capacities without employing Committees of Evidence.

DEFINITIONS

A Committee of Evidence:

A fact-finding body composed of impartial persons properly convened by a Convening Authority which hears evidence from persons it calls before it, arrives at a finding and makes a full report and recommendation to its Convening Authority for his or her action.

Convening Authority:

That duly appointed official of Scientology who appoints and convenes a Committee of Evidence to assist him in carrying out and justly exercising his or her authority, and who approves, mitigates or disapproves the Findings and Recommendations of the Committee of Evidence he or she appoints. The Convening Authority may not be a member of the Committee and may not sit with it and may not interfere with its conduct of business or its evidence, but may disband a Committee he or she convenes if it fails to be active in the prosecution of its business, and may convene another Committee in its place. The Convening Authority may not increase penalties recommended by the Committee he or she convenes.

No Convening Authority may be summoned before, appear before or be Chairman, Secretary or member of any Committee of Evidence he or she convenes.

No official authorized to act as a Convening Authority may be summoned before or named as an Interested Party to or witness before or serve on a Committee of Evidence at the level of Committee of Evidence he or she is authorized to convene or on any lower-level Committee; an official with the right to act as a Convening Authority may only be summoned by, appear before or become an Interested Party before Committees of Evidence of higher levels than he may authorize.*

Chairman of the Committee:

The Chairman is appointed at the discretion of the Convening Authority appointing the Committee. The appointment may be of a permanent nature, but again at the discretion of the Convening Authority. The Chairman may not appoint members to serve on the Committee. The Chairman presides over all meetings, conducts the largest part of the interrogation and sees that the Committee properly executes its duties in all respects in a dignified and expeditious manner. The Chairman may not interfere with the votes of the members and must include any divergences of opinion on the Findings by dissenting members. The Chairman sees to it that the Findings are based on majority opinion. The Chairman votes only in case of a deadlock. The Chairman may himself dissent from the majority opinion in the Findings but, if so, includes it as a separate opinion in the Findings like any other member dissenting and may not withhold Findings from the Convening Authority for this reason. If a Chairman is removed during the progress of any case before the Committee, the Findings are invalid and a new Committee must be convened and appearance before the incompleted hearings does not bar appearance before the newly convened Committee. However, a Chairman must be removed before Findings are being prepared before the Committee can be declared invalid and the removal must be for good and sufficient cause. The Chairman runs good S-C-S during all proceedings and gets evidence given rather than put in Itsa Lines. He gets the job done.

Secretary:

The Secretary is appointed specifically by the Convening Authority. The Secretary is a proper member of the Committee

---

The different levels of Committees of Evidence are contained and described in HCO Policy Letters and directives as issued by Senior HCO International.

and has a vote. The Secretary prepares and issues all notices to attend, attends all meetings, keeps all notes, collects all documentary evidence offered in the hearings, procures tapes and a tape recorder, does all the tape recording, and collects all members of the Committee for scheduled hearings. All this is in addition to usual staff duties.

Member:

Members of the Committee are specifically named by the Convening Authority. In addition to the Chairman and Secretary they may not number less than two or more than five. A member attends all hearings, may keep his own notes, passes on all Findings and votes for or against the Findings and their recommendations. A member must sign the Findings whether he approves of them or not but if disapproving may have the Chairman so note it. Interested Parties and witnesses may not object to any membership or composition of the Committee, it being taken for granted that the Convening Authority has been as impartial in this as is feasible. The member should conduct himself or herself courteously and with dignity toward other Committee members and particularly the Chairman, and should treat Interested Parties and witnesses as courteously as is possible with due recognition of the tension these may be under. By the member, any Interested Party who might be subject to charges is treated as not guilty until the last evidences have been heard and the Committee meets to discuss its Findings and their preparation. The member may question any Interested Party or witness but usually leaves this to the Chairman. The member may also write a question he or she wants asked and pass it to the Chairman. If a member truly does not understand some point of evidence toward the end of the hearings, he or she may demand the recall of anyone to clarify the matter but may not unduly extend the hearings by using this as a device. A member should not discuss the hearings abroad or form an early opinion and discuss it outside hearings as a fact.

No member should be permitted to express his own opinion as that of the Committee outside the hearings while they are in progress. A Chairman may discipline a member for failing to appear at his Committee's hearings, discourteous, foul or slovenly conduct or dishonesty when these imperil the functions or values of Committees of Evidence.

Evidence:

The spoken word, writings and documents are to be considered as evidence. The E-Meter is not to be used to procure evidence as it does not register lies on criminal types and, however vital and reliable as an auditing aid, is not always valid in detecting crime or acts. It can react on the flustered innocent and fail to react on the cold-blooded guilty. The reason for this is that it is inoperative during severe ARC breaks in which condition Interested Parties often are. Session withholds may not be used as evidence but evidence may not be refused because it also has been given in a session. Hearsay evidence (saying one heard somebody say that somebody else did) should not be admissible evidence, but statements that one heard another make damaging remarks or saw another act or fail to act are admissible.

Interested Party:

A person, plaintiff or defendant, called before a Committee of Evidence for whom penalties may be recommended or decisions awarded by the Committee. An Interested Party may not be called before another Committee or a later convened Committee for the same offense or complaint after having been summoned and heard for that offense or his complaint at one or more meetings of the current Committee. It may be that the Committee does not charge an Interested Party with an offense or award a decision but if so must either implicate or exonerate fully all Interested Parties to the hearing and recommend accordingly in its Findings. It is common to have more than one Interested Party named in any matter brought to a Committee. Being named as an Interested Party does not imply guilt but may result in becoming the subject of disciplinary recommendation or award by the Committee. To eventually be charged by the Committee or awarded a decision, a person must have been named as an Interested Party in the Bill of Particulars *before* the matter is heard by the Committee (except for failure to appear or false witness). An Interested Party is liable to penalty recommendation by the Committee. Refusal or failure of an Interested Party to appear results in a recommendation of the full penalty possible in the case for that Interested Party.

A person not named as an Interested Party in the original Bill of Particulars may not become an Interested Party to the action before the Committee by reason of new evidence. He or she would have to be specifically charged before a newly convened Committee.

Witness:

A witness is anyone who is called before the Committee to give evidence who is not an Interested Party. A witness may not be implicated or charged if not already named in the Bill of Particulars as an Interested Party except for failure to appear or when found to be a false witness. A witness who refuses to appear or refuses to testify may be separately charged for that failure and the Committee may recommend any fitting discipline for such a defaulting witness. For *false witness,* see below.

Bill of Particulars:

A written and signed appointment of a Committee of Evidence naming (1) the Chairman, Secretary and members of the Committee, (2) the Interested Party or Parties, (3) the matter to be heard and a summary of data to hand. It is duly signed by the Convening Authority and a copy of it is furnished to each person whose name appears in it and to local Legal Files.

Findings:

The full report of the Committee accompanied by a tape recording of the evidence given and a full recommendation to the Convening Authority for his action. The Findings is a document which gives a fast summary of the hearings, their result and a complete recommendation. It must be so written that it may be published without alteration by the Convening Authority. The summary states who appears to be at fault and who does not and why. The recommendation tells the Convening Authority exactly what disciplinary action should be taken and how, including any plea for leniency or insistence upon full penalty. The Findings is done after the last hearing and after the last Committee meeting that votes on the recommendation to be given. It is done by the Secretary from his or her notes but under the guidance of the Chairman. It is done as soon after the last Committee meeting as possible, is signed by Committee members and promptly forwarded to the Convening Authority. Only one copy is prepared and forwarded to the Convening Authority. No other copies are made or given anyone. Before forwarding to the Convening Authority, it is signed by every member of the Committee as well as the Chairman and Secretary. Accompanied by any tapes or documents, it is placed directly into the hands of the Convening Authority. It may not go by despatch line or mail. It is not accompanied by any other letter of transmission or by any delegation or by the Committee in person. It may be delivered by the Secretary or Chairman or their specially appointed messenger without further comment.

Endorsement:

The Findings now have added to them the endorsement by the Convening Authority. The Findings have no force until the endorsement is added. The Convening Authority makes the endorsement on the Findings in as brief a fashion as possible. The Convening Authority can (1) accept the Findings in full, (2) reduce the penalty recommended or

(3) suspend or cancel the penalty completely with a pardon. The Convening Authority may make no other endorsement, save only to thank the Committee and witnesses. The moment the Findings are endorsed they have the effect of orders as per the endorsement and all persons under the authority of the Convening Authority are bound to execute them and abide by them accordingly.

Publication:

The Findings and their endorsement are published according to the directions of the Convening Authority. They are first *mimeographed*. Publication is done in three ways: (1) By posting a *copy* on the staff board or public board and copies to executives; (2) By circulation in any area affected; (3) By continental magazine or other broad means. However it is published, a mimeographed copy goes to every Interested Party or witness and to each Committee member.

Files:

The original, all spare mimeograph copies and any documents and tapes are placed in a large envelope and filed in the Valuable Documents file of the organization. Their loss could prejudice the Convening Authority in any review. This envelope may be called for by any upper Committee reviewing the case.

344

Review:

Any Committee of Evidence Findings and Convening Authority Endorsement may be subject to review by any upper-level Committee. Review must be applied for by anyone named as an Interested Party but no other, and only if a penalty was recommended (whether endorsed or not). A Committee of Evidence for Review is convened and handled in exactly the same way as an ordinary Committee of Evidence but it cannot call new or even old witnesses or the Interested Parties. All it can do is listen to the tapes of the hearings, examine the evidence given in the original hearings and recommend to its own Convening Authority one of two things:

(1) That a new Committee be convened on the site by the upper Convening Authority to examine points thought to be in question; (2) That the penalty be changed. A Committee of Evidence Review can recommend to *increase* or decrease the penalty. In event of a Review, the Convening Authority of the Committee of Review endorses the Review Findings and this new endorsement now takes precedence over the old endorsement and must be complied with by the original Convening Authority. Review should be rapid. An applicant for Review should understand its risk.

False Witness:

Anyone found to be knowingly testifying falsely becomes at once an Interested Party to the hearings and may receive a penalty commensurate with that which would have been recommended for an Interested Party to that hearing.

Types of Bills:

A Committee may hear any civil or criminal matter or dispute within the realm of Scientology whether the parties are connected with an organization or not. Libel, estranging marital partners, dismissals, debt, theft, mayhem, violations of codes, deprivation of income or any dispute or harmful improper action of any kind may be heard. Plaintiffs and defendants are alike Interested Parties in any such hearing. It is only necessary that the Convening Authority issue a Bill of Particulars on the matter. The Convening Authority should always issue a Bill of Particulars on all matters harmful to persons under his or her sphere of influence rather than attempt to independently adjudicate the matter. Anyone can call such a matter to the attention of a Convening Authority or the Convening Authority may act to convene a Committee on his or her own observation without complaint being given to the Convening Authority. Independent, offhand justice by a Convening Authority should be held to a minimum and all such subjects should be made the business of a Committee of Evidence.

SUMMARY

Purpose:

A Committee of Evidence is convened by any major executive of Scientology, with or without anyone filing a complaint, in order to handle any and all personal or organizational or field matters requiring justice.

Formation:

The Committee is composed of a Chairman, Secretary and two to five Committee members appointed by the Convening Authority.

Procedure of Committee:

The Convening Authority sets out in its instruction to the Committee (Bill of Particulars) the matter to be investigated and supplies any information already available together with names of any person known to be involved or requesting justice (Interested Parties).

The Committee meets as soon as possible and at times which will cause the least interference with normal work. At the first meeting the instructions and information are examined and the Committee decides what further information it will require to arrive at a conclusion and what information requires confirmation. It then decides who shall be called to give evidence. The Secretary is instructed to warn witnesses and let them know when and where they will be required.

In subsequent short meetings, when witnesses appear before the Committee, the Chairman should put the questions and keep them to the point. When he has completed his questions, he invites other members to ask any questions they feel will help the Committee. They do not *have* to ask questions and should only ask relevant questions. Finally, the Chairman asks the witness if there is any more information he/she wants to give or if there is anything he/she wants to say to correct any wrong impression he/she feels the Committee may have.

The Secretary takes notes of these proceedings and in addition a tape record can be made if the Convening Authority or Chairman considers it advisable, which it usually is.

When the Committee has assembled all the evidence it needs, it has a final meeting to prepare a report. In practice it will be found best for one member (the Chairman, the Secretary or a member appointed by the Chairman) to prepare a draft report prior to the final meeting and for the Committee to use this as a basis for discussion. The report (the Findings) should include findings and a recommendation and is sent together with the evidence and any tapes to the Convening Authority.

Actions of Convening Authority:
From the evidence and Findings the Convening Authority judges whether or not the evidence is complete and if the Findings and Recommendations are in keeping with the evidence. He assumes that the Committee has done its job thoroughly and unless there is a blatant apparent miscarriage of justice, he endorses the Findings and instructs an appropriate executive to carry out the recommendations and how to publish the matter.

If anyone feels aggrieved by the Findings of a Committee, the aggrieved person may have the case reviewed by the next higher authority, but should be apprised of the risk. If after review they are still aggrieved, they can have the case reviewed by Senior HCO International and thence to L. Ron Hubbard.*

---

*For further levels of recourse, see chapter Conduct of Justice and Forms of Redress.

BOARD OF INVESTIGATION

he purpose of a Board of Investigation is:

To help LRH discover the cause in any conflict, poor performance or down statistic.

COMPOSITION

A Board of Investigation is composed of not less than three and not more than five members.

A majority of the members must be senior to the persons being investigated except when this is impossible.

CONDUCT

The Board may investigate by calling in a body on the persons concerned or by sitting and summoning witnesses or principals.

FUNCTION

A Board of Investigation is a much less serious affair than a Committee of Evidence.

Persons appearing before it are not under duress or punishment.

The whole purpose is to get at the facts.

No disciplinary measure may result except for false attestation.

The Board may recommend an Executive Ethics Hearing or an Ethics Hearing if Crimes or High Crimes are found but may take no action on Errors or Misdemeanors.

False attestation before a Board must result in an Executive Ethics Hearing or Ethics Hearing.

FINDINGS

The Findings of a Board of Investigation are sent to the Convening Authority and from this orders can be issued or the Convening Authority can request action or policy from higher authority. (The method of making policy is not changed.)

FORM

In all other ways the form of a Board, its orders, conduct and finding is the same as in a Committee of Evidence.

COMMITTEE OF EVIDENCE

A Committee of Evidence is convened on the subject of a known Crime or High Crime, as it has come to be looked on (and is) a trial by jury, there being a charge.

A Board may recommend a Committee of Evidence.

The complete body of Scientology Ethics and Justice Technology on Boards of Investigation includes regulations on who may convene and be subject to their authority. Any persons convening a Board of Investigation are required to abide by all policy on the subject and any individual subject to a Board has access to all policy on the subject.

COURTS OF ETHICS AND ETHICS HEARINGS

Court of Ethics may be convened by any Ethics Officer.

Any Scientologist of the status of Officer or below may be summoned before a Court of Ethics.

The summons is issued as an HCO Ethics Order. It must state when and where the person is to appear.

A Court of Ethics is convened on matters as follows:

1. Any Misdemeanor.

2. Any Crime.

High Crimes are not accorded a Court of Ethics but may be accorded an Ethics Hearing.

A Court of Ethics may direct discipline as follows:

A. Not to be trained or processed for ___ weeks or ___ months.

B. An Amends Petition be submitted.

C. Suspension for ___ weeks.

D. Repayment of loans or debts.

E. Restitution of wrongs.

F. Damages to be paid another of an equitable sum commensurate with the loss.

EXECUTIVE COURT OF ETHICS

Convened in the same way and with the same powers and disciplines, an Executive Court of Ethics is convened by the Office of LRH via the HCO Executive Secretary.

The presiding person must be at or above the rank of the person summoned.

A Court of Ethics may not summons a Director, a Secretary or an Executive Secretary.

An Executive Court of Ethics only may be convened on a Director, Secretary or Executive Secretary.

The Executive Ethics Court is presided over by a Secretary or Executive Secretary as appointed for that one Court and one purpose by the Office of LRH via the HCO Executive Secretary.

An Executive Ethics Court may also be convened at the request of a Secretary or Executive Secretary on any staff member by requesting same of the Office of LRH via the Ethics Officer, but another is appointed to preside and there is no necessity for the Office of LRH to comply with such a request.

ETHICS HEARING

An Ethics Hearing may be convened by an Ethics Officer to obtain data for further action or inaction.

The order is issued as an HCO Ethics Order. The time and place of the Ethics Hearing is stated in the order. The purpose of the Hearing is stated.

Interested Parties are named.

An Ethics Hearing may name witnesses but not the person's immediate superiors to appear against him in person but may consider a written statement by a superior.

An Ethics Hearing has no power to discipline but may advise on consequences.

If doubt exists in the matter of whether or not a Misdemeanor or Crime or suppression has occurred, it will be usual to convene an Ethics Hearing or Executive Ethics Hearing, not a Court of Ethics.

EXECUTIVE ETHICS HEARING

No one of the rank of Director or above may be summoned for an Ethics Hearing, but only an Executive Ethics Hearing, presided over by a person superior in rank. It is convened by the Office of LRH via the HCO Exec Sec. The same rank in a senior org is a senior rank.

STATISTICS

A Court of Ethics or Executive Court of Ethics is *not* a fact-finding Court.

One is convened solely on statistics and known evidence.

If adequate statistics do not exist, then an Ethics Hearing or a Committee of Evidence is convened to obtain or discount evidence.

The ordinary reasons for convening a Court of Ethics would consist of:

a. Too many reports on a person (see *Staff Member Reports*).

b. Observed commission of a Misdemeanor or a Crime.

c. Demand by a person's superior to handle a Crime.

d. Debt.

e. Disputes between two Scientologists of similar rank.

f. Continuing an Emergency.

NO DEMOTION, TRANSFER OR DISMISSAL

A Court of Ethics or an Executive Court of Ethics may not order transfer, demotion or dismissal. This may only be done by a Committee of Evidence duly convened.

A Court of Ethics or an Executive Court of Ethics may, however, suspend a staff member from post for a reasonable length of time. In a suspension, recourse may be had and restoration of pay lost if a Committee of Evidence is convened and reverses the decision.

NO RECOURSE FROM A COURT

There is no recourse from the decision of a Court legally rendered and based on statistics. If a staff member accumulates too many adverse reports or if his unit, section, department or division statistics have remained down or if a State of Emergency was continued, there is no acceptable evidence that refutes it that could be heard by a Committee of Evidence as evidence is evidence.

PTS AND SP

Potential Trouble Sources and Suppressive Persons are not necessarily accorded a Court or a Hearing. But they may have one if they request it, but the only action will be to determine or confirm the actual status and the action is already laid down by firm unalterable policy in any case.

CHAPLAIN'S COURT, CIVIL HEARINGS

s many matters come before Ethics which are not properly ethics but civil matters (i.e., between other persons), a Chaplain's Court is formed in the Public Division.*

A permanent presiding justiciary, who must be a minister, may be appointed (called an Arbiter) where activities warrant.

The Chaplain (or the permanent or part-time assisting Arbiter) presides over all Court Hearings and renders judgment.

The organization of this activity is similar to any civil proceedings and may, when conditions warrant, have clerks and other personnel.

The Court may charge reasonable fees and has these as its statistic.

Only civil matters may be heard or judged.

All ethics matters must be referred to Ethics.

JUSTICE

Reasonably priced and easily obtained justice are requisites to any civilization.

*In the Scientology system of Justice, the Chaplain's Court offers expedient resolution to civil matters of dispute between individual Scientologists, while keeping such outside of usual civil court proceedings. (Bringing civil court proceedings against another Scientologist is a violation of the Justice Codes of Scientology [see The Scientology Justice Codes and Their Application].) Further, the World Institute of Scientology Enterprises (WISE) was later established to specifically handle matters of business dispute among Scientologists. Membership in WISE is a requirement and failure to be a member of WISE does not, however, absolve an individual of the policy prohibiting suit against another Scientologist.

The purpose of the Chaplain's Court is to resolve matters of dispute between individuals.

Staff personnel, pcs, students and Scientologists may utilize this Court to resolve their own disputes or legal affairs.

Staff members may not be sued by reason of performance of their org duties, as this belongs to Ethics where such complaints may be made.

Any suit filed must be against the person who actually personally knew and damaged the individual suing by an action directed personally against the plaintiff, except for suits to remove Ethics Orders.

The org, a division, department or section may only be sued to obtain restoration of status, to revoke or alter Ethics Orders or obtain service which was denied, such as auditing time to right an omission. The org or any part of it may not be sued for financial damages or refund.

Preliminary hearings only can be given in divorce matters at this time as these must also have state action before any such findings can be considered legal in the eyes of the state. However, separation may be found, both parties consenting.

Collection of debt and remedy in defaulting on obligation may be sought from the Court.

REBUTTAL DAMAGES

If a person who is sued has reason, he can, as defendant, require damages in his rebuttal. And should the suit be fallacious and found against the plaintiff, such may be awarded.

COSTS

Costs may be recovered as part of damages, meaning costs of Court action.

EXTENT OF DAMAGES

Any damages assigned by the Court must be reasonable and in keeping with reality.

ETHICS RELATIONS

Ethics may route civil matters to the Chaplain's Court.

In return, in matters of perjury or the collection of damages awarded by the Court, the Court may refer the matter to Ethics.

REFUND SUITS

Suits for refund of donations may not be filed as this is an Ethics matter.

LRH SUITS

Suits against LRH, Board Members, Executive Secretaries or Secretaries are not accepted by the Court.

WRONGFUL ETHICS ACTIONS

HCO may be sued in the Court for erroneous issue of an Ethics Order and for no other action. Damages requested may not exceed $5 or an order apologizing or restoration of status.

BONUS ACTIONS

All bonus matters or disputes between or amongst Tech, Qual and Treasury or their personnel may be heard by the Court.

STAFF MEMBER DISPUTES

Personal disputes between staff members, even when org business is concerned, may be heard by the Chaplain's Court.

FAILURE TO ABIDE

Failure to abide by a Court finding may become an Ethics matter.

JURY

When requested and allowed by the Chaplain, a jury of three persons may be chosen and used. The persons chosen must be agreed upon by both litigants.

ATTORNEYS

Anyone may act as an attorney in the Court.

Professional attorneys may appear before it.

No attorney is required.

PROCEDURES

All procedures for the Chaplain's Court are developed by and all magisterial appointments are made by the Chaplain in the form of Public Division Executive Directives. All fees are set in this manner. The Chaplain and the Court and such Executive Directives may be overruled only as authorized by policy.

14

CONDUCT
OF JUSTICE
AND
FORMS OF
REDRESS

AN OPERATING STANDARD RULE

his is rigid policy, not advice:

No matter how stiff the ethics action is you have to apply to keep the show on the road, remember this:

You must keep the door open only if it's just a crack.

Expulsion without hope of reinstatement puts people into total hopelessness. It may even be the reason governments eventually experience revolt. Expulsion without recourse leads to desperation and revolt.

There must always be the hope of return to good graces and all Ethics Orders or actions must state what the person has to do to be reinstated in good standing.

Do not practice or permit discipline or expulsion with no hope of amends.

LEVELS OF ETHICS AND JUSTICE ACTIONS

thics actions in degree of severity are as follows:

1. Noticing something nonoptimum without mentioning it but only inspecting it silently.

2. Noticing something nonoptimum and commenting on it to the person.

3. Requesting information by Ethics personnel.

4. Requesting information and inferring there is a disciplinary potential in the situation.

5. Talking to somebody about another derogatorily.

6. Talking to the person derogatorily.

7. Investigating in person by Ethics.

8. Reporting on a post condition to Ethics.

9. Reporting on a person to Ethics.

10. Investigating a person by interrogating others about him.

11. Asking others for evidence about a person.

12. Publishing an interrogatory about a person that points out omissions or commissions of Ethics Offenses.

13. Assigning a lowered condition by limited publication.

14. Assigning a lowered condition by broad publication.

15. Investigating a person thoroughly in his or her own area.

16. Interrogation stated to be leading to a Court of Ethics.

17. Interrogation in a Court of Ethics.

18. Sentencing in a Court of Ethics.

19. Suspending a Court of Ethics sentence.

20. Carrying out a Court of Ethics discipline.

21. Suspension or loss of time.

22. A Committee of Evidence ordered.

23. A Committee of Evidence publicly ordered.

24. Holding a Committee of Evidence.

25. Findings by a Committee of Evidence.

26. Submitting Findings of a Committee of Evidence for approval.

27. Waiting for the Findings to be passed on or carried into effect.

28. Suspending Findings for a period for review.

29. Modifying Findings.

30. Carrying Findings into effect.

31. Publishing Findings.

32. Demotion.

33. Loss of certificates or awards.

34. Denial of auditing or training by a Comm Ev for a considerable period of time.

35. Dismissal.

36. Expulsion from Scientology.

The above is a rough guide to the severity of discipline.

Note that none of it carries any physical punishment or detention.

Short suspension of training or processing up to ninety days is considered under (18) above and is not to be compared with (34) where the time is measured in years.

Just issuing the Ethics Codes is itself a sort of discipline, but it is more broadly welcomed than protested as it means greater peace and faster accomplishment.

ETHICS REVIEW

Orders to auditing or training may not be made as a sentence or used in an Ethics Court or by a Comm Ev or any other reason. Auditing and training are awards.

A student who is disruptive of discipline and acts contrary to the Ethics Codes may not be ordered to Review by the Director of Processing, Director of Training or Ethics personnel or other persons in an org.

ORDERING STUDENTS AND PCS

Tech and Qualifications personnel, particularly the Tech Sec and Qual Sec and Director of Estimations, the Director of Processing and Director of Training, Director of Examinations and Director of Review and Director of Certifications may order students or pcs to Review or to course or to HGC or anywhere in and around these two divisions without any Ethics action being implied. It is just normal, done to get students and pcs on the road to higher levels.

Ethics actions may only suspend training or deny auditing.

Therefore, a student ordered to Ethics for discipline who does not then give adequate promise and example of good behavior and compliance must be thoroughly investigated even to his or her own area and in the meanwhile may not be trained or processed.

The student, however, may not be dismissed or expelled unless full ethics actions and procedures have been undertaken.

All sentences carrying a denial of training or processing must carry a means of the right to be trained or processed being restored in a specified time or under specified conditions.

STUDENTS AND PCS AND ETHICS

The routine action of Ethics is to request a reappraisal of behavior and a signed promise of good behavior for a specified time. If the student or pc refuses to so promise, then the next action of Ethics is an investigation of the student's course or pc's processing behavior. When then confronted with the data, if the student still refuses to promise, Ethics undertakes a full investigation in the student's or pc's own area. If the student or pc still refuses to cooperate, the student goes before a Court of Ethics which may pass sentence.

RECOURSE

Only after sentence has been passed by a legal body, such as a Court of Ethics or Committee of Evidence, or after an illegal disciplinary action may a student or pc ask for *recourse.*

Normally before asking for recourse a student or pc *petitions* the Office of L. Ron Hubbard if unwilling to accept the discipline, but this must be done at once.

If the petition is unfavorably acted upon, the student or pc may ask for recourse.

Recourse must be requested of the Convening Authority that had local jurisdiction over the student or pc and may not be requested of higher authority. A request to higher authority than the Ethics activity that passed sentence is a *petition,* not recourse.

COMM EV

A Committee of Evidence is considered the most severe form of ethics action.

One must not be idly threatened or requested.

Only a Comm Ev can recommend suspension or remove certificates or awards or memberships or recommend dismissal.

The Office of LRH passes on all Comm Ev Findings before they can go into effect.

A staff member may not be suspended or demoted or transferred illegally out of his division or dismissed without a Committee of Evidence.

Only after that action (or wrongful demotion, transfer or dismissal), as above, may recourse be requested.

Students or pcs, however, may be transferred, demoted in level or grade by a Court of Ethics. And the action of sending the student or pc to a Court of Ethics is, of course, a type of suspension which may be prolonged in the face of noncooperation.

A student or a pc is not a staff member in the Ethics sense of the word by simple enrollment on a course or in an HGC or Review.

A staff member who is temporarily a student or pc in the Academy or Review or the HGC is not covered as a student or pc by his staff member status. He may be transferred about or demoted as a student or pc by Tech and Qual personnel or suspended as a student or pc by Ethics. This, however, may not affect his staff member status as a staff member. Because he or she is transferred or demoted or suspended by Tech personnel or Ethics when a student or pc does not mean he or she may be transferred, demoted or dismissed from his or her regular staff post unless the person's staff status permits it.

POTENTIAL TROUBLE SOURCES

Staff members found to be Potential Trouble Sources are handled like any other Potential Trouble Source but, unless Provisional or Temporary, may not be affected by this in their staff post. They are, of course, denied auditing or training until they handle or disconnect, but this may not also suspend, transfer or dismiss them (unless of Provisional or Temporary status).

This Ethics action (the Potential Trouble Source) is in lieu of any discipline and disciplinary actions that go beyond temporary suspension of training or processing, until the matter is settled, must be undertaken by a Court of Ethics or a Comm Ev.

ARC BROKEN STUDENTS OR PCS

An ARC break is not an extenuating circumstance in Ethics or disciplinary matters and is only taken into account on the person of the auditor who made the ARC break and didn't repair it.

The plea of "ARC broken" is inadmissible in any Ethics matter as a defense or justification of Misdemeanors, Crimes or High Crimes.

LIGHT TOUCH

Scientology Ethics are so powerful in effect, as determined by observation of it in use, that a little goes a very long ways.

Try to use the lightest form first.

Students are quite caved in by it when it is applied, by actual observation.

Our lines are too powerful and direct and what we mean to a person's future, even while he or she is nattering, is so well understood down deep that Ethics action is a far worse threat than mere wog law.

The being who is guilty knows with certainty that he is offending against the future of all, no matter what his surface manifestations or conduct. Further, while wog law at the worst can only cause him or her some pain and a body, by execution, or one lifetime's loss of liberty, we threaten his eternity. Even while he screams at us, he knows this down deep.

My first instance of this was a very dangerous psychotic who was largely responsible for a great deal of the public commotion in 1950. This person desisted and caved in the moment the thought was suggested to her by a non-Dianetic friend that she was threatening all Mankind. She suddenly saw it as truth and instantly gave up all attacks and utterances.

Even the fellow who could push the button on atomic war knows, really, it's only one lifetime per person he is blowing up, only one phase in Earth's existence he or she is destroying. That we exist here could actually restrain him. The mere destruction of a planet might not as it's temporary.

Our discipline is quite capable of driving a person around the bend because of what he or she is attacking.

Therefore we can all too easily make a person feel guilty by just a whisper.

I've now seen a student, simply asked a question by Ethics, promptly give up and *ask* for his Comm Ev and expulsion. He hadn't done more than a poor auditing job. Nobody was talking about a Comm Ev or expulsion and he had not a bit of defiance in it. He just caved right in.

You are threatening somebody with oblivion for eternity by expulsion from Scientology. Therefore realize that an ethics action need not be very heavy to produce the most startling results.

Down deep they know this even when they are screaming at us.

One Suppressive Person who had committed a High Crime of some magnitude went quite insane after departing Scientology and then realizing what he had done.

Therefore, use ethics lightly. It is chain lightning.

INJUSTICE

ny staff member who does not know Ethics Policy is a clay pigeon. "Clay pigeons" are used to throw up in the air and shoot at.

The cycle is: Goofs are made. The real Why is not located or handled. And when this happens, angry executives, who have to pick up the ball, start shooting.

Staff members *are* expected to do their jobs and there are no excuses at all for not doing so.

But it sometimes happens that injustices occur. Goofs happen, then conditions are assigned, persons are removed from post or otherwise bashed about.

Usually this occurs because the staff member is pitifully ignorant of his rights.

Justice is expected and has definite use. When a state of discipline does not exist, the whole group caves in. It has been noted continually that the failure of a group began with a lack of or loss of discipline. Without it the group and its members die.

Most people think discipline is bad because most wog discipline is simply harsh injustice.

Most people do not even know that *justice* means fair and equitable treatment for both the group and individual.

Commercial firms and credit companies have a level of injustice that is hard to believe. One is never faced by his accusers and may not even know he is accused until he is shot.

Psychiatry, as exposed in the brilliant book *The Manufacture of Madness* by Dr. Szasz, uses the "justice" procedures developed in the days of witch burning; unknown accusers, opinions only, punished before being tried, etc. Psychiatric influence on contemporary court thinking may well be a major reason for the present disturbed condition of society.

Lord forbid we ever fall into such barbarism ourselves.

It is injustice that destroys discipline.

When you indicate the wrong bypassed charge on a case, the case caves in. When you accuse wrongly and punish unjustly, the group caves in.

The truth is, Man cannot really be trusted with "punishment." With it, he does not really seek discipline, he wreaks injustice.

Many governments are so touchy about their divine rightness in judicial matters that you hardly open your mouth before they burst into uncontrolled violence. Getting into police hands is a catastrophe in its own right in many places, even when one is merely the plaintiff, much less the accused. Thus social disturbance is at maximum in such areas.

Only where a group has a buffer against injustice is it safe to use discipline.

Posts are valuable to staff. Sudden removals, false condition assignments and other actions can do more harm than they achieve good.

Reversely, you can't expect a staff to fall all over a goofing staff member whose lack of performance upsets the lines and production. It does far more harm than good to let the situation continue without taking action.

Between the points of harsh injustice and required discipline there is a happy center ground where discipline, no matter how *severe,* is just and where goofs are not tolerated.

The achievement of this middle ground depends less upon educating and restraining executives than upon the staff member knowing his rights and himself using them.

This is hard to get across because some senior can say "that policy doesn't apply in this case" or "you report this and I'll have your head" or "I don't care what your rights are, you are *removed*!"

Then again, a Review Committee of Evidence can be so slow it never handles in time or it never gets held.

We are living—or trying to—in a very unjust culture. So most of our basic training was in injustice, not in correct discipline.

So you cannot look for a total perfection of justice. But we can make it better and less unjust.

RECOURSE

Recourse means "a turning or applying to a person or thing for aid or security."

Not only can one turn to a person, but one can turn to a thing or a procedure to set the matter right.

In investigating why certain persons who had been posted did not do their post, it was found they had been told to do something else instead. They had done this something else. They did not know they had any "recourse." Because they sought no recourse, it had to be assumed they had willingly accepted illegal orders and so were Comm Eved.

Now what is this point "they sought no correction" of this obviously illegal order? They simply did not make it known. They did not have to fly in the face of the person. They did not have to refuse.

The Comm Ev should have asked them, "Did you seek any recourse to being given an illegal order?" If the answer was *no,* they were a party to the damage. If the answer was *yes* and they could prove it, they would have to be found innocent of intent and the senior would have caught it.

What form would the recourse have taken?

A simple Knowledge Report to the Ethics Officer, "I have been given different orders in conflict with my post assignment and have made it known but am having to follow the illegal order," would have proofed them against severe action.

By *not* taking recourse, the junior *thereby made himself a party to the act.*

The above is not very effective as it does not correct the order and so *some* penalty would have leveled at the person.

At the other end of *maximum recourse,* there would have been a telex to the Senior HCO Continental or International stating, "Joe Blow ED will not let me take my post as HAS, as ordered, but has made me an auditor."

Whether this was acted on or not, it would absolve the person. He or she would have "blown the whistle on" his or her illegal orderer. He could not be punished for it or for taking the auditor post instead of the ordered HAS post.

To understand *recourse* one would have to know the seniority of orders. Policy (in HCO PLs) and HCOBs come first. Then there is International, Continental and local in descending order.

The org board tells one at a local level. The higher names are the more senior.

If a person does not *seek recourse* for a wrong condition, a removal, an illegal order, a Court or a Comm Ev and, no matter how *unjust* the action is, the person has had it.

You can't follow an illegal order and/or do other wrongs, get a Comm Ev and expect much help.

But if a Court or Comm Ev is wrong in its findings, a person has *recourse.* He can ask for a *Review Comm Ev* and *must* receive one.

OUT OF SEQUENCE

To remove a person from post and then give him a Court or Comm Ev him is out of sequence.

The person has to have a Court or Comm Ev *before* he can be removed.

To assign a condition and then also Comm Ev is also out of sequence. One assigns a condition or a Comm Ev.

DISMISSALS

Dismissals or offloads, once a person has been accepted as a staff member, require a Court or a Comm Ev.

If the Findings are protested, there can be a Review Comm Ev.

The Comm Ev can send the person to a Fitness Board or a Fitness Board can send a person to a Comm Ev.

A Fitness Board has the power to prevent taking someone on staff in the first place. That needs no Comm Ev to reject.

But the person so rejected can ask for a Review Comm Ev.

And if the person is on staff, one cannot be "removed from post, sent before the Fitness Board and dismissed." It requires a Court or Comm Ev to remove from post and/or to send before a Fitness Board.

STATISTICS

The best defense against *any* ethics action is good statistics. If one has no personal statistic, he is in a bad position and a very eligible clay pigeon if something goes wrong.

When personal statistics are challenged as "unreal" or "doesn't fit" or "falsified," one should have his section or department or divisional stat in very good shape indeed and point to that (and not permit it to be bad), as it is more visible and reliable.

REQUESTED COMM EV

Anyone can request a Comm Ev on himself for anything. An example would be an intern removed from course who does not believe he failed. He can request a Comm Ev. If he can prove he didn't, he has to be restored.

If one is being shot at or regarded with contempt through false accusations, his first action would be to ask the Ethics Officer for a Third Party investigation and, if that didn't work, request a Comm Ev to clear his name or repute. Or to get himself rightfully shot for that matter.

Example: Someone is being kicked around. He can't handle it himself. So he requests a Comm Ev.

This *must* be given him. And it must be *swift*.

SENIORS

A person has a right to be tried only by seniors in rank or status.

Example: A Class VIII, on a tech matter, could not be legally tried by a Comm Ev whose Chairman was a Class 0.

Example: The Tech Sec cannot be tried by a Comm Ev chairmaned by a D of P or a Court held by one of his auditors.

An Executive Director or LRH Comm have to be tried by the next senior org and cannot be tried in their own orgs at all.

There have been flagrant violations of all these things. An Executive Director and LRH Comm were once ripped off and sent home by being *told* it was "an LRH order," which it was not. They did *not* stay on post and do the normal things like "Let's see it in writing, signed." Or "We must query" or "We request a Comm Ev." By *not* staying on post, by letting themselves be ripped off, by not using *any* recourse, they were actually guilty of desertion of post. They caught it from all sides *by not using their rights*.

SUMMARY

This is not a full list of procedures and legalities.

All that is being set out here is that:

DISCIPLINE IS NEEDFUL IN A GROUP.

INJUSTICE INJURES DISCIPLINE.

INJUSTICE OCCURS WHEN PEOPLE PERMIT IT BY NOT KNOWING OR IGNORING THEIR RIGHTS AND NOT SEEKING RECOURSE OR REDRESS OF WRONGS.

It is a pitiful scene where executives and Ethics Officers don't know or use correct justice and where the staff members are ignorant of their rights or don't use them.

The result is a complete loss of discipline no matter how many get hanged! Or how many don't.

So where *ethics is out,* one really need only check out Execs and Ethics Officers on Ethics Policy and check out the staff on their rights and some semblance of order will occur in the most disturbed scene.

This is the remedy for better discipline and prosperity in a group. Not more shootings of clay pigeons.

It *can* be made a calm, happy scene.

376

JUSTICE: THIRD PARTY AND FALSE REPORTS

n an extension of Third Party Technology (see *The Third Party Law*), I have found that false reports and suppression are very important in Third Party Technology.

We know that a Third Party is necessary to any quarrel. Basically it is a three-terminal universe.

In reviewing several org upsets, I have found that the Third Party can go completely overlooked even in intensive investigation.

A Third Party adds up to suppression by giving false reports on others.

In several cases an org has lost several guiltless staff members. They were dismissed or disciplined in an effort to solve enturbulation. Yet the turbulence continued and the area became even more upset by reason of the dismissals.

Running this back further, one finds that the real Third Party, eventually unearthed, got people shot by *false reports*.

One source of this is as follows:

Staff member X goofs. He is very furious and defensive at being accused. He blames his goof on somebody else. That somebody else gets disciplined. Staff member X diverts attention from himself by various means including falsely accusing others.

This is a Third Party action which results in a lot of people being blamed and disciplined. And the real Third Party remaining undetected.

The missing point of justice here is that the disciplined persons *were not faced with their accusers* and were not given the real accusation and so could not confront it.

Another case would be a Third Party simply spreading tales and making accusations out of malice or some even more vicious motive. This would be a usual Third Party action. It is ordinarily based on false reports.

Another situation comes about when an executive who can't get an area straight starts to investigate, gets Third Party false reports about it, disciplines people accordingly and totally misses the real Third Party. This enturbulates the area even more.

The basis of all really troublesome Third Party activities is, then, *false reports*.

There can also be *false perception*. One sees things that don't exist and reports them as "fact."

Therefore we see that we can readily run back an investigation by following a chain of false reports.

In at least one case, the Third Party (discovered only after it was very plain that only he could have wrecked two divisions, one after the other) also had these characteristics:

1. Goofed in his own actions.

2. Furiously contested any Knowledge Reports or Job Endangerment Chits filed on him.

3. Obsessively changed everything when taking over an area.

4. Falsely reported actions, accusing others.

5. Had a high casualty rate of staff in his division or area.

These are not necessarily common to all Third Parties but give you an idea of what can go on.

———————

After a lot of experience with ethics and justice, I would say that the real source of upset in an area would be *false reports* accepted and acted upon without confronting the accused with all charges and his or her accusers.

An executive should not accept any accusation and act upon it. To do so undermines the security of one and all.

What an executive should do, on being presented with an accusation or down stats or "evidence," is conduct an investigation of false reports and false perceptions.

––––––

An area is downstat because of one or more of the following:

1. No personnel.

2. Personnel not trained.

3. Cross orders (senior orders unattended because of different junior orders).

4. Area doing something else than what it is supposed to do.

5. An adjacent area dumping its hat.

6. False perception leading to false stats.

7. False reports by rumor or misunderstanding.

8. False reports from single rare instances becoming accepted as the condition of the whole.

9. False reports on others defensively intended.

10. False reports on others maliciously intended (real Third Party).

11. Injustices cumulative and unremedied.

12. Actions taken on others without investigation and without confronting them with their accusers or the data.

This is a list of probable causes for an upset or downstat area.

SECURITY

The personal security of the staff member is so valuable to him apparently that when it is undermined (by false accusations or injustice) he becomes less willing and less efficient and is the real reason for a PTS condition.

JUSTICE

The only thing which can actually remedy a general insecure feeling is a renewed faith in justice.

Justice would consist of a refusal to accept any report not substantiated by actual, independent data, seeing that all such reports are investigated and that all investigations include confronting the accused with the accusation and, where feasible, the accuser, *before* any disciplinary action is undertaken or any condition assigned.

While this may slow the processes of justice, the personal security of the individual is totally dependent upon establishing the full truth of any accusation before any action is taken.

───────────

Harsh discipline may produce instant compliance but it smothers initiative.

Positive discipline is in itself a stable datum. People are unhappy in an area which is not *well* disciplined because they do not know where they stand.

An area where only those who try to do their jobs are disciplined encourages people to hide and be inactive.

But all discipline must be based on truth and must exclude acting on false reports.

Therefore we get a policy: *Any false report leading to the unjust discipline of another is an act of* Treason *by the person making the false report and the condition should be assigned and its penalties fully applied.*

A Condition of *Doubt* should be assigned any person who accepts and disciplines another unjustly on the basis of a report which subsequently turns out to have been false.

———

This, then, is the primary breakdown of any justice system—that it acts on false reports, disciplines before substantiation and fails to confront an accused with the report and his accuser before any discipline is assigned, or which does not weigh the value of a person in general against the alleged crime even when proven.

BOARD
OF REVIEW

ccasionally an administrative body takes an action or issues a directive or order that:

a. Results in lowered statistics.

b. Causes contraction of an area.

c. Results in an injustice.

This is usually the result of incomplete CSW, acting on rumor without proper investigation and violation of basic policy.

The function of a Board of Review is to look into injustices, technically incorrect findings and instances of flagrant injustice or out-ethics actions which are destructive to stats.

The Board is convened by any LRH Comm or Keeper of Tech (KOT) who appoints a Chairman and two other members. Members of the Board are appointed based on their own good statistics, high ethics level and knowledge of Ethics and Justice Policy. They are preferably Org Exec Course graduates.

A Board of Review can be originated by the LRH Comm or KOT or a CSW may be submitted to the LRH Comm or KOT requesting a Board be convened.

The Board, once convened, reviews the data concerning the matter using standard investigatory procedure and bases its decisions only on LRH policy. It has no authority to write or issue new policy or issue new directives or orders. The Board can only cancel an action, directive or order which has been found to:

a. Be impractical.

b. Lower statistics.

c. Cause contraction.

d. Result in an injustice.

e. Violate basic LRH policy.

It is expected that very few appeals will be lodged and few Boards will have to be convened as the function of Org Execs and Exec Councils is to implement the longstanding and successful programs already covered in HCO Policy Letters. Directives, orders and actions taken should be toward this end.*

*For higher levels of recourse, Boards of Review exist at each echelon of the Church of Scientology ecclesiastic structure. Their function, and who qualifies to avail themselves of such recourse and when they are available are made known in Church directives.

PETITION

he right to petition must not be denied.

It is the oldest form of seeking justice and a redress of wrongs and it may well be that when it vanishes, a civilization deteriorates thereby.

Therefore these policies apply:

1. Any one individual has the right to petition in writing any senior or official no matter how high and no matter by what routing.

2. No person may be punished for submitting a petition.

3. No two persons or more may simultaneously petition on the same matter and if so the petition must at once be refused by the person petitioned. Collective petition is a Crime under Ethics as it is an effort to hide the actual petitioner. And as there may be no punishment for a petition, collective petition has therefore no excuse of safety and is to be interpreted as an effort to overwhelm and may not be regarded as a petition.

4. No generality may be used in a petition, such as a report of collective opinion unspecified as to identities. This is to be interpreted as an effort to ARC break a superior and the petition must be refused.

5. Only one person may petition on one matter or the petition must be refused.

6. Threat included in a request for justice, a favor or redress deprives it of the status of "petition" and it must be refused.

7. Discourtesy or malice in a request for justice, a favor or redress deprives it of the status of "petition" and it must be refused.

8. If a "petition" contains no request it is not a petition.

9. There may be no special form for a petition beyond these policies.

10. A petition which cannot be deciphered or understood should be returned to the sender with a request that it be made legible or comprehensible, but this should not be interpreted as a refusal or acceptance of the petition.

11. A copy of a petition seeking justice against another person or group must be sent that person or group to qualify the request as a petition. No action may be taken by the person or group, but he or they should append the copy to their own statement of the matter and send it at once to the executive being petitioned.

12. Petitions are normally directed to the heads of activities such as the head of a portion of an org (HCO or the Org or the Public Divisions in the persons of the HCO Executive Secretary, the Organization Executive Secretary and the Public Executive Secretary) or senior orgs or L. Ron Hubbard.*

13. Petitions may not demand Committees of Evidence or punishment for executives, but may only state what has happened and request the matter be righted.

14. A petition is itself and is not a form of recourse and making a petition does not use up one's right to recourse.

15. All petitions delivered in person verbally or in person with a note, particularly when this restricts a senior's freedom of motion, must be refused.

*Ecclesiastic lines of authority are posted in Churches of Scientology and indicate the various echelons of recourse.

16. HCO Secretaries or Communicators receiving petitions directed to be forwarded to higher executives which do not comply with these policies should append a copy of this policy to the petition and return it to sender. The sender should then reform the petition into acceptable form and return it on the same channels. When receiving his petition back with this policy, the sender must not assume it has been refused and become apathetic. He or she should realize that a favor has been done—for a petition in violation of these policies would *have* to be refused by the person to whom the petitioner addressed it and that by rewording or complying with these policies, the petition now has a chance and will undoubtedly be given courteous attention. A petitioner should consider himself fortunate if a discourteous or collective or threatening petition is returned as it would not be regarded as a petition by the executive to whom it is addressed and might color his or her opinion of the petitioner, perhaps obscuring some real wrong which might well have received attention.

PETITIONS AND ETHICS ACTIONS

No person under sentence or awaiting a Committee of Evidence may validly petition the Office of LRH.

A petition may only be submitted before or after the full course of Scientology Ethics has been taken.

As all Ethics actions, such as a Committee of Evidence, are reviewed, in effect a line already exists due to the Ethics action and the facts will be on it.

Therefore a communication from a person under legal sentence from Ethics Officers or a person named in a Comm Ev may not petition. Ethics actions must be permitted to take their course.

A protest from Ethics actions worded as a petition routinely causes further investigation as the "petitioner" is actually only protesting Ethics actions and is handled as such.

AMNESTY POLICY

 mnesty:

A general pardon for past offenses; the granting of such a pardon; a forgetting or intentional overlooking; the rendering of punishment null and void for offenses earlier than the amnesty date, known or unknown; forgiveness of past criminal or anti-social actions; the removal of criminal names from police wanted files.

An amnesty is general in nature and when issued includes everyone.

An amnesty is issued under L. Ron Hubbard, Founder, or Chairman of the International Board, to signalize an event of extreme importance in Scientology.

Its secondary purpose is to end personal upsets and liabilities by reason of withholds and make it possible for them to be audited easily by auditors.

A tertiary purpose is to prevent the buildup of personal rancor against Scientology, orgs and individuals, as persons so disposed are always critical or vicious because of their own overt actions and consequent withholds, or simply because they fear what we can discover about them. It ends the cycle for such people.

It is plainly meant by an amnesty that acts of a criminal or punishable nature are forgiven and placed beyond our retaliation or punishment.

An amnesty specifically does not mean monetary or other obligations or acts of what are called a "civil" nature.

Criminal acts result in punishment.

Merely civil matters can result only in civil suits.

Amnesty is clearly intended to cover only anti-social or anti-Scientology acts and is clearly not intended to cover debts, contracts or such agreements or obligations.

Suspended certificates or classifications are restored by an amnesty.

All Committee of Evidence sentences except financial and certificate cancellation are removed completely by an amnesty.

Cancellation of certificates, classifications and awards *cannot* be cancelled by an amnesty and so an amnesty does not restore them.

Certificate and award cancellations occur only when the person has departed Scientology. This occurs because of lack of case gain. Case gain cannot occur in a person who commits continuously acts hostile to his fellow man. All chronic no-gain cases which do not advance in the face of any auditing are traceable to recurring hostile actions the person undertakes secretly against his fellows, not in the past, but in the present, during the time period of the auditing. So an amnesty is useless in cancellation matters. Such persons would have to first cease their continuous anti-social conduct and again be trained or processed.

Offenses occurring after midnight of the release date of an amnesty are not covered by the amnesty.

The frequency of amnesties is determined solely by the frequency of new triumphs of significant general importance to Scientology. Help them happen.

EPILOGUE

A NEW HOPE
FOR JUSTICE

cientology Ethics Tech works when it is applied, but applying it means that the conditions have to be correctly assigned and the formulas have to be honestly applied.

False reports and false data are the order of the day in this society and justice has too often been used for political gain or getting rid of rivals or forwarding the purposes of some clique. The thought of using justice to straighten up the individual or to safeguard the society doesn't seem to have occurred to anybody.

OBSERVATION

Societies today seem to be rigged so that any downstat creep can torpedo any upstat person and is even assisted in doing so by the powers that be.

This alone could cause a decline of a civilization, as the reward for being an upstat is made inadequate by the penalties capriciously machine-gunned about by downstat criminals, bums and degraded beings favored by their protectors and sponsors—"the justice system" and modern governments.

As they themselves are contaminated by their criminal associates, the police and court systems are, in the main, composed of downstats who couldn't make it in life any other way.

Societies traditionally cave in through their police and justice systems, since these provide a channel of contamination between the vicious and lawless, and decent people. Eventually such police and justice systems, aided by advice from criminal practitioners such as psychologists and psychiatrists, sink into a belief that all men are criminals. This at once justifies their own vicious practices and excuses their merciless injustices against all men.

The few decent officers and judges in these systems find themselves unable to cope with the scene, surrounded as they are by vicious colleagues and connected as they are in their daily work to the minority dregs of the society. They soon sink into a hopeless apathy and their sensible weight is seldom felt by others in the morass in which they wallow.

Police and courts offer an open-armed opportunity to the vicious and corrupt to establish themselves in a position of safety while satisfying their strange appetites of perverted viciousness toward their fellow man.

There is little thought of administering justice so that individuals can improve. There is every thought to punish and create misery.

Justice systems thereby become a sort of cancer which erode every splendid ambition and achievement of the decent citizen.

Man has never before invented a remedy for this corrosion in the name of "justice." Even the Spanish Inquisition was headed, at Isabella's demand, by her own tutor so as to keep it from becoming a blot on her reign. And who was the tutor? It was the man Torquemada, who sank to a point where he began to bind his books with human skin and whose name has come down through the ages as a synonym for cruel and senseless sadism. It was the Inquisition which did more to destroy the repute and power of the Catholic Church than any other single operation.

"Justice" apparently cannot be trusted in the hands of Man.

The FBI charter mews about safeguarding the populace, but hides and is utterly disregarded by an organization whose principles are carefully planned wholly on terrorism and conducts itself more lawlessly than any criminal it ever listed as Public Enemy #1. Who is Public Enemy #1 today? The FBI! Its obvious target is every opinion leader and public-spirited group in America!

To the FBI, their own charter is not only a subject for mirth, but the Constitution itself (which they are sworn in to uphold) is just "garbage" which impedes their headlong terror zeal. In the name of "justice" (and even calling themselves the *Justice* Department), they practice every conceivable perversion of injustice. With their terror tools, preferring lies to fact, they have created a police state in which no man, woman or child or even a politician is safe, neither from downstats *nor* the FBI. To the FBI, all men are guilty and can't be proven innocent and, behind her bandaged eyes, Justice herself weeps. In the name of "justice," they have condemned this society to death.

———

Tolerance, mercy, understanding and the actual handling of the individual by decent and effective Ethics Technology is a new hope for justice.

You cannot bestialize every man and expect any benefit to accrue to the society at large, even though this is what the contemporary justice systems are trying to do (which is of course its own brand of insanity).

We must safeguard against unjust practices and make haste to remedy all injustices. We must be accordingly committed or we will never make it.

Meanwhile, we must cope with the social morass in which we find ourselves and rise above it. For, factually, these generations have no hope, either as individuals or society, unless we do make it.

APPENDIX

EDITOR'S GLOSSARY
OF WORDS, TERMS AND PHRASES

Words often have several meanings. The definitions used here only give the meaning that the word has as it is used in this book. Dianetics and Scientology terms appear in bold type. Beside each definition you will find the page on which it first appears, so you can refer back to the text if you wish.

This glossary is not meant to take the place of standard language or Dianetics and Scientology dictionaries, which should be referred to for any words, terms or phrases that do not appear below.

—The Editors

∞ (infinity symbol): a mathematical symbol that represents infinity. Page 13.

abdicate: resign or give up (a high office) formally or officially. Page 154.

aberrated: subjected to or affected by *aberration*. Page 26.

aberration: a departure from rational thought or behavior. From the Latin, *aberrare*, to wander from; Latin, *ab*, away, and *errare*, to wander. It means basically to err, to make mistakes, or more specifically to have fixed ideas which are not true. The word is also used in its scientific sense. It means departure from a straight line. If a line should go from A to B, then if it is "aberrated" it would go from A to some other point, to some other point, to some other point, to some other point, to some other point and finally arrive at B. Taken in its scientific sense, it would also mean the lack of straightness or to see crookedly, as an example, a man sees a horse but thinks he sees an elephant. Aberrated conduct would be wrong conduct, or conduct not supported by reason. When a person has engrams, these tend to deflect what would be his normal ability to perceive truth and bring about an aberrated view of situations which then would cause an aberrated reaction to them. Aberration is opposed to sanity, which would be its opposite. Page 16.

able: showing talent, skill or knowledge. Page 149.

above the cut: a variation of the phrase "a cut above," meaning superior to others in some respect. Page 150.

absinthe: a very strong alcoholic drink made from wine mixed with a bitter, dark-green oil obtained from the wormwood plant (a shrub native to Europe). Absinthe was created by a French physician in the 1700s and was utilized as a medicine to aid digestion as well as for restoring strength and vigor. It became popular with French soldiers and consequently attained common use. This drink was very toxic and habitual; excessive use caused *absinthism,* a disease characterized by psychotic manifestations. Absinthe was banned in France in 1915, and then in the United States and other countries. Page 244.

absolute: 1. perfect or complete in quality or nature. Page 16.
2. free from restriction or condition. Page 156.

absolutes: those things, conditions, etc., which are perfect and complete in quality or nature. Page 22.

Academy: the department of a Church of Scientology organization where training courses are delivered, including auditor training, administrative training, co-auditing and other technical training actions. Page 231.

accrue: gather together in amount, especially over a period of time. Page 393.

Ad Comm: (Advisory Committee) a committee in each division of a Church of Scientology organization composed of the Department Heads of the division and chaired by the Divisional Secretary. The Advisory Committee takes up the statistics of the division in an effort to improve them, assigns conditions for its departments, sections and individuals in the division in accordance with statistics, and confirms any personnel appointments, transfers or dismissals. Page 238.

addressee: the person to whom something (such as a letter or despatch) is sent or addressed. Page 108.

Addresso: the section of a Church of Scientology organization which keeps address files of Scientologists up-to-date for mailings and furnishes addresses or addressed envelopes for other areas of the organization. The term *Addresso* comes from *Addressograph,* a trademark for a machine that automatically prints addresses on envelopes, etc. Page 313.

address plates: a reference to the plates used on an Addressograph machine where an address is pressed or placed onto it by the machine. The plate then receives ink and is pressed against a card, a sheet of paper or an envelope where the address is printed. Page 254.

adhered: followed a rule or instruction exactly or kept an agreement. Page 4.

adherents: those devoted to or supportive of a person, party or system; followers. Page 300.

admin: a contraction or shortening of the word *administration*. *Admin* is used as a noun to denote the actions involved in administering an organization. The clerical and executive decisions, actions and duties necessary to the running of an organization, such as originating and answering mail, typing, filing, dispatching, applying policy and all those actions, large and small which make up an organization. Page 137.

affinity: the feeling of love or liking for something or someone. Affinity is a phenomena of space in that it expresses the willingness to occupy the same place as the thing which is loved or liked. The reverse of it would be antipathy (dislike) or rejection which would be the unwillingness to occupy the same space as or the unwillingness to approach something or someone. It comes from the French, *affinité,* affinity, kindred, alliance, nearness and also from the Latin, *affinis,* meaning near, bordering upon. Page 39.

aggrieved: of the state of mind that one has been wronged in one's rights or position; affected by the action of another in a way to cause injury or grief. Page 36.

agin: an informal term for against; opposed to. Page 107.

Allies: a group of twenty-six nations, including Britain, the United States and the Soviet Union, who opposed the Axis—the countries, which included Germany, Italy and Japan, which fought together during World War II. Page 5.

alter-is: alteration; the action of altering or changing the reality of something. *Isness* means the way something is. When someone sees it differently he is doing an *alter-is,* in other words, is *altering* the way it is. Page 272.

Alter-isness: the consideration which introduces change, and therefore time and persistence, into an As-isness to obtain persistency. Page 64.

amalgamation: the action of combining distinct elements or associations, into one uniform whole. Page 222.

amassing: gathering for oneself; accumulating (a large amount of something) over a period of time. Page 24.

American Bill of Rights: an addition made to the Constitution of the United States in 1791, which guarantees certain rights to the people including freedom of speech and freedom of religion. It also prohibits the police and other government officials from searching people's homes or offices or seizing property without good reason and proper authority. Page 205.

anarchy: a state or condition of society where there is no ruler and where the various functions of the state are either badly performed or not at all. Hence, social and political confusion, lawlessness or chaos. Page 150.

Andes: the principal mountains of South America, one of the greatest mountain systems in the world, including some of the world's highest peaks. More than 50 of them soar higher than 20,000 feet (6,100 meters) above sea level (only the Himalayas of south central Asia are higher) and thus present a formidable barrier to east-west transportation and communication. The Andes extend for more than 5,000 miles (8,000 kilometers) in a narrow belt along the western edge of the South American continent, from the coast of the Caribbean Sea in the north to the island of Tierra del Fuego in the extreme south. The mountains reach into seven countries: Venezuela, Colombia, Ecuador, Peru, Bolivia, Chile and Argentina. Page 157.

approximates: is similar to something in nature, size or extent. Page 15.

apt: inclined; disposed to; given to; likely. Page 19.

arbitrary: based on judgment or useful selection rather than on the fixed nature of something. Page 12.

ARC: a word made from the initial letters of Affinity, Reality and Communication which together equate to Understanding. It is pronounced by stating its letters, A-R-C. To Scientologists it has come to mean good feeling, love or friendliness such as "He was in ARC with his friend." One does not, however fall out of ARC, he has an ARC break. Page 196.

ARC break(s): a sudden drop or cutting of one's affinity, reality or communication with someone or something. Upsets with people or things come about because of a lessening or sundering (breaking apart) of affinity, reality or communication or understanding. It is called an ARC break instead of an upset because if one discovers which of the three points, or understanding, have been cut one can bring about a rapid recovery in the person's state of mind. It is pronounced by its letters A-R-C break. Page 196.

around the bend: a slang expression meaning insane or crazy. Page 369.

ascertain: find out definitely; learn with certainty or assurance; determine. Page 128.

As-isness: the condition of existence that occurs when a person makes a perfect duplicate, which is creating a thing again in its same time, in its same space, with its same energy, mass, motion or continuance. All As-isness is doing is merely accepting the responsibility for having created something. Page 67.

Assistant Board Member: one of the three members (Assistant Chairman, Secretary or Treasurer) of a three-division organizational pattern that existed at org level in early 1965. This pattern paralleled that of the International Board (controlling board of all Scientology). The Assistant Board Members headed the three divisions: Chairman (Division 1, HCO); Secretary (Division 2, Training and Processing); Treasurer (Division 3, Materiel and Accounts). Assistant Board Members helped the International Board Members wear their hats. They did not have the power to make a resolution, but had the power to recommend one. And in their own right, on delegated authority, they had the right to run their own area divisions. *See also* **division** and **International Board.** Page 303.

at length: 1. after some time; eventually. Page 47.
2. in detail; fully. Page 308.

attend: take care of; treat. Page 24.

attendant upon: accompanying, connected with or immediately following as a consequence. Page 177.

attrition, war of: literally, *attrition* means the rubbing or grinding or wearing away of one thing against another. Hence, a *war of attrition* refers to one side wearing down and weakening the other side through continuous pressure, harassment, deprivation, etc., such as by siege. (A *siege* is the act or process of surrounding and attacking a fortified place in such a way as to isolate it from help and supplies so as to lessen resistance of the defenders, thereby making capture possible.) Page 153.

auditing: same as *processing,* the application of Scientology or Dianetics processes and procedures to someone by a trained auditor. The exact definition of auditing is: the action of asking a preclear a question (which he can understand and answer), getting an answer to that question and acknowledging him for that answer. Page 44.

auditor: a person trained and qualified in applying auditing to individuals for their betterment. *Auditor* means one who listens, from the Latin *audire* meaning "to hear or listen." He is a minister or minister-in-training of the Church of Scientology. Page 40.

Auditor's Code: the specific rules that an auditor follows while auditing someone to ensure that the preclear will get the greatest possible gain from auditing. It includes such points as not evaluating for or invalidating the preclear, keeping all auditing appointments once made, not processing a preclear who has not had sufficient rest or food, and administering only standard tech to a preclear in the standard way, as well as others. Page 300.

automaticity: anything that goes on running outside the control of the individual. Page 5.

avail: use or value to; advantage to. Page 102.

avail oneself of: to use to one's advantage. Page vii.

avowed: openly acknowledged or declared. Page 100.

Babylon: the capital of *Babylonia,* an ancient empire of southwest Asia (located in the area now called Iraq) which flourished ca. 2100–689 B.C. The most important city in western Asia during this time period, Babylon was famous for its magnificent temples and palaces. Page 184.

backtrack: the whole span of time comprising a being's existence prior to the current lifetime. Page 198.

bad hats: corrupt, worthless or good-for-nothing persons; people who are morally lax or who frequently engage in improper conduct. Page 256.

badlands: extensive areas of heavily eroded, uncultivatable land with little vegetation. Page 285.

balked: stopped, as at an obstacle, and refused to proceed or do something specified. Page 107.

Baltimore Orioles: a US professional baseball team formed in 1872 in Baltimore, Maryland. The team is named after the *oriole,* an orange and black bird commonly found in that region. Page 163.

bank: reactive mind, that portion of a person's mind which works on a totally stimulus-response basis (given a certain stimulus it gives a certain response), which is not under his volitional control, and which exerts force and the power of command over his awareness, purposes, thoughts, body and actions. (A *bank* is a storage place for information, as in early computers where data was stored on a group or series of cards called a bank.) Page 5.

basic personality: the individual himself. The basic individual is not a buried unknown or a different person, but an intensity of all that is best and most able in the person. Page 20.

battalions: large bodies of troops organized to act together. Page 161.

battle plan: a military term used to describe a plan of battle to achieve an overall strategy in a war. A battle is something that occurs in a short unit of time and many battles go into winning a war. From this idea, the term *battle plan* has come to be used informally in the field of administration for a list of targets an administrator or staff member intends to execute in the immediate short-term future (as in the coming day or week) that will implement or bring into reality some portion of a strategic plan for the organization. Page 127.

battle royal: a heated disagreement or dispute among several people or groups, especially one that is long and bitter; *royal* here means large in scale. Page 257.

batty: insane; crazy. Page 19.

bear, brought to: to have exerted or applied pressure or influence on, so as to have brought about an effect or attained something desired. Page 201.

Bedlam: an old insane asylum (in full, *St. Mary of Bethlehem*) in London, known for its inhumane treatment and filthy environment. Inmates were chained to the walls or floor and when restless or violent, beaten, whipped or dunked in water. Page 192.

beg off: to decline or back out from doing something. Page 191.

behooves, well: it is right, proper and appropriate to a great extent or degree for (somebody); very necessary for. Page 178.

beingness: the condition of being is defined as "the result of having assumed an identity." It could be said to be "the role in a game."

An example of beingness could be one's own name. Another example would be one's profession. Another example would be one's physical characteristics. Each or all of these things could be called one's beingness. Beingness is assumed by oneself, or given to oneself, or is attained. For example, in the playing of a game each player has his own beingness. Page 35.

benefactor: one who renders aid or kindly service to others, a friendly helper; one who advances the interests of a cause or institution, a patron. Page 41.

bent upon: strongly inclined; determined to take a course of action. Page 176.

bereft: deprived, stripped. Page 167.

bested: got the better of; defeated or outdid; gained or achieved a mastery over some circumstance, opponent or adverse situation. Page 157.

bestialize: to brutalize; reduce in quality or character; change into the nature of an animal. Page 393.

Bill of Rights, American: an addition made to the Constitution of the United States in 1791, which guarantees certain rights to the people including freedom of speech and freedom of religion. It also prohibits the police and other government officials from searching people's homes or offices or seizing property without good reason and proper authority. Page 205.

blackness of cases: a reference to a case that sees blackness with his or her eyes closed. The person doesn't see pictures. The case has a poor level of reality. Page 64.

blasphemy: something done or said that shows disrespect for God. Page 44.

Bligh, Captain: William Bligh (1754–1817), British admiral and captain of the ship *Bounty* who was overpowered and set adrift in a small boat by his crew who claimed Bligh's severity as a commanding officer as justification for their mutiny. Page 248.

blighting: destroying the promise of; ruining or spoiling. Page 23.

blind spot: an area or subject where one's vision, perception or understanding is lacking; something that one is unable or unwilling to confront or understand. Page 5.

blot: something that spoils the reputation of something; a disgrace. Page 392.

blown the whistle on: reported someone for doing something wrong or illegal. Page 373.

body cycle: a reference to the repeated cycle of birth, growth, decay and death. Page 150.

body politic: the people of a nation or any politically organized state, considered as a group. Page 248.

boots, (pair of): figuratively, a position or situation. The expression is a variation of the phrase *fill (someone's) shoes,* meaning to take the place of (a predecessor); to take over one's job or position and its duties or responsibilities satisfactorily. Page 122.

borne out: supported, backed up or confirmed. Page 46.

bourne: a boundary, limit. Hence, domain, area of activity or thought. Page 55.

braid, devoted to: *braid* is a band of material (often a gold or silver color) used to decorate a uniform and indicate a rank (usually high) as in the army or navy. The term *devoted to braid* means having enthusiasm for and dedication to status and decoration rather than action and duty. Page 151.

breach: 1. an opening made by breaking down a portion of a solid body such as a wall, riverbank, etc. Hence, a gap, rupture or break in anything. Page 158.
2. a violation or breaking of a trust, agreement, promise or obligation. Page 313.

breaks faith: violates one's promise or word; acts as a traitor. *Break* means to transgress or violate by disregarding or failing to observe (something); to fail to keep one's word or pledge. *Faith* means a verbal promise, vow or pledge; the duty of fulfilling an obligation. Page 23.

breeze: an effortless and very easy task. Page 270.

Bridge, the: the route to Clear and OT, also referred to as the Bridge to Total Freedom. In Scientology there is the idea of a bridge across the chasm. It comes from an old mystic idea of a chasm between where one is now and a higher plateau of existence and that many people trying to make it fell into the abyss. Today, however, Scientology has a bridge that goes across the chasm and is complete and can be walked. It is represented in the steps of the Grade Chart. Page 67.

brought to bear: to have exerted or applied pressure or influence on, so as to have brought about an effect or attained something desired. Page 201.

B routing: a method of routing communications in a Church of Scientology organization in which the particle goes via established channels. A communication on B routing goes up through the seniors in one's own area, across to the senior of the terminal the communication is addressed to, and down to the intended recipient. Page 271.

Bulgravia: a made-up name for a nondescript or unknown place. Page 165.

but good: thoroughly, completely, extremely. Page 260.

bypass: a condition whereby one is being ignored while someone else performs one's assigned duties. Page 105.

bypassed charge: charge that has been restimulated but overlooked by both the preclear and auditor. *Charge* is harmful energy or force accumulated and generated in the reactive mind, resulting from the conflicts and unpleasant experiences that a person has had. Page 202.

cabals: small groups of people involved in secret plans, as against a person or government, especially to obtain economic or political power. Also the secret plots and schemes of such groups. Page 156.

Callao: a fortress that guarded *Callao,* Peru's major seaport and gateway to Lima. It was the last stronghold of the Spanish royalist forces in South America. The Spanish General Rodil refused to surrender the fort, despite generous terms offered by Simón Bolívar. Rodil held the fortress until 1826 even though Peru achieved independence from Spain in 1821. Page 155.

call the lightning down on: to invoke lightning to strike someone. Used figuratively in reference to the action of reprimanding, rebuking, scolding, etc. Page 236.

cannonade: a continued discharge of cannon or artillery directed against an enemy. Page 156.

carbons: *carbon paper,* a type of paper used to make duplicate copies of written work. The paper is treated on one side with a dark-colored, waxy preparation, such as carbon or other material. It is placed between two sheets of plain paper and when pressure is applied to the top sheet in writing or typing, the preparation transfers to the bottom sheet making a duplicate copy of the original. Page 136.

carping: characterized by frequent ill-natured, disgruntled faultfinding. Page 46.

case(s): 1. a general term for a person about to be audited or actually being audited. Page 43.

2. all the content of the reactive mind. Page 49.

case gain: the improvements and resurgences a person experiences from auditing. Also, any case betterment according to the pc. Page 67.

Case Supervisor(s): an accomplished and properly certified auditor who is trained additionally to supervise cases. The C/S is the auditor's "handler." He tells the auditor what to do, corrects his tech, keeps the lines straight and keeps the auditor calm and willing and winning. The C/S is the pc's case director. Page 194.

caught it from all sides: a coined phrase meaning was punished, scolded or got in trouble from every direction. Page 375.

cave (oneself) in: *cave in* is a US Western phrase for mental or physical collapse as like being at the bottom of a mine shaft when the supports collapsed and left the person under tons of debris. To *cave oneself in* means to cause oneself to experience mental and/or physical collapse to the extent that one cannot function causatively. Page 5.

censured: found fault with; expressed strong disapproval. Page 188.

Central Files (CF): a file system in a Church of Scientology organization which has the purpose of collecting and holding all names, addresses, pertinent data about and correspondence to anyone and from anyone who has ever bought a book or donated for a service. Page 313.

Central Organization(s): the main Scientology organization founded in strategic areas of the world responsible for all Dianetics and Scientology activities in its geographical zone or area and which delivers first-rate training and processing to its public. Page 216.

chain lightning: something that is unusually powerful and rapid in effect or movement. *Chain lightning* is lightning that appears to move very rapidly in long zigzag or wavy lines and which gives off a brilliant light. Page 369.

Chaldea: the ancient name given to the lands at the head of the Persian Gulf, south of Babylon. The Chaldeans conquered

Babylon in the 600s B.C., establishing the Chaldean Empire (ca. 625–539 B.C.). Chaldea expanded and became the center of the civilized world until conquered by the Persians in 539 B.C. Page 285.

charge, bypassed: charge that has been restimulated but overlooked by both the preclear and auditor. *Charge* is harmful energy or force accumulated and generated in the reactive mind, resulting from the conflicts and unpleasant experiences that a person has had. Page 202.

checksheet: a list of materials, often divided into sections, that give the theory and practical steps which, when completed, give one a study completion. The items are selected to add up to the required knowledge of the subject. They are arranged in the sequence necessary to a gradient of increasing knowledge of the subject. After each item there is a place for the initial of the student or the person checking the student out. When the checksheet is fully initialed, it is complete, meaning the student may now take an exam and be granted the award for completion. Page 311.

chop: a sharp disapproval or reprimand. Page 238.

Christie: John Reginald Christie (1898–1953), English murderer. He was convicted and hung for the murder of his wife. He confessed to killing other women and was thought to have murdered as many as eight, whose bodies were found in the walls, under the floorboards and in the garden of his home. Page 178.

chute, down the: into a state of failure or ruin, deterioration or collapse. A *chute* is a descent or decline and alludes to an incline or steeply sloped channel used to convey water, grain, coal, etc., into a wagon, truck or other receptacle at a lower level. Page 5.

chute, up the: out of a state of failure or ruin, deterioration or collapse. This is a variation of *down the chute* with the opposite meaning. Page 5.

civic: of or relating to the duties or activities of citizens in contrast to military, etc. Page 151.

Class VIII: an auditor (Hubbard Specialist of Standard Tech) who has completed the Class VIII Course. The Class VIII Course trains the auditor to a standard of perfect understanding and application of the *basics* of auditing. On the course, the auditor develops an *exact, unvarying* standard of application of every *fundamental* of auditing and the mind, in order to achieve stellar results on *any* preclear. Page 375.

classic: standard or recognized as particularly appropriate or effective (to a given end). Page 61.

classifications: awards given auditors requiring certain actions and conditions be attained such as completing a course, passing an examination, and showing proficiency and results at that level of auditing. Page 299.

Class 0: an auditor who has completed Academy Level 0, the first of the auditor classification levels, and is able to audit others to ARC Straightwire Recall Release and Grade 0 Communications Release. Page 375.

clay demo: to make a *clay demonstration,* a model made out of clay to clarify studies, definitions or confusions. Page 141.

clay pigeon: a saucerlike disk of baked clay or other material that is hurled into the air by a machine called a "trap" and which serves as a moving target (somewhat like a bird in flight) for shooting practice or in the game or sport of trapshooting. Originally the targets shot at were live pigeons (or other birds) but were replaced with clay disks, hence their name. This term can also be used to refer to a person who, like a clay pigeon, has gotten himself into a vulnerable or disadvantageous position and is therefore open to being a "target," as for some criticism, action, discipline, etc. Page 370.

Clear: a being who no longer has his own reactive mind. Page 231.

clearing: (of the mind or spirit) the freeing or releasing of overts and withholds. Page 42.

coffee and cakes: more than enough money, wherewithal, etc.; luxuries. Page 243.

cognition: a pc origination indicating he has "come to realize." It's a "What do you know? I..." statement. A new realization of life. It results in a higher degree of awareness and consequently a greater ability to succeed with one's endeavors in life. Page 96.

coin, opposite side of the: the other side, aspect or point of view of something. This phrase comes from the fact that a coin has two sides, usually with a different appearance on each. Page 150.

colonialism: the system or principle whereby a company or body of people migrate to a new country or area to inhabit and cultivate its economic resources for themselves and the parent state. The word is frequently used in the sense of exploitation of backward or weak people by a larger power. Page 246.

colonies: countries or areas that are ruled or politically controlled by another country. Page 5.

color-flash paper: paper of the color designated for a specific division per the color-flash system used in Church of Scientology organizations. Each division uses a different color paper for its despatches, orders and letters. *Flash* in this sense means to make known or cause to appear with great speed. Page 271.

color (of an enemy): the flag (symbol) of the opposition in any fight or battle. The word *color* refers to a flag of a regiment or ship. Page 102.

come to grief: suffer misfortune or ruin. Page 31.

Comm Ev: 1. to call before a Committee of Evidence as an Interested Party. Page 229.
2. abbreviation for *Committee of Evidence*. Page 231.

Committee(s) of Evidence: in a Scientology organization, a fact-finding body composed of impartial persons properly convened by a Convening Authority which hears evidence from persons it calls before it, arrives at a finding and makes a full report and recommendation to its Convening Authority for his or her action. Page 289.

comm lag: short for *communication lag,* meaning the length of time from the moment an individual is asked a question to the moment when he actually replies to that exact question, regardless of what comes in between. Page 141.

comm line: short for *communication line,* the line on which particles flow; any sequence through which a message of any character may go. Page 104.

common denominator: something common to or characteristic of a number of people, things, situations, etc.; shared characteristic. Page 258.

communicators: those who keep the lines (body, despatch, letter, intercom, phone) moving or controlled for the executive. Page 107.

compounded the felony: made a situation worse; added to a difficulty, problem or crime. The phrase refers to a person having done something which made a crime more serious. Page 124.

compulsive: of or relating to *compulsion,* an irresistible impulse to perform an act that is contrary to one's own will. Page 60.

computation: of or relating to calculating or processing data (to come up with answers); of thinking, as in *"Logic is not good or bad in itself, it is the name of a computation procedure—the procedure of the mind in its effort to attain solutions to problems."* Page 17.

computation: calculation or evaluation held in the mind in order to deal with some situation or solve some problem. Page 45.

Confessional: a procedure in Scientology whereby an individual is able to confess his withholds and the overt acts underlying them as the first step toward taking responsibility for them and seeking to make things right again. Page 42.

Congressional committees: legislative groups composed of members of Congress (the highest lawmaking body of the United States) that conduct investigations and consider, evaluate and recommend action on legislation. Page 6.

Consort: the wife, husband or romantic companion to a monarch (a king or queen) or reigning leader. Page 149.

conspiracy(ies): 1. any coming together or conjunction in action or combination of causes in bringing about a given result or achieving some end. Page 166.
2. a secret plan by two or more people to agree to do something unlawful or harmful. Page 316.

Constantinople: former name for Istanbul which was the capital of the eastern part of the Roman Empire and survived the fall of Rome in the fifth century. Page 161.

Continental Executive Council: the Scientology body responsible for the coordination and expansion of all Church of Scientology organizations in its continent. Page 85.

Continental Justice Chief: the executive responsible for the standard application of Scientology Justice policies to staff and public in his or her continental zone. Page 316.

contra-survival: from *contra,* against, in opposition to, and *survival.* Hence, contra-survival is something in opposition to, against or contrary to survival. Page 6.

convalescences: gradual returns to good health after illnesses or medical treatment, or the periods spent recovering. Page 179.

corollary: a proposition that follows upon one just demonstrated and that requires no additional proof, but is a natural consequence or result. Page 205.

correction fluid: a usually white liquid that can be applied to paper to cover up writing or typing errors and provide a white surface on which to type or write over. Page 136.

countermanded: stopped or prohibited with a contrary order. Page 273.

counter-postulate: a postulate (a decision that something will happen) that is counter (against or opposed) to an existing postulate. Page 134.

Course Supervisor: the person in charge of a Dianetics or Scientology course who is responsible for the training of students and graduating auditors and other graduates at a high level of technology. Page 238.

court(s): 1. bodies of people before whom judicial cases are heard, also, the places where they meet. Page 24.
2. to act as though trying to provoke (something harmful, unpleasant, etc.); to invite unwisely. Page 59.
3. an enclosed area, a yard. Page 193.

Court of Ethics: a justice action convened for Misdemeanors or Crimes. It is not a fact-finding court. One is convened solely on statistics and known evidence. Page 235.

covetous: having a strong desire to possess something, especially something that belongs to another person. Page 23.

cowboys in the black hats: lawbreaking bad guys; unethical, morally corrupt persons. In many Western movies the good guys wore white hats and the villains or bad guys wore black hats. Page 173.

cowboys in the white hats: law-abiding good guys or heroes; ethical, morally upright persons. In many Western movies the good guys wore white hats and the villains or bad guys wore black hats. Page 173.

cowed: intimidated or dispirited into a state of submission, inactivity or fear. Page 179.

crevices: narrow cracks or openings. Page 53.

Crosby, Bing: (1904–1977) popular American singer and motion picture star. His more than 1,000 records have sold over 300 million copies and he also appeared in more than 50 films. Page 243.

crown, stars in your: figuratively, an acknowledgment of a great achievement. Originally a *crown* was a wreath worn about the head as a symbol of victory. From this, a crown became traditionally used to designate the power or authority of a king. A *star* is an award for excellence. Hence, to place stars on a crown is to further acknowledge something which is already recognized as outstanding, powerful, victorious, etc. Page 199.

C/S: abbreviation for *Case Supervisor.* Page 211.

C/S-1, PTS: Case Supervisor Instruction Number One, so called as it is the first action taken with the preclear before auditing is begun to handle the PTS condition. Case Supervisor Instruction Number One instructs the preclear on the basic definitions and procedures of an auditing action he is about to begin. Page 211.

CSW: abbreviation for *Completed Staff Work,* an assembled package of information on any given situation, plan or emergency forwarded to an executive sufficiently complete to require from the executive only an "approved" or "disapproved." Completed Staff Work (1) states the situation, (2) gives all the data necessary to its solution, (3) advises a solution, and (4) contains a line for approval or disapproval by the executive with his signature. Page 316.

curdling: turning bad, failing or going wrong; spoiling or making sour. *Curd* is the thick, soft, almost solid substance that separates from milk when it becomes sour, hence, curdling (turning bad) the esteem. Page 156.

cut, above the: a variation of the phrase "a cut above," meaning superior to others in some respect. Page 150.

cycle-of-action: the sequence that an action goes through, wherein the action is started, is continued for as long as is required and then is completed as planned. Page 180.

dark: characterized by absence of moral or spiritual light; characterized by wickedness of an unrelieved nature. Page 42.

Dark Ages: any period of severe decline within a civilization which is without knowledge or culture; a period characterized by lack of intellectual and spiritual activity, often referring especially to the period in European history from the A.D. 400s to the early 1300s, when society lacked many artistic and technical skills and the knowledge of the previous Greek and Roman civilizations had virtually disappeared. Page 243.

dark operations: a series of actions or an organized campaign that is evil, dishonest or deliberately harmful. Page 52.

datum: a single piece of information, as a fact. Page 16.

defaulting: 1. failing to make an appearance although being ordered to do so. Page 342.
2. a failure to meet an obligation, especially a financial one. Page 355.

degraded being(s): a person who is at effect to such a degree that he or she avoids orders or instructions in any possible covert or overt way because orders of any kind are confused with painful indoctrinations in the past. Page 391.

deified: made a god of; adored or worshiped (as one would a god). Page 150.

delusion: a fixed false belief; a perception that is perceived in a way different from the way it is in reality. Page 104.

democracy: a form of government in which the supreme power is vested in the people and exercised directly by them or by their elected agents. Page 47.

department: a portion or section of an organization with its own staff headed by an executive and responsible for the performance of certain functions or production of certain products. For example, the Communications Department. Page 72.

depraving: making worse in character or quality; corrupting or perverting. Page 150.

determinism: power of choice or decision. Page 3.

devil, as the: to an excessive degree, exceedingly. Page 123.

devoted to braid: *braid* is a band of material (often a gold or silver color) used to decorate a uniform and indicate a rank (usually high) as in the army or navy. The term *devoted to braid* means having enthusiasm for and dedication to status and decoration rather than action and duty. Page 151.

Dev-T: abbreviation for *Developed Traffic*. It is condemnatory. The symbol Dev-T means on a despatch, "This despatch exists only because its originator has not handled a situation, problem or an executive order." It also means "Responsibility for your post very low." Also it means "You should be handling this without further traffic." It also means "You are manufacturing new traffic because you aren't handling old traffic." Also it means "For Gawd's Sake!" Every time traffic is developed somebody has flubbed. *"Developed"* Traffic does *not* mean usual and necessary traffic. It means *unusual and unnecessary traffic.* Page 107.

Dianetics: from Greek *dia,* through, and *nous,* mind or soul; what the soul is doing to the body. See *Dianetics: The Modern Science of Mental Health* and *Science of Survival.* Page 3.

did the trick: accomplished or resulted in something. Page 54.

die in the ditch: literally to end one's life in a trench dug in the earth used to carry off water and other waste. Used figuratively to mean left abandoned and unwanted, to die. Page 155.

Dillinger: John Dillinger (1902?–1934), an infamous American bank robber and murderer who was declared "public enemy number one" by the Federal Bureau of Investigation (FBI) in 1933 for his role in numerous bank robberies and a string of murders. In July 1934, FBI agents gunned him down. Page 177.

diminishes: lessens, reduces or becomes smaller and less important. Page 196.

Diogenes: (ca. 412–323 B.C.) Greek philosopher who was said to have lived in poverty, begged for food and used a tub for shelter to show his disregard for possessions. According to tradition, he once lit a lamp in broad daylight and went through the streets of Athens looking for an honest man. Page 173.

Director of Certifications: the Department of Certifications and Awards, Department 15 in the Qualifications Division, is headed by the Director of Certifications. Page 365.

Director of Estimations: the head of Department 10 on the 1965 Technical Division org board, responsible for interviews and testing. Preceding Department 11 (Training) and Department 12 (Processing), all students and preclears entered and exited the Tech Division through the Department of Estimations. Page 365.

Director of Examinations: on the 1965 org board the Department of Examinations (Department 13) in the Qualifications Division is headed by the Director of Examinations. Page 365.

Director of Processing: the head of the Department of Processing in the Technical Division, under whom come all public cases and who is responsible for auditing rooms, auditors and assignment of pcs to auditors. Page 226.

Director of Review: the head of the Department of Review in the Qualifications Division, responsible for the repair and correction of auditing and training difficulties. Page 226.

Director of Training: the head of the Department of Training in the Technical Division, responsible for producing effectively trained people who can skillfully apply what they have learned and will apply it. Page 226.

discernment: the act of distinguishing; perception of the difference between (things). Page 15.

disdaining: treating with contempt as being of little worth or consequence or as unworthy of oneself. Page 248.

dispensary: a room or shop in which medicines are dispensed or served out, as a hospital dispensary. Page 166.

Dissem Sec: short for *Dissemination Secretary,* the head of the Dissemination Division, the division of a Church of Scientology that sees that Dianetics and Scientology materials are widely disseminated and readily available, sees that public are procured for service and that records and files of parishioners, the backbone of procurement, are kept accurate and orderly and are used. Page 257.

diverge: deviate from a standard; stray or turn away from an acceptable course. Page 310.

divergent group: a group of people or an organization that has taken a different route, line of action or of thought than Scientology. Page 312.

divine rightness: a reference to the divine right of kings, the belief that kings and queens had a God-given right to rule, that they could do no wrong and were accountable only to God for their actions and not to the people they ruled. Used figuratively. Page 6.

division: 1. of or concerning one of the nine divisions of a Church of Scientology organization responsible for one of the major functions of the organization. A division is composed of either three or four departments and headed by a Divisional Secretary. Page 85.

2. a reference to any one of the three divisions of the International Board (controlling board of all Scientology) in early 1965. Each division was headed by a member of the Board and consisted of their staff and all staff of that division in all orgs. Division 1 (HCO) was run by the Chairman, Division 2 (Training and Processing) was run by the Secretary and Division 3 (Materiel and Accounts)

was the Treasurer. The three-division organizational pattern was duplicated in all orgs and personnel acting as assistants to the board members headed these divisions in each org. *See also* **Assistant Board Member** and **International Board.** Page 299.

does one(self) in: injures gravely; ruins. Page 5.

D of P: abbreviation for *Director of Processing,* the head of the Department of Processing in the Technical Division, under whom come all public cases and who is responsible for auditing rooms, auditors and assignment of pcs to auditors. Page 226.

D of T: abbreviation for *Director of Training,* the head of the Department of Training in the Technical Division, responsible for producing effectively trained people who can skillfully apply what they have learned and will apply it. Page 226.

dog-eat-dog: marked by a destructive or ruthless competition; without self-restraint, ethics, etc. From an old saying, implying a dog would have to be savage and cruel to eat another dog. Page 154.

do-gooder: a person who seeks to correct social ills in an idealistic, but usually impractical or superficial, way. Page 61.

dope: drugs to induce a state of extreme excitement and happiness or to satisfy an addiction; illegal drugs. Page 24.

downstat: in Scientology, a coined word meaning characteristic of a person or area which has low, declining statistics. Page 268.

down the chute: into a state of failure or ruin, deterioration or collapse. A *chute* is a descent or decline and alludes to an incline or steeply sloped channel used to convey water, grain, coal, etc., into a wagon, truck or other receptacle at a lower level. Page 5.

drafts, sleeping: drinks containing a drug that is meant to help somebody sleep. (Also spelled *draughts.*) Page 194.

dramatize(s): imitate, express or act out something, as an actor would in a drama or play acting out his scripted part. Page 6.

dregs: the least valuable or most unpleasant part of something, especially a group of people. Page 392.

driven: forced someone or something into a particular state or condition, often an extremely negative one. Page 29.

drives: inner urges that stimulate activity, energy and initiative. Page 12.

drum, beat the: to vigorously promote or loudly publicize (something); to advertise something, give one's support or argue noisily (for something). Page 246.

dull-faced: gloomy looking; deeply shaded. *Faced* refers to the appearance of something or how it looks. Page 55.

dwindling spiral: the worse someone (or something) gets, the more capacity they have to get worse. *Spiral* here refers to a progressive downward movement, marking a relentlessly deteriorating state of affairs, and considered to take the form of a spiral. The term comes from aviation where it is used to describe the phenomenon of a plane descending and spiraling in smaller and smaller circles, as in an accident or feat of expert flying, which if not handled can result in loss of control and a crash. Page vii.

ebb: a point or condition of decline or depression. From the literal meaning, the flowing back of the tide (ocean level at the shore) as the water returns to the sea. Page 59.

ecclesiastical: of or relating to a church especially as a formal and established institution. Page 313.

ED: abbreviation for *Executive Director,* the head of a Church of Scientology organization, responsible for the planning and running of the organization as well as its statistics and viability. Page 129.

eke out: manage to get or achieve something but only on a small scale and with a great deal of effort. Page 240.

element: one of the factors playing a part in or determining the outcome of some process or activity. Page 76.

embroiled: involved in conflicts and problems. Page 32.

Emergency, State of: a state assigned to an organization or portion thereof when it has consistently down statistics or numerous noncompliances or offenses. This can be assigned to a unit, subsection, section, department, division or the entire organization. It is not assigned to a person. To end an Emergency Condition, the portion of Scientology to which it is assigned must follow closely the Emergency Formula. Page 110.

E-Meter: a specially designed instrument which helps the auditor and preclear locate areas of spiritual distress or travail. Page 42.

E-Meter check: a check performed by an Ethics Officer, using an E-Meter. The Ethics Officer sets up the meter, hands the cans to the staff member. No question is asked of the staff member. The Ethics Officer records the position of the Tone Arm and the condition of the needle and that is all. Page 300.

empire: the country, region or union of states or territories under the control of an emperor or other powerful leader or government. An *empire* is a collection of conquered or colonized states, each with its own government under the empire as a whole. A *colony* is a country or area separate from but ruled by another country. Page 242.

end-all in itself: a purpose or goal desired for its own sake (rather than to attain something else). Page 6.

End Phenomena: those indications in the preclear and meter which show that a process or action is ended. Page 315.

enfilade: the firing of a gun or guns so as to sweep the length of a target such as a column of troops. Page 155.

engineered: planned something or brought it about, especially in an ingenious or secretive manner. Page 159.

engrams: mental image pictures which are recordings of moments of pain and unconsciousness. These recordings can be later brought into play by a similar word or environment and cause the individual to act as though in the presence of danger. They force the individual into patterns of thinking and behavior which are not called for by a reasonable appraisal of the situation. See *Dianetics: The Modern Science of Mental Health* and *Science of Survival*. Page 196.

enjoined: commanded to behave in a certain way; imposed authoritatively. Page 150.

enmist: cause (something) to be dim or obscure. *En-* means to bring or put into a certain state or condition. *Mist* is a thin gray cloud of water droplets that condenses in the atmosphere just above the ground limiting the view. Page 55.

enterprise: industrious activity, especially when directed toward survival. Page 182.

enterprising: showing initiative and resourcefulness, boldness or readiness in ventures or activities. Page 161.

entheta: a compound word meaning *enturbulated theta,* theta in a turbulent state, agitated or disturbed. (*Theta* is the energy of thought and life. Theta is reason, serenity, stability, happiness, cheerful emotion, persistence and the other factors which Man ordinarily considers desirable. The complete description of theta is contained in *Science of Survival*.) Page 203.

enturbulation: agitation or disturbance; commotion and upset. Page 233.

enturbulence: the state or condition of turbulence, agitation, disturbance or commotion. Page 220.

E/O: abbreviation for *Ethics Officer,* the person in a Scientology organization who has the following purpose: To help Ron clear organizations and the public if need be of entheta and enturbulation so that Scientology can be done. Page 254.

eons: an immeasurably or indefinitely long period of time. Page 27.

epic: a lengthy narrative poem, elevated in language and celebrating the heroic and noble achievements of a legendary hero in a way that is larger than life in size and magnitude. Page 167.

erstwhile: in the past; at a former time; formerly. Page 165.

estranged: 1. separated from a spouse. Page 159.
2. destroyed one's confidence in; aroused ill will or antagonism where there had been originally love, affection or friendliness. Page 198.

Ethics: the Ethics Section of an organization and all of its technology. Page vii.

Ethics Authority Section: the section in the Office of LRH in a Church of Scientology whose duties include the authorization of local ethics issues and handling of petitions that pertain to ethics matters. Page 280.

Ethics Hearing: an Ethics Hearing may be convened by an Ethics Officer to obtain data for further action or inaction. It has no power to discipline but may advise on consequences. Page 238.

Ethics Officer(s): the person in a Scientology organization who has the following purpose: To help Ron clear organizations and the public if need be of entheta and enturbulation so that Scientology can be done. Page vii.

evaluated: examined or judged the significance and condition of. Page 16.

evaluated: told someone what was wrong with him or what to think about his case. Page 60.

Executive Council: the highest governing council in a Church of Scientology organization composed of the Executive Director and the three Executive Secretaries (the HCO Executive Secretary, the Organization Executive Secretary and the Public Executive Secretary) which is responsible for the successful conduct of the org as a whole. Page 252.

Executive Directive(s): a type of issue used by executives in Church of Scientology organizations which contains various immediate orders, programs, etc. They are blue ink on blue paper. Page 357.

Executive Director: the head of a Church of Scientology organization, responsible for the planning and running of the organization as well as its statistics and viability. Page 85.

Executive Secretary: any of the three executives in a Church of Scientology organization, directly under the Executive Director, who are expert in and head the main portions of the org: the HCO Executive Secretary (over Divisions 7, 1 and 2), the Org Executive Secretary (over Divisions 3, 4 and 5) and the Public Executive Secretary (over Divisions 6A, 6B and 6C). Page 85.

exhume: restore someone to a former standing. Literally, to dig out or remove (something buried) from beneath the ground. Page 256.

Expanded Dianetics: that branch of Dianetics which uses Dianetics in special ways for specific purposes. Some pcs, particularly heavy drug cases, or who are physically disabled or who are chronically ill or who have had trouble running engrams (to name a few), require specially adapted technology. Expanded Dianetics is very specifically adjusted to the preclear. Page 199.

extort: obtain something from another, especially money, by intimidation or abuse of legal or official authority. Page 154.

extenuating: lessening the real or apparent seriousness of something (such as a crime, offense or fault) or the extent of a person's responsibility, by affording a basis for excuses; serving to make (a fault, offense, etc.) seem less serious. Page 368.

ex-wolves: a reference to people with the cruel, greedy and ferocious character of a wolf, and who harmed the organizations of Scientology. As former (ex-) wolves, they are thought to have changed and to no longer be vicious and evil. Page 259.

faith, breaks: violates one's promise or word; acts as a traitor. *Break* means to transgress or violate by disregarding or failing to observe (something); to fail to keep one's word or pledge. *Faith* means a verbal promise, vow or pledge; the duty of fulfilling an obligation. Page 23.

fallacious: deceptive, misleading or false. Page 355.

fancied: of or pertaining to an idea or opinion with little foundation; illusionary. Page 172.

fancy: imagination or fantasy. Page 42.

FBI: abbreviation for *Federal Bureau of Investigation,* a United States government agency established to investigate violations of federal laws and to safeguard national security. Page 181.

FCDC: abbreviation for *Founding Church of Scientology, Washington, DC,* established in 1955. (A *founding church* is one from which other churches have their origin or derive their authority.) Page 222.

felony, compounded the: made a situation worse; added to a difficulty, problem or crime. The phrase refers to a person having done something which made a crime more serious. Page 124.

ferret out: to search out, discover, bring to light. A *ferret* is a small weasel-like animal used to hunt rabbits and rats by chasing them out of the ground. Page 132.

fidelity: the quality of being faithful; having firm and unchanging loyalty to a person. Page 158.

fiduciary: designating or of a person who holds or manages money or property for another or a group of people. Page 313.

field: the general (geographical) areas, individuals and groups serviced by a Church of Scientology organization. Page 43.

Fitness Board: an official group of persons which exists in the Sea Organization to determine the mental and physical fitness of its personnel. Page 374.

flies in the teeth of: is in direct, forceful opposition to or defiance of. Page 44.

Floyd, Pretty Boy: Charles Arthur Floyd (1904–1934), American gangster, bank robber and killer. He was nicknamed "Pretty Boy" because he wore his hair slicked back and was never without a pocket comb. At the age of eighteen Floyd committed his first major crime, and went on to rob more than thirty banks, murdering at least ten men, half of whom were police officers. In 1934, US government agents shot him to death. Page 177.

folded up: broke down; collapsed; failed. Page 19.

fold, into the: into a group or organization providing spiritual salvation. Literally from the fenced enclosure (fold) for sheep. Page 259.

footing: a foundation or basis for further advancement or development. Page 98.

for it: about to suffer unpleasant consequences, especially of one's own actions or omissions. Page 108.

forsworn: vowed to stop doing, having or using something. Page 221.

frame of mind: a person's mental attitude towards something. Page 139.

French revolt: a reference to the *French Revolution,* a revolt in France from 1789 to 1799 which overthrew the royal family and the aristocratic class and system of privileges they enjoyed. The revolution was in part a protest against France's absolute monarchy, entrenched (firmly established) and unproductive nobility and the consequent lack of freedom for the middle classes. During the revolution, 300,000 people were arrested and 17,000 were beheaded under the guillotine. Page 152.

Freud: Sigmund Freud (1856–1939), Austrian founder of psychoanalysis who emphasized that unconscious memories of a sexual nature control a person's behavior. Page 60.

front up: face; confront; appear before or meet face-to-face. Page 273.

fruits: the benefits or advantages of an activity. Page 24.

game condition: a condition similar to a game. By *game* we mean contest of person against person, team against team. A game consists of freedoms, barriers and purposes. Participation in any game (whether it be a game of tennis, football or arguing with one's neighbor) is preferable to not having a game. All aberrative games must contain the element of unknowingness. Page 45.

General Sherman tank: a tank of the United States armed forces, as well as French and English forces, in World War II (1939–1945). It was named after William Tecumseh Sherman (1820–1891), a famous general in the American Civil War (1861–1865). General Sherman tank is also used figuratively in reference to the real reason behind a situation or somebody who is trying to stop things. Page 235.

Genghis Khan: (1162–1227) Mongolian general and emperor. He conquered large portions of China and southwestern Asia. His army ruthlessly eliminated any enemy; they were known to systematically slaughter the population of entire cities that resisted them. Page 251.

get away with murder: figuratively, to commit an act for which one could be censured (have expressed strong disapproval or harsh criticism), without being punished. Page 238.

get the show on the road: to get (an organization, plan, project, etc.) started and operating; to put (a strategy, idea, etc.) into motion. Page 237.

getting the wheels going: a variation of the phrase *set the wheels in motion,* which means to cause an activity to make forward progress or plans to go into effect. Page 164.

geysers: throws forth or gives out rapidly and in great quantity like a *geyser,* an intermittent hot spring throwing up water as a fountainlike column. Page 53.

gifted: (said of someone) given a special quality or ability, thought of as naturally possessed or imparted (rather than obtained through work, practice or drill). Page 167.

gifts: special qualities or abilities that are thought of as naturally possessed or imparted to someone (rather than obtained through work, practice or drill). Page 151.

given pause: caused to hesitate or reconsider, as from surprise or doubt. Page 61.

glow (something) right: a coined phrase meaning to make something happen or be successful merely by the magnetism of one's presence rather than by organizational or preparatory steps necessary to political or personal achievements. Used in a derogatory sense. Page 151.

gnaw the rug: a coined variation of the phrase *chew the carpet,* meaning to react to something with great or uncontrolled anger, wrath or anxiety. Page 173.

go bust: fail completely. Page 72.

godos: a Spanish word used in South America as a derogatory term for Spaniards, especially during the war of independence between South America and Spain in the early 1800s. The word literally means Gothic, and originally referred to members of the rich and powerful Germanic tribe that invaded the Spanish peninsula in the fifth century A.D. and ruled until the eighth century. Page 155.

go for broke: exert oneself or employ one's resources to the utmost. Page 46.

going concern: an activity that is flourishing and actively operating to full capacity. Page 104.

"good roads, good weather": communication about things, activities or subjects of which everyone is in favor. Page 198.

gossamer: a fine, filmy cobweb seen on grass or floating in the air in calm weather. Page 53.

grace, reinstated to: *grace* is a state or condition of being regarded with favor by someone. *Reinstated to grace* would be to return to a former condition, as if having been forgiven for one's transgressions. Page 259.

Grade Chart: the Classification, Gradation and Awareness Chart of Levels and Certificates, the route to Clear and OT (also called the Bridge to Total Freedom, or the Bridge). First released in 1965, it is the master program for every case. Classification refers to training and the fact that certain actions are required, or skills attained, before an individual is classified for a particular training level and allowed onto the next class. *Gradation* refers to the gradual improvement that occurs in Scientology auditing. *Awareness* refers to one's own awareness, which improves as one progresses up. Scientology contains the entire map for getting the individual through all the various points on this gradation scale, getting him across the Bridge and to a higher state of existence. Page 67.

Great Depression: the great slowdown in the American economy, the worst in the country's history, which began with the enormous decrease in the price of stocks on the stock exchange in October 1929, and lasted through the 1930s. During this time, business, employment and stock market values declined severely and remained at a very low level. Many banks and businesses failed, and millions of people lost their jobs. Page 243.

group engram(s): a mutual engram of a group. The anatomy of a group engram is false orders, false reports and false perceptions. They cause a group to go downtone and downstat. Page 337.

Guayaquil: a seaport in Ecuador, historically noteworthy as the meeting place in July 1822 of Simón Bolívar and General José de San Martín (South American revolutionary leader and protector of Peru). Guayaquil was the only good port for thousands of miles. Whoever controlled it controlled the whole of Ecuador and Great Colombia (inclusive of what is now Colombia, Panama, Venezuela and Ecuador). Bolívar was determined to have Guayaquil; however, San Martín held the power in Peru and was also pledged to his government to gain Guayaquil. Both men had the common interest of liberation from Spain, but Bolívar would not assist Peru with San Martín in charge. San Martín thus resigned his post, leaving Bolívar in full command to gain Guayaquil and to liberate Peru. Page 157.

hand in hand: in the manner of things that are inseparably interrelated; in union. Page 20.

harbinger: one who gives warning of something about to happen. Page 179.

hardbound: unyielding, rigid and inflexible, used in reference to rules, standards, customs, etc. Page 40.

HAS: abbreviation for *HCO Area Secretary.* Page 373.

has his head down: a variation of the phrase *have one's nose down,* to work very hard and steadily at something. Page 254.

hat: slang for the title and work of a post in a Church of Scientology organization. Taken from the fact that in many professions such as railroading the type of hat worn is the badge of the job. Page 111.

hat pack: a term used to describe the write-ups, checksheets and packs that outline the purposes, know-how and duties of a post. It exists in folders and packs and is trained in on the person on the post. Page 142.

HCO: abbreviation for *Hubbard Communications Office.* HCO is the division of the org that builds, holds, maintains, mans and controls the organization. It hires personnel, assigns posts and gets staff hatted, routes incoming and outgoing communications, and maintains ethics and justice among Scientologists on staff and in the area. Page 42.

HCO Area Secretary (HAS): the head of the Hubbard Communications Office. The HAS is responsible for hats (write-up, checksheet and pack) and hat folders, org boards, personnel assignments, personnel procurement and readying personnel for posts, routing of bodies through the shop and routing forms for them, and she or he is responsible for internal and external communication, transport of people and goods as well as vehicles, inspecting the org, comm lines, posts and activities, for compiling the stats and posting them in OIC and for ethics being in, in the org, and all ethics actions. Page 279.

HCOB: abbreviation for *HCO Bulletin*. Page 132.

HCO Bulletin(s): a technical issue written by L. Ron Hubbard. These are the technical issue line. They are valid from first issue unless specifically cancelled. All data for auditing and courses is contained in HCOBs. They are red ink on white paper, consecutive by date.

HCO Exec Sec: abbreviation for *HCO Executive Secretary*. Page 276.

HCO Executive Letter: a type of issue written by L. Ron Hubbard between 1964 and 1966. HCO Executive Letters were usually a direct executive order or a request for a report or data or news or merely information. They were not policy. They are blue ink on green paper. Page 280.

HCO Executive Secretary (HCO Exec Sec): the executive in charge of the functions of the first three divisions of a Church of Scientology organization: Division 7 (Executive Division), Division 1 (Hubbard Communications Office) and Division 2 (Dissemination Division). Page 290.

HCO PL: abbreviation for *HCO Policy Letter*. Page 255.

HCO Policy Letter(s): a type of issue written by L. Ron Hubbard. This is a permanently valid issue of all Third Dynamic organization and Administrative Technology. These, regardless of date or age, form the know-how in running an organization or group or company. The bulk of hat material is made up from HCO PLs. They are printed in green ink on white paper. They are filed by consecutive date. Page 66.

HCO Secretary: another name for the *HCO Area Secretary*. Page 324.

head down, has his: a variation of the phrase *have one's nose down,* to work very hard and steadily at something. Page 254.

head-of-state: of the highest position in a national government. Page 184.

healing arts: professions in which one cures, heals or restores (someone or something) to good health. Examples include medical practitioners, physicians, surgeons, dentists, chiropractors, etc. *Art* here means a craft or profession, employment of a skilled nature (from the Latin *ars,* meaning skill). Page 216.

HE&R: abbreviation for *Human Emotion and Reaction*. Page 199.

hearing(s): in law, a preliminary examination of basic evidence and charges to determine whether a case should proceed to trial (a formal examination of the facts and law before a court of law in order to determine an issue), as in *"Persons attempting to sit in judgment on Scientology in hearings or attempting to investigate Scientology should be given no undue importance."* Page 219.

Hearing(s): any Scientology Justice proceeding in which data is obtained for further action or inaction, or evidence is presented for the purpose of establishing guilt or innocence, as in *"the condition is not over when the Hearings are over. It is over when that portion of the org has visibly statistically recovered."* Page 132.

heaven, to high: to an unusual or excessive level or degree. Alludes to something being so loud that it can be heard in a place as far away as heaven. Page 207.

heavy energy patterns: a reference to incidents on the track where strong electrical energy was used to overwhelm, impress and entrap a thetan. Page 175.

heckling: harassing with questions, challenges or objections designed to embarrass and disturb. Page 305.

hectares: units of land or a surface equal to 10,000 square meters or 2.471 acres. Page 164.

Hell's spent: one's pain or misery or its cause has been depleted of its strength or force so it no longer has the power to affect one. Page 56.

hem and haw: to hesitate or stammer in speaking; to avoid giving an answer. *Hem* is a representation of the sound made when one makes a sort of half-cough or clears his throat, and which is used to get someone's attention, warn someone or express hesitation or doubt. *Haw* is a sound expressing hesitation. Page 141.

Hershey: Milton Hershey (1857–1945), American businessman and philanthropist who founded the company that became the world's largest manufacturer of chocolate products. In 1903 Hershey built a factory in Pennsylvania to manufacture five-cent chocolate bars; the business so prospered that "Hershey" became virtually synonymous with chocolate in the US. In order to maintain his constantly expanding need for reliable workers, he began to build an entire town near the factory, including stores, schools, recreational facilities and a large amusement park. In 1909 he built

428

a trade school for orphan boys. Hershey was often criticized for his paternalism and for running a "company town." Page 40.

HGC: abbreviation for *Hubbard Guidance Center,* the Department of Processing in a Church of Scientology organization where auditing is delivered to preclears. Page 129.

high wine: wine which has a high percentage of alcohol. Used figuratively to refer to anything having a highly intoxicating or exhilarating effect. Page 152.

Hitler: Adolf Hitler (1889–1945), German dictator who dreamed of creating a master race that would rule for a thousand years. He began World War II (1939–1945), murdered millions of Jews and others considered "inferior" and left Germany in ruins. He committed suicide in 1945 when his defeat was imminent. Page 5.

hoarded: accumulated things of value and carefully guarded over them to keep them away from others. Page 153.

hocus-pocus: unnecessarily mysterious or elaborate activity or talk to cover up a deception. Page 41.

hold the fort: to act as a temporary substitute, to maintain a state of affairs. Page 228.

hold the line: maintain or support a position, viewpoint or the like, especially by being firm under pressure to change. Page 252.

Homo sapiens: human beings, especially in an aberrated state. Page 67.

Human Emotion and Reaction: the counter-emotions and reactions which aberrated human beings express when they are guided toward survival objectives. They are usually below 2.0 on the Tone Scale. Page 199.

humanoid(s): literally, someone resembling or having the form or appearance of a human. Page 150.

immemorial: extending back beyond memory, record or knowledge. Page 3.

imperialism: often used negatively to refer to the policy of extending a group's or nation's authority by territorial acquisition or by the establishment of economic and political authority over other individuals, groups or nations. Page 221.

improvident: failing to provide for future needs, lacking an anticipatory or future perception of things. Page 161.

in: things which should be there and are or should be done and are, are said to be "in," i.e., "We got scheduling in." Page 3.

inborn: existing in a person; native or natural. Page 58.

incapacitating: depriving of ability or strength; making incapable or unfit; disabling. Page 20.

indexes: scales that represent the level of something in comparison to something else or an earlier time; indicators or signs of something. Page 49.

indigence: extreme poverty in which the basic necessities of life are lacking. Page 47.

infanticide: the practice of killing newborn babies. Page 19.

infinity: 1. a quality or state of unlimited extent of time, space or quantity. Page 13.
2. the quality of having limitless duration. Page 16.

infinity symbol (∞): a mathematical symbol that represents infinity. Page 13.

info: short for *information*. Page 108.

info addressee: the person to whom information (such as a copy of a despatch) is sent to or addressed. Page 108.

infos: short for *informs*. Page 278.

in full bloom: a phrase meaning at its peak or point of highest development, strength; in full operation. This expression alludes to a flower that is in full bloom meaning fully open. Page 258.

inkling: a hint or imperfect or vague idea or notion of something; a slight suggestion or indication. Page 150.

in practice: in the realm of action; practically, actually, as a fact. Page 201.

Inquisition: referring to the *Spanish Inquisition,* a court appointed by the Roman Catholic Church to discover and suppress heresy (religious beliefs that the Roman Catholic Church considered to be false) and to punish heretics (those who practiced heresy). The Spanish Inquisition was in operation from the late 1400s until 1834, and was marked by the extreme severity and cruelty of its proceedings. Torture was used to obtain "confessions" and evidence against the accused. Thousands of people branded heretics were flogged, strangled to death or executed by burning, often on the dubious evidence of enemies. Page 183.

insidiously: having a gradual, cumulative and usually hidden destructive effect. Page 32.

insight: the ability to see clearly into the nature of a situation or subject. Page 139.

Inspection Officer: the post in the Department of Inspection and Reports in the Hubbard Communications Office whose duty is to inspect the status of various projects and orders and to report this to the Secretary of the division concerned. Page 274.

instant hatted: (said of someone put onto post and taking the load of it) told what his post title is and what he is supposed to be doing on that post, placed on the org board, work space, supplies, what his title is and what it means, org communication system and what he is supposed to produce on his post. The staff member is gotten producing what he is supposed to produce in some volume at once. Page 141.

intern(s): an auditor who is apprenticing under an experienced Case Supervisor in order to become a flubless auditor. An *intern* is an advanced graduate or a recent graduate in a professional field who is getting practical experience under the supervision of an experienced worker. Page 314.

International Board: the controlling board of all Scientology, in the mid-1960s. It was composed of three board members, the Chairman, Secretary and Treasurer, and had three divisions. Each member was the head of a division: the Chairman (Division 1, HCO); the Secretary (Division 2, Training and Processing); and the Treasurer (Division 3, Materiel and Accounts). Assistant Board Members were in charge of these same divisions in every Scientology organization. *See also* **Assistant Board Member** and **division.** Page 303.

International Justice Chief: the executive in Senior HCO International responsible for the standard application of Scientology Justice policies to staff and public. He is a protector of the Church and its tenets and membership. His duties include reviewing and approving (or not approving) any major justice actions to ensure that no injustice is done. He is assisted by Continental Justice Chiefs in each Continental Senior HCO. Page 269.

in the long run: in the end; in the course of time or experience. Page 217.

in the name of: under the designation or excuse of. Page 180.

into the fold: into a group or organization providing spiritual salvation. Literally from the fenced enclosure (fold) for sheep. Page 259.

intravenous: administered by injecting into the veins. Page 193.

Introspection Rundown: an auditing rundown which helps a preclear locate and correct those things which cause him to have his attention inwardly fixated. He then becomes capable of looking outward so he can see his environment, handle and control it. Page 194.

invalidating: depriving something or someone of its (their) force, value or effectiveness; making less of or nothing of. Page 171.

inveigh against: to speak or write against with great hostility in criticism of something. Page 264.

irresponsibility: denial of past participation, agreement or authorship. Page 37.

irrevocable: that cannot be changed; unalterable. Page 163.

Isabella: Isabella I (1451–1504), queen of Castile (a former kingdom comprising most of Spain) and wife of Ferdinand V (1452–1516), king of various Spanish regions in the late 1400s and early 1500s. In 1480, Ferdinand and Isabella instituted the Inquisition in Spain, putting it under royal control. Page 392.

-ism(s): a distinctive belief, theory, system or practice, from words with the ending "ism" such as colonialism, parasitism and the like. Page 246.

item(s): one of a pair of things, people, ideas, significances, purposes, etc., of equal mass and force, the significance of which the thetan has in opposition to his own intentions. Page 62.

Itsa Line(s): communication lines to the auditor where the preclear is saying what is, what is there, who is there, where it is, what it looks like, ideas about, decisions about, solutions to, things in his environment. Page 339.

javelin: a long thin piece of wood or metal with a pointed end, used as a weapon; spear. Page 42.

jockey: to direct or maneuver by cleverness or skill. Page 115.

jolly well: a chiefly British term meaning most certainly; used to add emphasis. Page 73.

judo: a Japanese system of combat and self-defense in which one uses balance and body weight, with minimal physical effort, to throw or hold one's opponent. From the Japanese *ju,* gentle and *do,* way. Page 250.

juggernaut: a large irresistible force or object that overrides everything in its path. Page 167.

jurisprudence: a system or body of law; a legal system. Page 337.

Justice: the action taken on the individual by the group when he fails to take actions himself to "get his own ethics in." Ethics consists simply of the actions an individual takes on himself. It is a personal thing. When one is ethical or "has his ethics in," it is by his own determinism and is done by himself. Page vii.

justiciary: one who maintains or executes justice; an administrator of justice. Page 354.

justification: a social mechanism a person uses when he has committed an overt act and withheld it. It is a means by which a person can relieve himself of consciousness of having done an overt act by trying to *lessen the overt.* This is done by finding fault or displacing blame. It is explaining away the most flagrant wrongnesses. The reasons overts are not overts to people are *justifications.* Page 36.

Justinian I: (A.D. 483–565) Roman emperor from A.D. 527 to 565, known as "Justinian the Great," and famous for his codification of Roman law and his regaining of earlier lost Roman territories. When he became emperor, he made his wife, Theodora, joint ruler. Page 161.

Keeper of Tech: short for *Keeper of Tech and Policy Knowledge,* the post in the Executive Division with the purpose to help LRH establish tech and policy in orgs fully and accurately and in full use and keep it there. Page 382.

key (someone) out: to cause someone to release or separate from the reactive mind or some portion of it. Page 198.

KGB: abbreviation for *Komitet Gosudarstvennoj Bezopasnosti* (Russian for "Committee for State Security"), the former Soviet Union's secret police, espionage and security agency. Its responsibilities included covert intelligence operations, the protection of Soviet political leaders and border patrol (to keep intruders out and citizens in). Page 256.

kicks in: activates; goes into effect. Page 5.

last-ditch: done finally in desperation to avoid defeat, failure, etc. Page 61.

leadership-survey-grade: of or related to one's score on a *leadership survey,* a test developed to help guide personnel appointments within Church of Scientology organizations. It consists of questions which test a person's current and potential leadership ability. Page 133.

learn the ropes: become familiar with the special procedures or techniques involved in something; the customary actions or practices of some area, field, etc.; the ways to get around and do things or get things done. This term derives from the days of sailing ships, wherein a sailor or apprentice had to become thoroughly familiar with handling the ropes that control the sails of a ship. Page 122.

legal test of sanity: a reference to a "test" used by many courts of law to determine the criminal responsibility of a defendant who claims insanity. Per this test, to be "sane" and thus responsible, the person must have been able to distinguish between right and wrong at the time of the commission of the criminal act. Page 58.

legion: a very large number of things. Originally a *legion* was a highly disciplined group of between 3,000 and 6,000 Roman soldiers. Page 159.

leisure class: the social strata consisting of those people who can afford not to work; the rich or wealthy. Page 243.

Lenin: Vladimir Ilyich Lenin (1870–1924), Russian leader of the communist revolution of 1917 who, through force and terror, then became dictator of the USSR (Union of Soviet Socialist Republics, a former group of Russian controlled states) from 1917 to 1924. Page 287.

Letter Registrar: the staff member in the Dissemination Division with the purpose to help LRH guide individuals by letter into correct channels to obtain Scientology and to increase the size of organizations. Page 238.

leveled: aimed, directed, pointed. Page 242.

libel: the action of publishing false and malicious statements about someone. Page 42.

Liberatress: a female liberator. A *liberator* is one who frees, such as a country from an oppressive government or domination or control by a foreign power. Page 149.

license: abusive disregard for what is considered right, proper, etc.; excessive liberty. Page 25.

light: manner in which something is regarded, taking into consideration what has just been said. Page 41.

lightning down on, call the: to invoke lightning to strike someone. Used figuratively in reference to the action of reprimanding, rebuking, scolding, etc. Page 236.

light of day, seen the: been brought forth or come into existence. Page 7.

lights go out: (the) end has come. Page 60.

light-year: a very long way in time, distance or some other quantity or quality. A *light-year* is the distance light travels in one year which is 5.88 trillion miles (9.46 trillion kilometers). Page 146.

line, hold the: maintain or support a position, viewpoint or the like, especially by being firm under pressure to change. Page 252.

line up: bring into line; straighten out. Page 200.

list: 1. (the auditor) writing down items said by the preclear in response to a question by the auditor. Page 197.
2. a prepared list, an assembly of the majority of things which can be wrong in a case, an auditing action or a session. The general types of prepared lists include: (a) *An analysis list:* This is a type of prepared list which analyzes a case broadly or analyzes a session. (b) *A direct auditing list:* Prepared lists exist which deliver direct auditing commands or questions which, run on the preclear, produce an auditing result. (c) *A correction list:* This type of list corrects an ongoing action. Page 330.

List One: a list of Scientology items which includes Scientology, Scientology organizations, an auditor, clearing, auditing, Scientologists, a session, an E-Meter, and so forth. Persons who Rock Slam on Scientology or associated items are security risks. A *List One* means an actual R/S on one of the items on this list. Page 261.

litigants: persons in a lawsuit or dispute. Page 356.

litigation: a contest in a court of law with the purpose of seeking a remedy, enforcing a right or settling a dispute. Page 154.

livingness: going along a certain course impelled by a purpose and with some place to arrive. Page 71.

lock: an analytical moment in which the perceptics of the engram are approximated, thus restimulating the engram or bringing it into action, the present time perceptics being erroneously interpreted by the reactive mind to mean that the same condition which produced physical pain once before is now again at hand. Locks are fully described in *Science of Survival*. Page 198.

locked in mortal combat: engaged in a struggle or fight to the death; *mortal* means intended to continue until someone dies. Used figuratively. Page 221.

lodged: made a formal complaint or appeal by handing the documents to the appropriate authority. Page 383.

logical: of or having to do with *logic,* a gradient scale of association of facts of greater or lesser similarity made to resolve some problem of the past, present or future, but mainly to resolve and predict the future. Logic is the combination of factors into an answer. Page 15.

long-arm: having policing duties that are far-reaching. Literally, *long-arm* means an arm that is lengthy, and thus can reach far. *Long-arm of the law* refers figuratively to the control or power of the authorities, especially when it seems to stretch over a wide area. Page 227.

long run, in the: in the end; in the course of time or experience. Page 217.

lost on him: have no effect or influence on him, such as through no understanding, perception, etc. Page 264.

LRH Comm: short for *LRH Communicator,* the executive in the Executive Division who ensures that the Church adheres to the policies and technical materials of L. Ron Hubbard. The LRH Communicator of each church also keeps the Office of LRH properties inventoried, safe and in good condition as a mark of respect for the Founder of the religion. Page 375.

lumberjack fighting: a rough fight between *lumberjacks,* men whose hard, physically demanding work consists of cutting down trees and transporting the wood (lumber) for use in building. A lumberjack fight is often portrayed as one that has no special rules, a participant using throws, kicks, punches and any other maneuvers to overcome his opponent. Page 250.

machine age: an era notable for its extensive use of mechanical devices, replacing human labor and homemade goods. Page 51.

Madison Avenue: a street in New York City that once was the address of many of the major advertising agencies and public relations firms of the United States. Over the years Madison Avenue has come to be synonymous with the advertising industry in general and the methods, practices, principles and attitudes of mass communications and advertising. Page 243.

magnet: a person that attracts. Page 180.

magnetize: to subdue or win by personal charm. Page 151.

majority rule: decision according to the wishes or votes of the majority members of a group or organization. Page 182.

make out: succeed; do well; accomplish what is planned. Page 246.

malaria: an infectious disease transmitted by the bite of infected mosquitoes, common in hot countries and characterized by severe chills and fever. If not treated it can cause death. Page 6.

malefactor: a person who does harm or evil, especially one who commits an offense against the law. Page 61.

Man: the human race or species, humankind; Mankind. Page vii.

man: 1. a human being, without regard to sex or age; a person. Page 4.
2. an adult male person, as distinguished from a boy or a woman. Page 11.

manner of the day: the current mode of action or fashion of procedure. Page 182.

masses: short for *mental masses. Mental mass* is the mass contained in the mental image pictures in the reactive mind. It has weight; very tiny, but it has weight, and it actually has size and shape. Its proportionate weight would be terribly slight compared to the real object which the person is making a picture of. Page 67.

mayhem: infliction of violent injury on a person or thing; deliberate violent destruction. Page 302.

mechanical arts: occupations requiring manual or mechanical skill and training; crafts in which skilled workers are employed. *Art* here means a craft or profession, employment of a skilled nature (from the Latin *ars,* meaning skill). Page 186.

Mechanical Definition: called "mechanical" as it is defined in terms of distance and position. *Mechanical* in this sense means interpreting or explaining the phenomena of the universe by referring to causally determined physical forces; mechanistic. Mechanical also applies to "acting or performing like a machine—automatic." Thus, a Mechanical Definition would be one which defined in terms of space or location such as "the car over by the old oak tree" or "the man who lives in the big house."

Here "the old oak tree" and "the big house" are fixed objects and the unfixed objects ("car," "man") are a sort of viewpoint. One has identified things by location. Page 64.

mechanism: 1. the agency or means by which an effect is produced or a purpose is accomplished, likened to the structure or system of parts in a mechanical device for carrying out some function or doing something. Page 5.
2. a structure or system (of parts, components, etc.) that together perform a particular function as would occur in a machine. Page 150.

mentalists: psychiatrists. Page 175.

MEST: a compound word made up of the first letters of Matter, Energy, Space and Time. A coined word for the physical universe. Page 13.

mews: makes the tiny, high-pitched sound of a cat or kitten. Page 392.

minion: a follower who gains favor or grace by unworthy means such as by being willing to do whatever demeaning actions are required by someone else. Page 154.

mis-emotional: exhibiting or displaying mis-emotion. *Mis-* means mistaken, wrong, incorrect. To say that a person was *mis*-emotional would indicate that the person did not display the emotion called for by the actual circumstances of the situation. Being mis-emotional would be synonymous with being irrational. Page 209.

mission: Scientology missions deliver the introductory and beginning services of Dianetics and Scientology in certain districts and territories. They are a front-line dissemination activity that exists to minister the religion at the grass-roots level. Page 302.

mock-up: to create. In Scientology, the word *mock-up* is used to mean, in essence, something which a person makes up himself. The term was derived from the World War II phrase which indicated a symbolized weapon or area of attack. Page 5.

moment: special importance or significance. Page 280.

monogamous: being married to only one person at a time. Page 205.

moral: able to know right from wrong in conduct; deciding and acting from that understanding. Page 3.

moral code: an agreed-upon code of right and wrong conduct. It is that series of agreements to which a person has subscribed to guarantee the survival of a group. The origin of a moral code comes about when it is discovered through actual experience that some act is more non-survival than pro-survival. The prohibition of this act then enters into the customs of the people and may eventually become a law. Page 25.

morals: a code of good conduct laid down out of the experience of the race to serve as a uniform yardstick for the conduct of individuals and groups. Page 3.

morass: a section of low, soft watery ground; a marsh or swamp. Used figuratively here for a confusing or unmanageable situation; something that traps or impedes one. Page 392.

mortal combat, locked in: engaged in a struggle or fight to the death; *mortal* means intended to continue until someone dies. Used figuratively. Page 221.

motivator(s): acts received by the person or individual causing injury, reduction or degradation of his beingness, person, associations or dynamics. A motivator is called a "motivator" because it tends to prompt an overt. It gives a person a motive or reason or justification for an overt. When a person commits an overt or overt of omission with no motivator, he tends to believe or pretends that he has received a motivator which does not in fact exist. This is a *false motivator.* Beings suffering from this are said to have "motivator hunger" and are often aggrieved over nothing. Page 5.

muck: a state of confusion, uncertainty or disorganization; a fouled-up condition. Page 145.

murder, get away with: figuratively, to commit an act for which one could be censured (have expressed strong disapproval or harsh criticism), without being punished. Page 238.

nail, on the: immediately and at once; when due, without any delay. From a practice used in the open markets of the Middle Ages, where it was customary to place all payments on a short pillar (known as a nail) in the presence of witnesses, so all could see that the money and change given was accurate and all agreements were kept. Hence, all payments made were "on the nail." Page 165.

Napoleon: Napoleon Bonaparte (1769–1821), French military leader. He rose to power in France by military force, declared himself emperor and conducted campaigns of conquest across Europe until his final defeat by armies allied against him in 1815. Half a million men died in the Napoleonic Wars (1799–1815). Page 27.

nationalism: the policy or doctrine of asserting the interest of one's own nation, viewed as separate from the interest of other nations or the common interests of all nations. *Nationalism* is often associated with the belief that one country is superior to all others. Page 243.

nattering: grumbling or complaining about something; finding fault with or griping about a person, place, situation, etc. Page 166.

nattery: inclined to complain or grumble. Page 67.

nay: a literary word used to introduce a stronger statement of truth, with the meaning not only so but; not only that but also. Page 59.

ne plus ultra: the utmost limit to which one can go or has gone; the furthest point reached or capable of being reached. The phrase is Latin and literally means no more beyond. Page 151.

neurotic: describing a person who is mainly harmful to himself by reason of his aberrations, but not to the point of suicide. Page 49.

Niagara Falls: a famous waterfall located on the Niagara River which is partly in Canada and partly in the US. Niagara has been the site of a number of dangerous stunts, including people going over the falls in a barrel. *Niagara Falls* is also used figuratively in such phrases as *to carry (something) over Niagara Falls,* meaning to lead (something) into ruin. Page 259.

noble: showing admirable qualities or high moral principles and ideals. Page 41.

non-survival: from *non,* implying negation or absence of and *survival.* Hence, *non-survival* is a negation or absence of survival, the act of remaining alive, of continuing to exist, of being alive. Page 19.

Not-isness: trying to create out of existence, by postulate or force, something which one knows priorly exists. Page 45.

notoriety: a state of being widely and publicly known; famous. Page 219.

nought: alternate spelling of *naught,* nothing at all. Page 53.

obliquely: (said of speech, action, etc.) in a manner that is roundabout, indirect and not straightforward, likened to being divergent from a straight line or course. Page 159.

oblivion: a state of being completely unaware and unconscious. Page 59.

obsessive: pertaining to or resembling an obsession (the domination of one's thoughts or feelings by a persistent idea, image, desire, etc.). Page 176.

occasioned: brought about; caused. Page 106.

offhand: without previous thought, study, preparation or research. Page 345.

Office of LRH: the department in the Executive Division headed by the LRH Communicator, responsible for seeing that the organization adheres to the policies and technical materials of L. Ron Hubbard so that the organization expands. Part of its duties include authorizing the orders, directives, programs and promotion necessary to expansion, as well as the Findings of locally convened justice bodies. Page 279.

officer: a reference to an executive in a Scientology organization. An *executive* is defined as anyone in charge of an org, part of an org, a division, a department or a section. Page 289.

off-line: a form of Dev-T generated when a despatch is sent to the wrong person, most commonly when a staff member writes a despatch to himself but routes it to somebody else. It is also despatches or orders passed in a manner to deny information on record. Page 272.

offloads: acts or instances of removing or discharging persons from service. Page 374.

off-origin: a form of Dev-T generated when a terminal originates something not its hat. Page 272.

off-policy: 1. pertaining to not applying Scientology procedures. Page 269.
2. a form of Dev-T generated when a despatch is originated by or forwarded by someone who should know that the matter is already covered by policy. Page 272.

off the rails: out of the correct, normal or usual condition; not functioning, working or acting correctly. This phrase alludes to a train that has run off the railway tracks and is literally off the rails. Page 4.

ogres: man-eating monsters in fairy tales, hence persons who are like monsters. Page 173.

OIC: abbreviation for *Organization Information Center,* a large display of the graphs of each of the key statistics of a Scientology org and is a solution to the problems of running a multi-department organization. It is updated weekly and used by executives to get a complete picture of the org, forecast emergencies, correct small bogs, etc. Page 228.

oil crisis: a shortage of oil occurring in the United States and certain European countries beginning in the early 1970s. The shortage was caused mainly by restrictions placed on oil trade by the Organization of Petroleum Exporting Countries (OPEC), which regulated the amount of oil produced by its member countries and set the prices for its export. The restrictions were intended to punish the United States and some of its allies for supporting Israel in its 1973 conflict with the Arab states. The situation caused widespread panic, severe shortages of gasoline and extremely inflated prices. The crisis continued at varying levels through the 1970s and by 1980 oil prices were ten times those of 1973. Page 22.

old-old-*old* hat: very, very behind the times; extremely old-fashioned. Page 246.

one for one: in every single case or instance. Page 144.

1.1: a numerical value assigned to the emotional state on the Tone Scale of covert hostility. Page 46.

on every hand: on all sides; all around. Page 48.

on the nail: immediately and at once; when due, without any delay. From a practice used in the open markets of the Middle Ages, where it was customary to place all payments on a short pillar (known as a nail) in the presence of witnesses, so all could see that the money and change given was accurate and all agreements were kept. Hence, all payments made were "on the nail." Page 165.

on the way out: going down in status or condition; dying. Page 19.

opposite side of the coin: the other side, aspect or point of view of something. This phrase comes from the fact that a coin has two sides, usually with a different appearance on each. Page 150.

order of the day: the characteristic or dominant custom, feature or activity of a particular time. Page 391.

org: abbreviation for *organization,* by which is meant a Church of Scientology. Page 72.

organism: a living thing or any organized body resembling a living thing. Page 15.

Organization Exec Sec (OES): the executive in a Church of Scientology organization who is in charge of the functions of Division 3 (Treasury Division), Division 4 (Technical Division) and Division 5 (Qualifications Division). Page 258.

org board: short for *organizing board,* a board used in Churches of Scientology that displays the functions, duties, sequences of action and authorities of the organization. It is laid out in an exact pattern that consists of nine divisions with each division subdivided into three or four departments which are in turn composed of a number of sections and then units. Page 141.

Org Rudiments: the basic administrative and technical organizational actions that when implemented put an org there and cause it to rapidly expand. There are seventeen Org Rudiments and they are done in order, getting one in before going on to the next. Page 255.

OT: short for *Operating Thetan,* a being who is knowing and willing cause over life, thought, matter, energy, space and time. Page 67.

OT Levels (sections, courses, etc.): the advanced Scientology training and auditing actions that enable a Clear to reach the state of Operating Thetan. Page 264.

out: things which should be there and aren't or should be done and aren't, are said to be "out." Page 5.

out-ethics: an action or situation in which an individual is involved, or something the individual does, which is contrary to the ideals, best interests and survival of his dynamics. Page 5.

outmoded: not acceptable by present standards; obsolete. Page 25.

outpoints: plural of *outpoint,* any one datum that is offered as true that is in fact found to be illogical. "I am a Swiss citizen" as a statement from someone who has had a German passport found in his baggage would be an example. Page 139.

"outsight": to have or use the capacity of seeing that which is external. Page 151.

overt: a harmful act or a transgression against the moral code of a group is called an "overt act" or an "overt." When a person does something that is contrary to the moral code he has agreed to, or when he omits to do something that he should have done per that moral code, he has committed an overt act. An overt act violates what was agreed upon. It is an act by the person or individual leading to the injury, reduction or degradation of another, others or their beingness, persons, possessions, associations or dynamics. It can be intentional or unintentional. Page 35.

overt act–motivator sequence: when a person commits an overt, he will then believe he's got to have a motivator or that he has had a motivator. For instance, if he hits somebody, he will tell you immediately that he has been hit by the person, even when he has not been. Or when one has a motivator, he is liable to hang himself by committing an overt. If Joe hits Bill, he now believes he should be hit by Bill. More importantly, he will actually get a somatic to prove he *has* been hit by Bill, even though Bill hasn't hit him. He will make this law true regardless of the actual circumstances. And people go around all the time justifying, saying how they've been "hit by Bill, hit by Bill, hit by Bill." Page 36.

overt of omission: a failure to act resulting in the injury, reduction or degradation of another or others or their beingness, persons, possessions or dynamics. Page 36.

PABs: abbreviation for *Professional Auditor's Bulletins,* a series of bulletins written by L. Ron Hubbard between 10 May 1953 and 15 May 1959. The contents of the bulletins carried the newest technical advances, reprints of the latest processes and technical issues released. Their intent was to give the professional auditor and his preclears the best possible processes and processing available at the moment it became available. Page 329.

painted white: made to look *white,* morally pure and innocent, as by being painted, covered over with a coating or layer that conceals. Page 259.

pamphleteered: wrote and/or issued pamphlets. *Pamphlets* are printed works consisting of a few pages stitched or stapled together. The term can also mean a short essay or writing on a controversial subject of temporary interest which excites public attention at the time of its appearance; hence, a writing intended to publish one's own views on a particular question, or in some cases to attack the views of another. Page 160.

parasitic: of or relating to something that survives by taking its power from another source while contributing nothing in return. Page 222.

parasitism: the practice of living on or at the expense of another. Page 246.

parked: placed in a certain position for a period of time. Page 249.

part and parcel: an indivisible element in something. Page 23.

passivity: the quality or condition of submitting or obeying without resisting. Page 251.

pathology: any condition that is a deviation from the normal healthy condition, such as a disease. Page 196.

pause, given: caused to hesitate or reconsider, as from surprise or doubt. Page 61.

Pavlov: Ivan Petrovich Pavlov (1849–1936), Russian physiologist, noted for his dog experiments. Pavlov presented food to a dog, while a bell was sounded. After repeating this procedure several times, the dog (in anticipation) would salivate (produce saliva) at the sound of the bell, whether or not food was presented. Pavlov erroneously concluded that all acquired habits, even the higher mental activity of Man, depended on such conditioned reflexes (automatic and involuntary movements as the result of some stimuli). Page 60.

pay: give or offer, as in return or exchange for something received, as in *"they pay only with death."* Used figuratively. Page 251.

pc: abbreviation for *preclear,* from pre-Clear, a person not yet Clear; generally a person being audited, who is thus on the road to Clear; a person who, through Scientology and Dianetic processing, is finding out more about himself and life. Page 46.

peddle: sell something illegal, especially drugs. Page 24.

peer: equal standing in rank, quality and ability. Page 150.

penny soldier: a coined phrase meaning a soldier who is paid a small amount or the least amount of money for his services. *Penny* means costing a penny or of the value or price of a penny; a very little or least amount of wealth, money, etc. Page 155.

period to, put: a variation of *put a period to,* meaning to cause to end, stop or cease. Page 251.

permissiveness: the quality or state of complete tolerance or lenience without control, such as letting someone do whatever he or she wishes. Page 267.

perpetrated: committed or performed. Page 26.

phantom: that can be felt or experienced, but which is not physically there. Page 53.

Phase I: when beginning a new activity an executive single-hands while he trains his staff. When he has people producing, functioning well and hatted, he then enters the next phase, Phase II—running an established activity; an executive gets people to get the work done. By "single-handing" one means do it himself, being the one responsible for actually handling things. Phase I occurs when an executive is forming up his personnel. Page 106.

phenomenon: an observable fact or event. Page 39.

plaintiff: one who begins a lawsuit against another person (defendant) in a court of law to obtain a remedy for an injury to his rights. Page 6.

play it all the way out: to bring something to an end wholly and completely. Page 46.

Policy Letter(s): *HCO Policy Letter,* a type of issue written by L. Ron Hubbard. This is a permanently valid issue of all Third Dynamic organization and Administrative Technology. These, regardless of date or age, form the know-how in running an organization or group or company. The bulk of hat material is made up from HCO PLs. They are printed in green ink on white paper. They are filed by consecutive date. Page vii.

politician Jiggs: a made-up name for a politician. A *politician* is a seeker or holder of public office who is often more concerned about winning favor or retaining power than about maintaining principles. Page 165.

portfolio: originally a movable (portable) receptacle for holding loose papers, maps, music, drawings, documents, etc. Figuratively, a minister of state, as he would possess the portfolio of the position and have the documents, papers, etc., connected with that sphere of responsibility. By extension, then, any such official position. Page 159.

postulates: conclusions, decisions or resolutions made by the individual himself on his own self-determinism on data of the past, known or unknown. Postulates are always known. They are made upon the evaluation of data by the individual or on impulse without data. They resolve a problem of the past, decide on problems or observations in the present or set a pattern for the future. Postulates are described in *Advanced Procedure and Axioms.* Page 45.

posturing: behaving in a way that is artificial or affected as when intending to impress others. Page 162.

Potential Trouble Source (PTS): somebody who is connected with a Suppressive Person who is invalidating him, his beingness, his life. The person is a Potential Trouble Source because he is connected to the Suppressive Person. Potential Trouble Source means the person is going to go up and fall down. And he is a trouble source because he is going to get upset and because he is going to make trouble. And he really does make trouble. That's very carefully named. Page 171.

power push: a variation of the expression *power play,* meaning a strategy or maneuver employed by an individual or group, using influence and pressure to gain control, authority or command of something. Page 304.

powers that be: those in command; the authorities. Page 391.

practice license: to engage in abusive disregard for what is considered right, proper, etc.; to take excessive liberty. Page 25.

precipitated: brought on quickly or abruptly. Page 40.

preclear (pc): from pre-Clear, a person not yet Clear; generally a person being audited, who is thus on the road to Clear; a person who, through Scientology and Dianetic processing, is finding out more about himself and life. Page 39.

pre-OT: a thetan beyond the state of Clear who, through upper-level auditing, is advancing to the full state of Operating Thetan (OT). Page 67.

present time: of or relating to the time which is now and which becomes the past almost as rapidly as it is observed. It is also a term loosely applied to the environment existing in now as in "the preclear came up to present time," meaning the preclear became aware of the existing matter, energy, space and time of now. Page 97.

present time problem (PTP): a special problem that exists in the physical universe "now" on which the preclear has his attention fixed. It is any set of circumstances that so engages the attention of the preclear that he feels he should be doing something about it instead of being audited. Page 218.

process: 1. a systematic and technically exact series of steps, actions or changes to bring about a specific and definite result. In Scientology, a precise series of techniques or exercises applied by a practitioner to help a person find out more about himself and his life and to improve his condition. Page 37.

2. to apply Dianetics and Scientology processes to. Page 48.

Process Check: another name for a *Confessional,* a procedure in Scientology whereby an individual is able to confess his withholds and the overt acts underlying them. Page 56.

processing: a *process* is a systematic and technically exact series of steps, actions or changes to bring about a specific and definite result. In Scientology, *processing* is applying a precise series of techniques or exercises by a practitioner to help a person find out more about himself and his life and to improve his condition. Page 41.

profiteer: one who gains some advantage or acquires something of value—most often something material. In its use here, it refers to someone who takes advantage of a period of scarcity (such as during natural disasters, war, etc.) to make excessive profit from those items considered vital or necessary to survival, such as weapons, food, medical supplies, etc. Page 153.

prone: having a natural tendency or inclination to something; likely to (do something). Page 182.

proneness: tendency; character or quality that makes it likely something will happen. Page 199.

proofed: made resistant or not capable of being affected. Page 373.

pro-survival: from *pro,* in favor of, and *survival.* Hence, *pro-survival* is something in favor of or in support of survival, the act of remaining alive, of continuing to exist, of being alive. Page 25.

protracted: lasting or drawn out for a long time. Page 317.

provident: foreseeing wants and needs and making plans and provisions to supply them; wise and careful in providing for future needs; economical. Page 153.

Provisional: the status of a staff member who has completed study and examination of Staff Status 1 (basic policy on the organizing board and staff regulations). A staff member given a Provisional rating may have recourse to Ethics and have an Ethics Hearing if dismissed. He may be transferred to other divisions without a Hearing if his division is overmanned. Page 367.

psychopathic: characterized by severe anti-social behavior and obsessive desire to destroy. Page 251.

psychos: short for *psychotics. See* psychotic. Page 264.

psychotic: describing a person who is physically or mentally harmful to those about him out of proportion to the amount of use he is to them. Page 49.

PTP: abbreviation for *present time problem,* a special problem that exists in the physical universe "now" on which the preclear has his attention fixed. It is any set of circumstances that so engages the attention of the preclear that he feels he should be doing something about it instead of being audited. Page 308.

PTS C/S-1: Case Supervisor Instruction Number One, so called as it is the first action taken with the preclear before auditing is begun to handle the PTS condition. Case Supervisor Instruction Number One instructs the preclear on the basic definitions and procedures of an auditing action he is about to begin. Page 211.

PTS (Potential Trouble Source): somebody who is connected with a Suppressive Person who is invalidating him, his beingness, his life. The person is a Potential Trouble Source because he is connected to the Suppressive Person. Potential Trouble Source means the person is going to go up and fall down. And he is a trouble source because he is going to get upset and because he is going to make trouble. And he really does make trouble. That's very carefully named. Page vii.

Public Division(s): the portion of a Church of Scientology organization which is responsible for a wide, expanding and controlled field. These three divisions are Division 6A, which is a contact activity that interests people, delivering free introductory services, selling books and recorded LRH lectures; Division 6B, which delivers paid services, as well as offering courses and auditing to Scientologists to keep them active, interested and involved; and Division 6C, which runs all kinds of groups and Field Staff Members, staging events, handling PR and caring for the many aspects of keeping a field active and interested. Page 330.

Public Executive Secretary (PES): the executive in charge of the functions of the Public Divisions: Division 6A, Division 6B and Division 6C. Page 385.

pueblo: in Spanish America, a town or village. Page 153.

pulverized: subjected (someone) to a crushing defeat. Literally, *pulverize* means to crush or grind something into a powder. Page 250.

put period to: a variation of *put a period to,* meaning to cause to end, stop or cease. Page 251.

Qualifications: short for *Qualifications Division,* the division of a Church of Scientology organization which examines correctly students and pcs to ensure they have actually made it, issues the certificates to those who actually have and reviews those who haven't until they can make it, cares for staff as individual staff members, corrects the whole org by correcting its staff with the result of high quantity and quality production to the realization of an expanding org. Page 326.

Qual Sec: short for *Qualifications Secretary,* the head of the Qualifications Division. The Qual Sec corrects the whole org and its products and field by manning the Qual Division and training Qual staff and by making every Qual function actually occur. Page 365.

quandary: a state of uncertainty. Page 188.

quick knife: a coined term for a person who rapidly uses a knife to do away with someone. Page 160.

quinine: a bitter-tasting drug used to treat certain forms of malaria (an infectious disease that can cause death if not treated). Page 6.

rails: denounces, protests against, or attacks somebody or something in bitter or harsh language. Page 336.

rancor: bitter hate or ill will; resentment. Page 387.

ransomed: made to pay a sum of money demanded for the release of a prisoner, kidnapped person, captured goods, etc. Page 161.

ratifier: one who gives formal approval to something so as to make it valid and legally operative. Page 154.

rationale: the reasoning or principle that underlies or explains a particular course of action or phenomenon. Page 171.

rationality: power to draw conclusions that enable one to understand the world about him and relate such knowledge to the attainment of personal and common ends; power to reason or being in accordance with what reason dictates as being right, wise, sensible, etc. Page 4.

Reach and Withdraw: a process in which a person reaches for things and then withdraws from them. Reach and Withdraw is a method for getting a person familiarized and in communication with things in the environment so that he can be more at cause over and in control of them. Page 143.

reactively: irrationally; in a manner that shows one is affected by the reactive mind. Page 26.

reactive mind: that portion of a person's mind which works on a totally stimulus-response basis (given a certain stimulus it gives a certain response), which is not under his volitional control, and which exerts force and the power of command over his awareness, purposes, thoughts, body and actions. Page 319.

reasonable: 1. such an amount as is judged to be appropriate or suitable to the circumstances or purpose. Page 15.
2. using or showing reason or sound judgment; sensible. Page 19.
3. being or remaining within the bounds of reason; not extreme; not excessive. Page 216.
4. characterized by giving or accepting faulty explanations. People who are "reasonable" cannot recognize outpoints when they see them and so try to make everything illogical seem logical. Page 231.

rebuked: uttered sharp and direct disapproval of; beat down, silenced or restrained by sharp or severe criticisms or disapprovals. Page 157.

recants: makes an open confession of error. Page 316.

recluse: a person who lives alone and avoids going outside or talking to other people. Page 163.

recovers: recoveries. Page 199.

recriminations: accusations made against someone who has brought previous accusations. Page 288.

Reges: short for *Registrars*. Page 129.

registered post: a reference to *registered mail,* a method of sending mail where it is recorded at the post office, and at each successive point of handling, to guarantee safe delivery. Mail sent in this manner is insured against loss, theft or damage during transmission. *Post* is another word for *mail* (chiefly a British use). Page 300.

Registrars: staff members in the Dissemination Division who enlighten individuals about Dianetics and Scientology services and sign them up for training and auditing. Page 120.

reinstated to grace: *grace* is a state or condition of being regarded with favor by someone. *Reinstated to grace* would be to return to a former condition, as if having been forgiven for one's transgressions. Page 259.

render: to make, to cause to be or become of a certain nature, quality, etc. Page 26.

reprehensibly: in a manner deserving strong disapproval or criticism. Page 23.

repressed: forcibly subdued; kept under control. Page 174.

responsibility: the nonrecognition and denial of the right of intervention between oneself and any being, idea, matter, energy, space, time or form, and the assumption of full right of determination over it. Full Responsibility is not *fault,* it is recognition of being *cause.* Page 37.

Responsibility (Process): a process which addresses one's ability to be responsible. Page 43.

restimulation: the reactivation of a past incident by the appearance of a similarity to the content of the past incident. Page 47.

restimulator(s): an approximation of the reactive mind's content or some part thereof perceived in the environment of the organism. Page 150.

review: an action done in the *Department of Review* to repair or correct auditing or training difficulties. Page 132.

Review: short for *Department of Review,* that department in the Qualifications Division which has the entire purpose of repair and correction of auditing and training difficulties. Page 132.

rigging: assembling and adjusting to make ready for operation. Page 248.

rocket ride: the condition wherein someone or something rises or soars rapidly, likened to a rocket. Page 116.

Rock Slam: the crazy, irregular, *left-right* slashing motion of the needle on the E-Meter dial. Rock Slams repeat left and right slashes unevenly and savagely, faster than the eye easily follows. The needle is frantic. A Rock Slam (R/S) means a hidden evil intention on the subject or question under auditing or discussion.

Rock Slammers: individuals who Rock Slam on an E-Meter. Page 261.

Rodil, General: José Ramon Rodil (1789–1853), Spanish general and commander of the last stronghold (Callao fortress) of the Spanish royalist forces in South America, during its liberation from Spain in the 1800s. The stronghold guarded the major seaport of Callao in Peru. Although Peru had been liberated from Spanish control in 1821 by Simón Bolívar, Rodil, who took command of the fortress in 1824, refused to give up his position. Bolívar offered generous terms of surrender, but Rodil refused. Bolívar thus engaged in a siege of the fortress until Rodil was finally defeated in 1826. Page 155.

Rodriguez, Simón: a priest and beloved teacher of Simón Bolívar. Rodriguez lived in many countries and was a master of many languages. He dabbled in revolution while a priest and was caught and exiled. Possessing a high degree of learning, Rodriguez met Bolívar at an early age and became his tutor. Bolívar said of his teacher, "Rodriguez formed in my heart the ideas of liberty, justice, greatness and beauty." Page 152.

roll: move forward; proceed or continue successfully. Page 146.

roller coaster: to move (steeply) up and down, rise and fall. From the literal meaning, a steep, sharply curving elevated railway with small open passenger cars that is operated at high speeds as a ride in an amusement park. Page 117.

Roller Coaster: the state or condition of a case that betters then worsens. The person is doing well or he is not doing well, and then is doing well, and then is not doing well. That is a Roller Coaster. And when he is not doing well he is sometimes ill. A Roller Coaster is *always* connected to a Suppressive Person and will not get steady gain until the Suppressive is found on the case. Page 172.

romantic novels: novels representing heroic or marvelous deeds, romantic exploits, usually in a historical or imaginary setting. Page 23.

Roosevelt: Franklin Delano Roosevelt (1882–1945), thirty-second president of the United States (1933–1945). The early part of his presidency is remembered for a group of government programs known as the New Deal, designed to improve conditions for people during the economic depression in the US (which began in 1929 and lasted through the 1930s). These programs expanded governmental control over the American economy, but did not bring about the desired economic recovery. Page 243.

round the bend: an expression meaning insane, crazy. Page 226.

Rousseau: Jean Jacques Rousseau (1712–1778), French writer and political philosopher. He believed that Man was essentially good and equal in his natural state, but had been corrupted by civilization (the introduction of science, commerce, property and so forth). Rousseau believed there was a general will which rational men would choose for the common good. Government then would bring about a coordination or harmony of this general will with the wishes of the people—but the sovereignty and power of the government would reside with the people. Rousseau's principles inspired the revolutionaries who toppled the French monarchy, justifying a reign of terror and bringing eventual chaos to France. Page 158.

route, go the: to go all the way, to go the full distance; to continue to the end. Page 128.

royalists: persons who support government by a monarch, instead of by an elected parliament, particularly in times of a rebellion or civil war. In this case, the supporters of the Spanish king. Page 152.

ruling passion: a chief or predominating object of intense interest in a particular subject or activity. Page 19.

rumormonger: one who spreads false or damaging reports concerning the character or reputation of others. *Monger* literally means one who trades or sells something. Page 179.

rundown: a series of steps which are auditing actions and processes designed to handle a specific aspect of a case and which have a known End Phenomena. Example: Introspection Rundown. Page 194.

sabered: struck, hit or injured with a saber (a heavy, one-edged military sword, especially used by cavalrymen). Used figuratively, to express something brought about or created with much effort, force, or even violence as would be done using a saber. Page 164.

sadism: a type of behavior in which pleasure is obtained from hurting others and making them suffer physically or mentally. Page 6.

salt: to intersperse with; scatter among. Page 247.

sanity, legal test of: a reference to a "test" used by many courts of law to determine the criminal responsibility of a defendant who claims insanity. Per this test, to be "sane" and thus responsible, the person must have been able to distinguish between right and wrong at the time of the commission of the criminal act. Page 58.

San Martín: José de Martín (1778–1850), Argentinian revolutionary leader who led an army across the Andes and overthrew the

Spanish in Chile in 1818. In 1820 he conducted an expedition to liberate Peru. He defeated the Spanish army and occupied Lima, the capital, where he declared independence and was appointed protector of the country. But further Spanish resistance a year later forced him to request military aid from Simón Bolívar. Page 157.

Santander: Francisco de Paula Santander (1792–1840), Colombian revolutionary who served under Simón Bolívar to liberate Colombia from Spanish rule. He was later the vice-president and undermined Bolívar's authority, stirred up mutiny and was behind a failed attempt to assassinate him. Page 154.

scathing: bitterly severe. Page 46.

science: knowledge; comprehension or understanding of facts or principles, classified and made available in work, life or the search for truth. A science is a connected body of demonstrated truths or observed facts systematically organized and bound together under general laws. It includes trustworthy methods for the discovery of new truth within its domain and denotes the application of scientific methods in fields of study previously considered open only to theories based on subjective, historical or undemonstrable, abstract criteria. The word *science,* when applied to Scientology, is used in this sense—the most fundamental meaning and tradition of the word—and not in the sense of the *physical* or *material* sciences. Page 297.

Scientology: Scientology addresses the thetan (the spirit). Scientology is used to increase spiritual freedom, intelligence, ability and produce immortality. It is further defined as the study and handling of the spirit in relationship to itself, universes and other life. Page 3.

Scientology Axioms: statements of natural laws on the order of those of the physical sciences. There are fifty-eight Scientology Axioms in addition to the one hundred and ninety-four Axioms of Dianetics which preceded them. Page 63.

Scotland Yard: the general term for the headquarters of the London Metropolitan Police, situated in central London, England. The original site of the headquarters was a twelfth-century palace used for visiting Scottish royalty; thus the police facilities became known as *Scotland Yard.* Page 256.

S-C-S: abbreviation for *Start-Change-Stop,* the three parts of control. To "run good S-C-S" means to control something positively and well. Page 339.

Sea Organization: a fraternal religious order consisting of Scientologists who have pledged themselves to eternal service to Scientology and achieving the goals and purpose of the religion. The Sea Organization derives its name from its beginnings in 1967 when L. Ron Hubbard, having retired from his position as Executive Director in 1966, set to sea with a handful of veteran Scientologists to continue his research into the upper levels of spiritual awareness and ability. Initially, Sea Org members lived and worked aboard a fleet of ships. Today the majority of Sea Organization members are located on land. Appropriate to their high level of dedication and commitment, Sea Org members bear a responsibility unique within Scientology. They are the only Scientologists entrusted to minister the advanced levels of training and auditing and the only individuals who may hold the senior ecclesiastic positions in the Scientology hierarchy. No formalized structure exists for the Sea Org. Rather, each member is subject to the established lines of corporate and organizational seniority and authority of the church organization in which the member works. Despite its name, the Sea Organization is neither an "organization" nor "entity." It is, instead, the manifestation of a commitment.

Search and Discovery: a procedure used to find the suppressions the person has had in life. It locates the Suppressives on the case and is used to nullify the influence of Suppressive Persons or things on a case so the person will be able to be processed and will no longer be PTS. Page 181.

Secretary: a title designating the head of a division in a Church of Scientology organization. Page 279.

sedatives: drugs that are primarily used to induce drowsiness and sleep. Sedatives are habit-forming and can cause severe addiction problems. Page 29.

seen the light of day: been brought forth or come into existence. Page 7.

send to find: have a messenger go (or a message be delivered) in order to inquire about something. Page 108.

Senior HCO: a network that exists to establish, protect and maintain HCOs and ensure LRH policy concerning HCO's functions is applied. The Senior HCO Network is headed by the Senior HAS International and consists of Senior HCO International and Senior HCO offices in each continent. Page 339.

sequestrated: seized property of an enemy. *Sequester* is to separate and possess an owner's property or to seize the property of an individual for the state. Page 160.

session(s): an *auditing session,* a period in which an auditor and preclear are in a quiet place where they will not be disturbed. The auditor gives the preclear certain and exact commands which the preclear can follow. Page 39.

shifts: any available means used to handle a difficult circumstance. Page 153.

shoot: figuratively, to direct disciplinary action, censure, etc., at someone. Page 231.

shore patrolmen: members of the *shore patrol,* the military police organization of the US Navy responsible for the conduct of sailors on land. This organization assists military personnel, protects them from harm and investigates accidents or offenses in which they may be involved. Page 166.

show on the road, get the: to get (an organization, plan, project, etc.) started and operating; to put (a strategy, idea, etc.) into motion. Page 237.

single-handing: the action of doing the work oneself, being the one responsible for actually handling things. Page 110.

skipper: a casual name given to the captain or master of any vessel, especially a small trading, merchant or fishing vessel. Informally used to refer to anyone who is the head of any activity. Page 166.

slander: a false tale or report maliciously uttered with the intent to injure the reputation of another. Page 42.

slanging matches: exchanges of insults and abuse between two parties. To *slang* means to attack with abusive language. A *match* is a contest or competition of some kind. Page 278.

sleeping drafts: drinks containing a drug that is meant to help somebody sleep. (Also spelled *draughts.*) Page 194.

smoke out: force out into public view or knowledge; reveal. Page 253.

snap and pop: a coined phrase meaning to move swiftly or briskly; to act quickly, with energy, alertness and efficiency. This is formed from the word *snap,* which refers to the condition of being vigorous in spirit, mind or body; alert, energetic, and *pop* which means to move quickly and swiftly with agility; to dart or jump. Page 113.

socialism: an economic system in which the production and distribution of goods are controlled by the government rather than by individuals. Page 221.

socialized: established or developed according to the theories or principles of socialism. *Socialized medicine* is a system of medical care that is financed and administered by the state. Page 221.

soggy stream that's history: spiritless, heavy, dull or stupid series of events that make up history. Page 53.

somatic: *somatic* means, actually, *bodily* or *physical.* Because the word *pain* is restimulative, and because the word *pain* has in the past led to a confusion between physical pain and mental pain, the word *somatic* is used to denote physical pain or discomfort of any kind. It can mean actual pain, such as that caused by a cut or a blow; or it can mean discomfort, as from heat or cold; it can mean itching—in short, anything physically uncomfortable. It does not include mental discomfort such as grief. Hard breathing would not be a somatic. *Somatic* means a non-survival physical state of being. Page 36.

song, what a: a coined phrase used to show that something is extremely easy or effortless. Page 122.

sordid: demonstrating the worst aspects of human nature such as immorality, selfishness and greed. Page 45.

sortie: a sudden or rapid issuing of a body of troops from a besieged location, attacking those who are besieging. Generally applied to any rapid attack or harassment by troops (in a defensive position) against an attacking enemy. Page 155.

SP: abbreviation for *Suppressive Person,* a person who suppresses other people in his vicinity. A Suppressive Person will goof up or vilify any effort to help anybody and particularly knife with violence anything calculated to make human beings more powerful or more intelligent. The whole rationale of the Suppressive Person (SP) is built on the belief that if anyone got better, the SP would be for it as the others could overcome him, then. He is fighting a battle he once fought and never stopped fighting. He is in an incident. Present time people are mistaken by him for past, long-gone enemies. Therefore, he never really knows what he is fighting in present time, so just fights. Page vii.

Spanish Inquisition: a court appointed by the Roman Catholic Church to discover and suppress heresy (religious beliefs that the Roman Catholic Church considered to be false) and to punish heretics (those who practiced heresy). The Spanish Inquisition was in operation from the late 1400s until 1834, and was marked by the extreme severity and cruelty of its proceedings. Torture was used to obtain "confessions" and evidence against the accused. Thousands of people branded heretics were flogged, strangled to death or executed by burning, often on the dubious evidence of enemies. Page 392.

sparks will fly: excited action, activity, friction or heated words are going to occur as a result of some circumstance, situation, confrontation, etc. Page 198.

species: a group or class of animals or plants having certain common and permanent characteristics which clearly distinguish it from other groups and which can breed with one another. Page 21.

square one: the initial stage or starting point. Page 145.

squirrel(s): 1. somebody who goes off into weird practices or alters Scientology. Page 299.

2. go off into weird practices or alter Scientology. Page 309.

3. of or pertaining to materials, procedures, etc., which have been alter-ised and thus are unworkable. Page 311.

stable datum: that one factor, particular (fact, detail) or datum selected which keeps things from being in a confusion and on which other datums are aligned. Page 380.

Staff Section Officer (SSO): the staff member in the Qualifications Division with the purpose to help Ron make real staff members. The Staff Section Officer has total authority over who will be processed and what they will be processed on, who will be trained and what they will be trained on, and has authority over all persons who are engaged on those duties or at the time they are engaged on those duties. Page 262.

staff status: a number giving the value and promotion *eligibility* of a staff member in a Church of Scientology organization. The numbers run from zero to ten. They designate the type of post to which a person may be promoted or the status of the person. The status numbers most important to a new staff member are 0 (zero),

1 and 2 (0 = Temporary, 1 = Provisional and 2 = Permanent). Above that are the promotional numbers which must be earned by study and experience in the organization. Page 367.

stamp: 1. extinguish, do away with or destroy as if by stamping (pounding down on) with the foot. Page 240.

2. to impress or mark (something) with a device. Page 242.

stamp, all of a: all of a similar kind or type. Page 246.

star-rated: describing a very exact checkout which verifies the full and minute knowledge of the student of a portion of study materials and tests his full understanding of the data and ability to apply it. Page 314.

stars in your crown: figuratively, an acknowledgment of a great achievement. Originally a *crown* was a wreath worn about the head as a symbol of victory. From this, a crown became traditionally used to designate the power or authority of a king. A *star* is an award for excellence. Hence, to place stars on a crown is to further acknowledge something which is already recognized as outstanding, powerful, victorious, etc. Page 199.

static: a fixed or stationary condition, lacking movement or motion. Page 114.

stealthily: moving in a deliberately slow, careful and quiet way so as not to be seen or heard. Page 54.

step echelon: a stage in a progression or series of administrative or organizational levels in a government, country or the like. Page 153.

strained: 1. of personal relations, a situation, etc., subjected to a dangerous degree of tension, forced to a point of threatened disharmony. Page 32.

2. full of tension as if on the verge of hostility. Page 46.

strangulation: the action or process of constricting, choking off or killing natural, normal or desirable growth, development or activity. Page 47.

Study Tech: the term given to the methods developed by L. Ron Hubbard that enable individuals to study effectively. It is an exact technology that anyone can use to learn a subject or to acquire a new skill. It provides an understanding of the fundamental principles of how to learn and gives precise ways to overcome the barriers and pitfalls one can encounter during study such as going by misunderstood words or symbols. Page 329.

stumbling block: an obstacle or hindrance to progress or understanding. Page 195.

subordinate: to make subservient (of lesser importance); place in a position dependent upon or under the domination of. Page 51.

suborn: to bribe or induce unlawfully or secretly to perform some misdeed or to commit a crime; to induce by underhanded or covert means to do something immoral or illegal; to draw away from allegiance, corrupt the loyalty of. Page 154.

summarily: in a prompt and direct manner; immediately and without delay. Page 319.

sun, moon and stars, under the: a variation of *under the sun,* meaning "on earth; in the whole world," used to add emphasis to a statement. Page 116.

sun motes: numerous tiny specks of dust or other similar material floating in the air (called motes) which are visible in a shaft of sunlight. Page 53.

Supervisor: short for *Course Supervisor,* the person in charge of a Dianetics or Scientology course who is responsible for the training of students and graduating auditors and other graduates at a high level of technology who can apply the materials they have learned. Page 226.

suppress: to squash, to sit on, to make smaller, to refuse to let reach, to make uncertain about his reaching, to render or lessen in any way possible by any means possible to the harm of the individual and for the fancied protection of the suppressor. Page 20.

suppression: a harmful intention or action against which one cannot fight back. Thus, when one can do *anything* about it, it is less suppressive. Suppression in its most fundamental sense is knocking out the beingness or location of another or others. Page 134.

Suppressive Person (SP): a person who suppresses other people in his vicinity. A Suppressive Person will goof up or vilify any effort to help anybody and particularly knife with violence anything calculated to make human beings more powerful or more intelligent. The whole rationale of the Suppressive Person (SP) is built on the belief that if anyone got better, the SP would be for it as the others could overcome him, then. He is fighting a battle he once fought and never stopped fighting. He is in an incident. Present time people are mistaken by him for past, long-gone enemies. Therefore, he never really knows what he is fighting in present time, so just fights. Page 171.

sustain: maintain; make something continue to exist. Page 254.

swan song: last act or manifestation of someone or something before dying, from the belief that the dying swan sings. Page 184.

Szasz, Dr. Thomas: (1920–) American psychiatrist, university professor and writer, well known for his highly critical views of the practices of psychiatry. Szasz has written over 200 articles and several books, one of which is *The Manufacture of Madness* (1971). Page 371.

tantamount: equivalent in effect or value; nearly or almost the same as. Page 44.

tart: an offensive term for a woman thought to be a prostitute or to behave like one. Page 40.

TB (tuberculosis): a serious infectious disease in which swellings appear on the lungs and other parts of the body, once ranked among the most common causes of death in the world. Page 42.

tech: short for *technology.* Page 5.

Tech: short for *Technical Division.* Page 190.

Tech Director: the former name of the executive over the Technical Division of the org who coordinated all training and processing activities. Page 293.

Tech Division: short for *Technical Division,* the division in a Church of Scientology organization which schedules students and pcs for service, effectively and rapidly trains students on courses up to the class of the org, turns out competent auditors and course graduates, delivers high-quality intensive auditing to pcs on all levels and actions up to the class of the org and creates an abundance of fully trained and interned Case Supervisors and auditors. Page 229.

technology (tech): the methods of application of an art or science as opposed to mere knowledge of the science or art itself. In Scientology, the term *technology* refers to the methods of application of Scientology principles to improve the functions of the mind and rehabilitate the potentials of the spirit, developed by L. Ron Hubbard. Page vii.

techno-space society: a society that is technologically advanced to the point of space travel. *Techno* means technology. Page 51.

Tech Sec: short for *Technical Secretary,* the head of the Technical Division, the division of a Church of Scientology that gives high-volume, high-quality training and auditing with excellent results on every pc and student so that the org standardly delivers in high volume. Page 325.

telex: an urgent communication concerning operations. The word *telex* is formed from the words *teletypewriter* (telegraph instrument resembling a typewriter used for transmitting messages by typing) and *exchange. Telex* also means the message itself sent out by telex machine or computer. Page 304.

Temporary: the status of a staff member newly hired in a Church of Scientology organization. The person is classed as *Temporary* until he or she obtains a slip from their immediate senior saying they are doing fine on post and presents this to the HAS. The HAS may require they have a knowledge of the org board and comm lines and their own department before passing them. While Temporary, a staff member may be dismissed with or without cause by his immediate superior or by the HAS or a Secretary or anyone senior to a Secretary. Page 193.

temporizing: complying with the time or occasion or with the desires of another; yielding temporarily to the current opinion or immediate circumstances. Page 151.

tenement: a run-down and often overcrowded apartment house. Page 21.

term: a limited period for which something lasts or is intended to last. Page 15.

terminal: any person who receives, relays or sends communications. Page 45.

tertiary: third in order or importance; preceded by two others. Page 387.

"theater": an exterior or outward dramatization, spectacle or show for some effect, lacking true substance or reality. From the regular use of *theater,* meaning a building or structure of some kind set aside where actors carry out dramatic performances. Page 156.

theetie-weetie: a slang term from England, meaning sweetness and light. The person can't face MEST or any outness. Page 257.

Theodora: (A.D. 502?–548) wife and advisor of Justinian I, Roman emperor from A.D. 527 to 565. Daughter of an animal trainer in a circus, Theodora was an actress and prostitute when she met

Justinian. She soon became his mistress, wife and then empress when Justinian took the throne in 527. Page 161.

there's the frying pan—there's the fire: a variation of the phrase *out of the frying pan into the fire,* meaning to be clear of one difficulty only to find oneself in a greater one. An allusion to a fish leaping out of a frying pan only to fall into the cooking fire. Page 132.

theta: the energy of thought and life. *Theta* is reason, serenity, stability, happiness, cheerful emotion, persistence and the other factors which Man ordinarily considers desirable. Page 222.

thetan(s): the person himself—not his body or his name, the physical universe, his mind, or anything else; that which is aware of being aware; the identity which *is* the individual. Page 45.

Third Party: to act as a *Third Party,* one who by false reports creates trouble between two people, a person and a group, or a group and another group. Page 259.

three-terminal universe: a reference to the discovery of the fact that while it is commonly believed to take two to make a fight, a Third Party must exist and must develop it for actual conflict to occur. Page 377.

threw a fish: expressed contempt or ridicule. The expression comes from theater slang, where "Throw him a fish!" was formerly used as a call of ridicule towards an inept performer. Page 161.

thwart: prevent someone or someone's plans or purposes from being successful. Page 183.

Time Machine: a system for keeping track of an executive's orders and ensuring they are complied to. The Time Machine consists of a series of baskets. A copy of the executive's order is placed in today's basket and is advanced one basket every day. When the original order comes in complied with, it is matched up with the copy, clipped together and sent to the executive who issued the order. If the original does not arrive at the Time Machine, the copy will fall off it by appearing in the basket being emptied today. (It was filled one week ago and advanced once each day.) Orders that fall off the Time Machine are copied and sent to Ethics for filing in the staff member's ethics folder. Page 236.

tinsel: of or like someone who has a deceptively brilliant or valuable appearance with little real worth; showy or attractive but lacking real value. *Tinsel* is a thread, strip of paper, plastic or metal used to produce a sparkling or glittery effect. Page 161.

Tone Scale: a scale of emotional tones which shows the levels of human behavior. These tones, ranged from the highest to the lowest, are, in part, enthusiasm, boredom, antagonism, anger, covert hostility, fear, grief and apathy. The Tone Scale is fully described in *Science of Survival*. Page 57.

Torquemada: Tomás de Torquemada (1420–1498), Spanish monk who was confessor and advisor to Queen Isabella I from her childhood. Torquemada, a fanatic, organized and was the head of the Spanish Inquisition. His severity soon alarmed the pope and other church leaders, but he disregarded their complaints and tortured, jailed, banished or otherwise damaged tens of thousands of people. More than two thousand people were burned at the stake during his reign and the name *Torquemada* has come to symbolize ruthless persecution. Page 392.

track: short for *time track*, the consecutive record of mental image pictures which accumulates through the preclear's life or lives. Page 121.

travail: pain or suffering resulting from mental or physical hardship. Page 176.

treasure: money. Page 221.

Treasury: the division in a Church of Scientology organization which is responsible for receiving and recording donations to the organization, paying its bills and caring for its assets. Page 107.

trifle: a slight amount; a little. Page 335.

triggered: initiated or set off; caused (some situation or condition) to happen as if acted on by a trigger. Page 5.

triple flow: (of a process) addressing three flows (a being has a minimum of three flows). By *flow* is meant a directional thought, energy or action. The three flows are: (1) inward to oneself; (2) outward to another or others; and (3) crossways, others to others. An example would be: Flow 1, to self, drinking; Flow 2, self to another or others, preclear giving them drinks; Flow 3, others to others, people giving other people drinks. Page 196.

tripped up: caused to fail; hindered or obstructed. Page 102.

troth: one's faith as pledged in solemn agreement or undertaking; a promise. Page 54.

undercut: the action of going to a more basic, lower or less advanced level or stage than that which is being referred to. Page 137.

unfrocked: literally the word means deprived of one's *frock,* a garment with large sleeves worn by a monk. Hence, to deprive a priest, monk, etc., of his churchly authority or rank. Page 152.

unknownness: incomprehensibility of something; it is also the consideration that something cannot be known. Page 64.

unmock: make nothing of. Page 131.

unmolested: not interfered with, disturbed or harmed. Page 193.

unpalatable: unpleasant and not easy to accept, as facts or ideas. Literally, means not agreeable to the palate (roof of the mouth, popularly considered as the part of the mouth where one experiences taste). Page 6.

untold: too numerous to be counted or measured. Page 210.

unwittingly: unknowingly; without awareness. Page 20.

up against a (brick) wall, put (someone): to defy or confront (someone) with severity. Page 249.

upstat(s): 1. one who has high statistics. Page 249.
2. characteristic of a person or area which has high, rising statistics. Page 268.

utterances: things expressed, as words, whether written or spoken. Page 368.

utters: expresses, as words, whether written or spoken. Page 42.

Vallejo: General Mariano Guadalupe Vallejo (1808–1890), military and political leader in California, serving the Mexican government until 1846. In 1836 Vallejo supported his nephew in rebellion, which resulted in the proclamation of the "free state" of California. Page 155.

Veronal: a brand name for a drug that is used as a sedative. Regular use of such can cause addiction and an overdose can cause a coma and death. Page 42.

Victorian England: the period in English history during the reign of Queen Victoria, from 1837 to 1901, the longest reign in English history. The British Empire, which began in the sixteenth and seventeenth centuries with the establishment of colonies in North America, reached its greatest extent at the end of the Victorian Age and included Australia, Canada, India, New Zealand, large portions of Africa and many smaller territories throughout the world. This expansion and Britain's vast holdings overseas were largely fueled by the desire for profitable commercial trade routes as well as for the resources of the colonies acquired. Page 246.

Vietnam: a tropical country in Southeast Asia, site of a major war from 1954 to 1975 between South Vietnam and communist-controlled North Vietnam. The United States became involved in the mid-1960s, lending its support to the South. By the late 1960s, due to the length of the war, high US casualties, and US participation in war crimes against the Vietnamese, American involvement became increasingly unpopular in the US and was strongly protested. In 1973, despite continuing hostilities between North and South Vietnam, the US removed all its troops. By 1975, the communists had overrun South Vietnam and the war was officially ended. Page 22.

vilified: made less valuable or important; attempted to degrade by slander and/or abusive utterances; spoke evil of. Page 150.

villainy: evil conduct; extreme wickedness. Page 24.

wake: the visible trail (of agitated and disturbed water) left by something, such as a ship, moving through water. Hence, a condition left behind someone or something that has passed; following as a consequence. Page 54.

wall, put (someone) up against a (brick): to defy or confront (someone) with severity. Page 249.

war of attrition: literally, *attrition* means the rubbing or grinding or wearing away of one thing against another. Hence, a *war of attrition* refers to one side wearing down and weakening the other side through continuous pressure, harassment, deprivation, etc., such as by siege. (A *siege* is the act or process of surrounding and attacking a fortified place in such a way as to isolate it from help and supplies so as to lessen resistance of the defenders, thereby making capture possible.) Page 153.

warranted: justified (by the circumstances). Page 145.

way out, on the: going down in status or condition; dying. Page 19.

weight: influence, importance or authority. Page 324.

well behooves: it is right, proper and appropriate to a great extent or degree for (somebody); very necessary for. Page 178.

what a song: a coined phrase used to show that something is extremely easy or effortless. Page 122.

what matter: a phrase used to indicate that something is of no importance or consequence. Page 295.

wheels going, getting the: a variation of the phrase *set the wheels in motion,* which means to cause an activity to make forward progress or plans to go into effect. Page 164.

whips: persons or things causing mental or physical pain or acting as a stimulus to action. Page 48.

whistle on, blown the: reported someone for doing something wrong or illegal. Page 373.

whistling past the graveyard: a variation of the phrase *whistling in the dark,* which means being cheerful or optimistic in a situation that doesn't warrant cheer or optimism. The phrase comes from the literal idea of whistling in a dark or scary place to show that one is not concerned or frightened. Page 174.

Why: the real basic reason for a situation which, being found, opens the door to handling; the basic outness found which will lead to a recovery of statistics. A Why is not a mere explanation of why a nonoptimum situation exists. It is the major outpoint which explains all the other outpoints as a common denominator. And it is always some huge, enormous piece of stupidity. If you can still ask "How come?" of a Why found, it couldn't be a bottom-level Why. Anytime you can ask a "How come?" you haven't got a Why. The *real* Why when found and corrected leads straight back to improved stats. Page 146.

willy-nilly: whether one chooses it or not; willingly or unwillingly. Page 132.

wipe out: remove or eliminate something completely. Page 280.

witch hunts: investigations carried out, supposedly to uncover and expose disloyalty, dishonesty or the like, usually based on doubtful or irrelevant evidence. From the witch hunts of Salem, Massachusetts, in 1692, which led to the execution of twenty people, based on little evidence, for allegedly practicing witchcraft. Page 182.

withhold: an unspoken, unannounced transgression against a moral code by which the person is bound is called a "withhold." A withhold is an overt act that a person committed that he or she is not talking about. It is something that a person believes that if revealed will endanger his self-preservation. Any withhold comes *after* an overt. Page 37.

with trimmings: things added as accessories or extras; with nothing missed or omitted. Page 238.

witness: used to introduce something that gives evidence of a fact or demonstrates a statement just made. Page 205.

wog: a slang term which was originally used by the Royal Air Force (in reference to Egyptians) to mean "worthy oriental gentleman." There was nothing derogatory in being called a wog. In Scientology this means a common, ordinary, run-of-the-mill, garden-variety humanoid, by which is meant an individual that considers that he is a body and does not know that he is there as a spirit at all. Page 248.

woman scorned: a variation of the phrase *hell hath no fury like a woman scorned,* meaning no one has more fury or wrath than a woman whose love has been rejected, or who thinks her worth or dignity has been insulted, slighted, etc. Page 46.

word clear: the action of clearing away the ignorance, misunderstoods and false definitions of words and barriers to their use. Page 64.

worksheet: the complete running record of the session from beginning to end. A worksheet is always on 8" x 13" or 8½" x 14" paper. It is written on both sides of the page, 2 columns on each side and with every page numbered front and back. The pc's name is written on each separate sheet. Page 269.

wreaks: brings about (harm); causes, inflicts. Page 6.

wrested: gained with difficulty by or as if by coercive force, violent action or steady determined labor. Page 154.

write (something) over into: to transfer or alter the meaning, idea, etc., of one thing over into another. Page 6.

wrongheaded: stubborn in adherence to wrong opinion or principles. Page 45.

yardstick: a standard used to judge the quality, value or success of something. Page 25.

yoke: an agency of restraint, suppression and servitude; something that is oppressive, imposing a harsh or cruel form of domination. From the sixteenth to the nineteenth century, South America was ruled by Spain, hence under the *"yoke of Spain."* Literally, a *yoke* is a device laid over the necks of farm animals that are pulling a load or over the neck of a defeated person, slave or the like, indicating his suppression. During the period of Simón Bolívar, South America was under the control and dominance of Spain. Page 149.

zingo: a variation of *bingo,* a word used to express satisfaction at a sudden positive event or outcome. Page 255.

INDEX

C

E

F

G

game

ending of limited, 163

when over, must be new, 165

game condition

overt act mechanism, 45

generalities

Anti-Social Personality and, 178

never buy rumors as, 235

petition and, 384

Social Personality and, 185

SPs speaking in, 247

General Sherman tank, 235

Genghis Khan, 251

glow things right, 151

goal

constructive and destructive, 175

violent shift in goals pattern and illness, 175

God Dynamic

definition, 13

good

being more right than one is wrong, 21

definition, 21

evil and, 20–23

fixation on making "everybody good," 248

Man and basic, 20, 63

same being at different lifetimes is evil and, 175

good news

Social Personality and, 185

"good roads and good weather"

PTS handling and, 199

good standing

what to do to be reinstated in, 361

gossip

Anti-Social Personality and, 179

government, 241

Anti-Social Personalities and, 184

application of Dev-T Policies to, 295

decay of Western, 240

decide on your type of, 164

reverse the conduct of declining, 243

violence and, 6

Grade Chart

grades, Technical Degrades and, 315

truth and, 67

gradient

definition, 15

gradient scale

right and wrong, 15–17

graph, 75–91

definition, 75

example of trends, 86–90

how to scale, 75–78

of logic, 17

reading of statistical, 72

slant of line on a, condition and, 79

"upside down," 83–84

Great Depression

cause of, 243

greatest good for the greatest number of dynamics, 101

group

Anti-Social Personality supporting only destructive, 180

control of fellows by individual member in, 270

discipline needful, 376

enforcement of mores, 268

Ethics Officer and safeguard, 258

K

N

OT

honesty and, 68

Levels, psychos going berserk about, 264

out-basics, 137

production and, 139

out-ethics

caved in and, 27

Danger Formula and, 111

definition, 19

dynamics, 29–32

justice and, 26

known of by others, 268

more destructive than constructive, 21

Second Dynamic and, 31

situation and bank triggered by, 5

society, 19

Outline of Full PTS Handling, 211–215

outnesses

no good reasons for, except, 256

outpoints

inspect area by, 139

out-tech, 330

overt(s)

act, definition, 35, 57

kept afloat in universe, 45, 63

lessening of, 44

mutual action and, 54

no responsibility and not conceiving overt as, 37

not all destructive actions or omissions are, 57

of omission, 36

proceeding from irresponsibility, 37

PTSness and, 208

stop committing present time, 316

unburdening considered to be, 45

what one does against his will operating as, 46

writing up, *see* **O/W write-up**

overt act–motivator sequence, 36, 54

definition, 36

see also **motivator; overt(s)**

overt of omission

definition, 36

overts and withholds

writing up, relief, responsibility and, 63

see also **O/W write-up**

overworked executive

answer to, 131

O/W write-up, 63–66

basic theory, 63–64

format, 64–66

Junior Danger Formula and, 111

P

pain

evil and, 16

goodness versus, 54

immortality versus, 19

truly evil love, 249

parasitism, 246

pc, *see* **preclear**

peace

antagonistic terminal seeking to make, 215

on Earth, fully trust each other and, 52

productive, 154

to all the world, 225

penalties

Code of Discipline and, 298

Convening Authority and, 338

Recommendations

    Comm Ev and, 338, 340, 347

recourse, 361, 372–373

    definition, 372

    failure to use, 375

    illegal orders and, 373

    none from Court, 353

    of auditor, 323

    petition and, 385

    Review Comm Ev, 373

    sentence passed and, 366

redress, 359

    forms of, 359–388

    of wrongs, petition and, 384

refund, 312, 355

    Sources of Trouble and, 220

    suits, 356

relief

    writing up overts and
      withholds and, 63

remorse

    Anti-Social Personality and,
      180

removal

    from post, sequence, 374

reporters

    efforts to be helpful to, 219

    why they should not be
      audited, 219

reports

    deemed incorrect, handling,
      278

    description, 271

    disputed Ethics Chits,
      278–279

    failure to make, 270, 271

    five accumulating, 273

    job endangerment and, 271

    most serious ones, 273

    staff member reports,
      271–274

Tech and Qual Ethics Chits,
    275–277

    withdrawal of chits, 278

    see also **Knowledge
      Reports**

responsibility, 47–49

    Anti-Social Personality and,
      180

    definition, 37

    doingness without any, 48

    get over idea one is forced
      into, 47

    of declaring Danger, 131

    of leaders, 149–167

    overt acts and, 37, 208

    power of choice and, 47–49

    processing and, 41

    rehabilitating on any case,
      49

    religious confession, no real
      stress of, 44

    return of, 63

    Social Personality and, 186

Responsibility (Process), 43

**responsible-for-condition
  case**

    definition, 218

restimulation

    Type II PTS and, 192

Review

    find disagreements with
      meter, 132

    may send to Ethics, 227

**Review Committee of
  Evidence**, 344, 373

    see also **Committee of
      Evidence (Comm Ev)**

rewards

    Bolívar and no, 152

    down statistics and, 240

    good performance and, 307

    penalties and, 240–246

rich or influential

    auditing because, 219

T

witness

    Committee of Evidence and false, 345

    definition, 342

word

    keeping one's, 23

    Word Clearing Tech, 329

        Axiom 28 and, 331

work

    filing and real trick of Ethics, 235

    forcing people to, 47

    on a bypass, Danger and, 131

World Institute of Scientology Enterprises (WISE), 354

wrong

    no absolute, 58

    not necessarily definable for everyone, 57

    right and, 20–23

    those who specialize in, 188

wrongness

    "admit-you-are-wrong," 61

    cure of compulsive repetition of a, 60

    degradation and making another, 60

    effort to make others, 58

    first accidental, then repeated, 59

    gradient approaching infinite wrongness, 15

    gradient scale of right and, 15–17

wrong target

    Anti-Social Personality and, 180

Y

yawn

    file complaints with a, 238

Z

zero

    influence, 27

GUIDE TO THE MATERIALS

YOU'RE ON AN ADVENTURE!
HERE'S THE MAP.

- All books
- All lectures
- All reference books

All of it laid out in chronological sequence with descriptions of what each contains.

Your journey to a full understanding of Dianetics and Scientology is the greatest adventure of all. But you need a map that shows you where you are and where you are going.

That map is the Materials Guide Chart. It shows all Ron's books and lectures with a full description of their content and subject matter so you can find exactly what *you* are looking for and precisely what *you* need.

Since each book and lecture is laid out in chronological sequence, you can see *how* the subjects of Dianetics and Scientology were developed. And what that means is by simply studying this chart you are in for cognition after cognition!

New editions of all books include extensive glossaries, containing definitions for every technical term. And as a result of a monumental restoration program, the entire library of Ron's lectures are being made available on compact disc, with complete transcripts, glossaries, lecture graphs, diagrams and issues he refers to in the lectures. As a result, you get *all* the data, and can learn with ease, gaining a full *conceptual* understanding.

And what that adds up to is a new Golden Age of Knowledge every Dianeticist and Scientologist has dreamed of.

To obtain your FREE Materials Guide Chart and Catalog, or to order L. Ron Hubbard's books and lectures, contact:

WESTERN HEMISPHERE:
**Bridge
Publications, Inc.**
4751 Fountain Avenue
Los Angeles, CA 90029 USA
www.bridgepub.com
Phone: 1-800-722-1733
Fax: 1-323-953-3328

EASTERN HEMISPHERE:
**New Era Publications
International ApS**
Store Kongensgade 53
1264 Copenhagen K, Denmark
www.newerapublications.com
Phone: (45) 33 73 66 66
Fax: (45) 33 73 66 33

*Books and lectures are also available direct from Churches of Scientology.
See **Addresses**.*

ADDRESSES

S cientology is the fastest-growing religion in the world today. Churches and Missions exist in cities throughout the world, and new ones are continually forming.

To obtain more information or to locate the Church nearest you, visit the Scientology website:

www.scientology.org
e-mail: info@scientology.org

or

Phone: 1-800-334-LIFE
(for US and Canada)

You can also write to any one of the Continental Organizations, listed on the following page, who can direct you to one of the thousands of Churches and Missions world over.

L. Ron Hubbard's books and lectures may be obtained from any of these addresses or direct from the publishers on the previous page.

CONTINENTAL CHURCH ORGANIZATIONS:

UNITED STATES

**CHURCH OF SCIENTOLOGY
CONTINENTAL LIAISON OFFICE
WESTERN UNITED STATES**
1308 L. Ron Hubbard Way
Los Angeles, California 90027 USA
info@wus.scientology.org

**CHURCH OF SCIENTOLOGY
CONTINENTAL LIAISON OFFICE
EASTERN UNITED STATES**
349 W. 48th Street
New York, New York 10036 USA
info@eus.scientology.org

CANADA

**CHURCH OF SCIENTOLOGY
CONTINENTAL LIAISON OFFICE
CANADA**
696 Yonge Street, 2nd Floor
Toronto, Ontario
Canada M4Y 2A7
info@scientology.ca

LATIN AMERICA

**CHURCH OF SCIENTOLOGY
CONTINENTAL LIAISON OFFICE
LATIN AMERICA**
Federacion Mexicana de Dianetica
Calle Puebla #31
Colonia Roma, Mexico D.F.
C.P. 06700, Mexico
info@scientology.org.mx

UNITED KINGDOM

**CHURCH OF SCIENTOLOGY
CONTINENTAL LIAISON OFFICE
UNITED KINGDOM**
Saint Hill Manor
East Grinstead, West Sussex
England, RH19 4JY
info@scientology.org.uk

AFRICA

**CHURCH OF SCIENTOLOGY
CONTINENTAL LIAISON OFFICE AFRICA**
5 Cynthia Street
Kensington
Johannesburg 2094, South Africa
info@scientology.org.za

AUSTRALIA, NEW ZEALAND & OCEANIA
CHURCH OF SCIENTOLOGY
CONTINENTAL LIAISON OFFICE ANZO
16 Dorahy Street
Dundas, New South Wales 2117
Australia
info@scientology.org.au

**Church of Scientology
Liaison Office of Taiwan**
1st, No. 231, Cisian 2nd Road
Kaoshiung City
Taiwan, ROC
info@scientology.org.tw

EUROPE
CHURCH OF SCIENTOLOGY
CONTINENTAL LIAISON OFFICE EUROPE
Store Kongensgade 55
1264 Copenhagen K, Denmark
info@scientology.org.dk

**Church of Scientology
Liaison Office of Commonwealth
of Independent States**

Management Center of Dianetics
and Scientology Dissemination
Pervomajskaya Street, House 1A
Korpus Grazhdanskoy Oboroni
Losino-Petrovsky Town
141150 Moscow, Russia
info@scientology.ru

**Church of Scientology
Liaison Office of
Central Europe**

1082 Leonardo da Vinci u. 8-14
Budapest, Hungary
info@scientology.hu

**Church of Scientology
Liaison Office of Iberia**

C/Miguel Menendez Boneta, 18
28460 – Los Molinos
Madrid, Spain
info@spain.scientology.org

**Church of Scientology
Liaison Office of Italy**

Via Cadorna, 61
20090 Vimodrone
Milan, Italy
info@scientology.it

BECOME A MEMBER
OF THE INTERNATIONAL
ASSOCIATION OF SCIENTOLOGISTS

The International Association of Scientologists is the membership organization of all Scientologists united in the most vital crusade on Earth.

A free Six-Month Introductory Membership is extended to anyone who has not held a membership with the Association before.

As a member, you are eligible for discounts on Scientology materials offered only to IAS Members. You also receive the Association magazine, *IMPACT,* issued six times a year, full of Scientology news from around the world.

The purpose of the IAS is:

"To unite, advance, support and protect Scientology and Scientologists in all parts of the world so as to achieve the Aims of Scientology as originated by L. Ron Hubbard."

Join the strongest force for positive change on the planet today, opening the lives of millions to the greater truth embodied in Scientology.

513

JOIN THE INTERNATIONAL
ASSOCIATION OF SCIENTOLOGISTS.

To apply for membership,
write to the International
Association of Scientologists
c/o Saint Hill Manor, East Grinstead
West Sussex, England, RH19 4JY

www.iasmembership.org

FROM CLEAR TO
ETERNITY

*I*n this time and in this place—for possibly just a little while, we have this chance. To go free and to make it. Planets and cultures are frail things. They do not endure.

I cannot promise you that you will make it. I can only provide the knowledge and give you your chance.

The rest is up to you.

I strongly advise you to work hard at it—don't waste this brief breath in eternity.

For that is your future—ETERNITY.

It will be good for you or bad.

And for you, my dearest friend, I've done what I could to make it good for you.

L. Ron Hubbard

TAKE YOUR NEXT STEP
ON THE BRIDGE